PARTNERS AND RIVALS

PARTNERS AND RIVALS

REPRESENTATION IN U.S. SENATE DELEGATIONS

WENDY J. SCHILLER

PRINCETON UNIVERSITY PRESS

PRINCETON, NEW JERSEY

Library of Congress Catalog Card Number: 99-069513

ISBN 0-691-04886-X (cloth : alk. paper). —
ISBN 0-691-04887-8 (pbk. : alk. paper).

This book has been composed in Sabon

The paper used in this publication meets the
minimum requirements of
ANSI/NISO Z39.48-1992 (R 1997)
(*Permanence of Paper*)

www.pup.princeton.edu

Printed in the United States of America

10 9 8 7 6 5 4 3 2 1

10 9 8 7 6 5 4 3 2 1
(pbk.)

To Frances Levine, Sidney Levine, and Joan Schiller

CONTENTS

LIST OF ILLUSTRATIONS   ix

ACKNOWLEDGMENTS   xi

INTRODUCTION   3

CHAPTER 1
A Theory of Dual Representation   12

CHAPTER 2
Choosing Different Institutional Career Paths   33

CHAPTER 3
Diversification and Media Recognition   63

CHAPTER 4
Reputation and Constituent Evaluation   88

CHAPTER 5
Expanding the Boundaries of Electoral Coalitions   113

CHAPTER 6
Economic Interests and Campaign Contributions   143

CHAPTER 7
Rethinking Senate Representation   161

APPENDIX A
Measurement of Variables   175

APPENDIX B
Questionnaire Mailed to Newspaper Editors and Reporters   177

APPENDIX C
Newspaper Articles by Subject Matter, State, and Senator   179

REFERENCES   185

INDEX   193

ILLUSTRATIONS

TABLES

2.1   Roll-Call Voting Unity within Senate Delegations, 1991–1992:
      Nonparty Votes   40
2.2   Roll-Call Voting Unity within Senate Delegations, 1991–1992:
      All Votes   42
2.3   Shared Committee Assignments within Senate Delegations,
      1987–1992   45
2.4   Shared Committee Assignment within Senate Delegations,
      1987–1992 (logistic regression)   47
2.5   Overlap between Appropriations Subcommittee Assignments and
      Authorizing Committees for Senators from Same State   51
2.6   Overlap between Authorizing Committees and Appropriations
      Subcommittee Assignments for Senators from Same State   52
2.7   Bill Sponsorship Overlap within Senate Delegations, 1989–1990   55
2.8   Bill Cosponsorship within Senate Delegations, 1987–1992   57
2.9   Amendment Cosponsorship within Senate Delegations, 1987–1992   58
2.10 Scale of Legislative Similarity within Unified Party Senate
      Delegations   59
2.11 Scale of Legislative Similarity within Divided Party Senate
      Delegations   60
2.12 Scale of Legislative Similarity within Senate Delegations that
      Changed Composition   61
2.13 Similarity in Legislative Behavior within Senate Delegations,
      1987–1992   61
3.1   Sample of State Newspapers   66
3.2   Content of Newspaper Coverage: Georgia   70
3.3   Content of Newspaper Coverage: Massachusetts   73
3.4   Content of Newspaper Coverage: Illinois   75
3.5   Content of Newspaper Coverage: Kentucky   78
3.6   Selected Determinants of State Newspaper Coverage of Senators,
      1987–1992   81
3.7   Determinants of State Media Coverage of Senators in Specific Issue
      Areas, 1987–1992   84
4.1   Selected Determinants of the Number of Constituent Mentions
      about Senators   100
4.2   Effects of State Media Coverage on Constituent Recognition of
      Senators in Issue Areas   102
4.3   Overlap in Like and Dislike Mentions for Senators from
      Same State   106
5.1   Predicting Differences in Share of Senate Vote by County for
      Incumbent Senators, 1987–1994: Same-Party Delegations   129

5.2	Predicting Differences in Share of Senate Vote by County for Incumbent Senators, 1987–1994: Split-Party Delegations	130
6.1	State-Based PAC Campaign Contributions to Senate Incumbents, 1987–1992	151
6.2	Total Amount of State-Based PAC Campaign Contributions to Senators, 1987–1992	157
6.3	Total Number of State-Based PACs that Contributed to Senators, 1987–1992	159

FIGURES

3.1	Newspaper Coverage of Senators in Georgia	69
3.2	Newspaper Coverage of Senators in Massachusetts	72
3.3	Newspaper Coverage of Senators in Illinois	74
3.4	Newspaper Coverage of Senators in Kentucky	77

MAPS

5.1	Oklahoma Senate Election Returns	119
5.2	Ohio Senate Election Returns	122
5.3	New York Senate Election Returns	126
5.4	Oregon Senate Election Returns	133
5.5	Pennsylvania Senate Election Returns	134
5.6	Michigan Senate Election Returns	135
5.7	Wyoming Senate Election Returns	136
5.8	Nebraska Senate Election Returns	137
5.9	Florida Senate Election Returns	139
5.10	Texas Senate Election Returns	140
5.11	South Carolina Senate Election Returns	141

ACKNOWLEDGMENTS

THERE ARE many individuals to whom I owe a great deal of thanks for supporting this project. Because they are geographically dispersed, I shall name them by their place of origin. My colleagues at Brown University have provided enormous support, especially Darrell West, who has offered his valuable advice and criticism at every single stage of this book. He is what every academic mentor should aspire to be.

In my parallel universe, Washington, D.C., Michael Baker, Sarah Binder, Dorian Freidman, Bob Katzmann, Curtis Kelley, Frances Lee, Matt Levine, Forrest Maltzman, Mark Patterson, Steve Porter, Jordana Schwartz, and Kent Weaver provided round-the-clock intellectual and moral support.

Among my fellow Congress jocks and jockettes, and those in other assorted subfields of political science, I am especially grateful to Douglas Arnold, Larry Bartels, Bill Bianco, Larry Evans, Dick Fenno, Corinna-Barbara Francis, Fiona McGillivray, Bruce Oppenheimer, Marsha Pripstein, Elaine Swift, and Eric Uslaner for their steadfast support of my work.

Brown University and the Howard Foundation provided the financial support that made this project possible. I also wish to thank Thomas Mann and the Brookings Institution for allowing me to invade their space once again. For their hard work and toil as research assistants, I also want to thank Shalisha Francis, Jill Frankfort, Sara Goldreich, and Kevin Johnson. I would also like to thank the editorial staff at Princeton University Press for all their hard work.

Finally, to the Bennett, Friedman, Miller, and Schiller clans, words do not do justice to the tremendous support I get from having a family like ours.

PARTNERS AND RIVALS

INTRODUCTION

> Pilfering laugh lines is a public speaking practice that goes
> back at least to Demosthenes. Most perpetrators escape
> unscathed, but occasionally one does not. A month ago in
> New York City, Senator Alfonse D'Amato heard his
> Democratic colleague, Senator Daniel Patrick Moynihan,
> respond to a laudatory introduction with this line: "Lyndon
> Johnson used to say, I wish my mother and father could
> have heard that introduction. My mother would have
> believed it, and my father would have enjoyed it." Three
> weeks later before a different audience, Senator Moynihan
> used the same opening with success and left before Senator
> D'Amato arrived. The Republican began his remarks,
> obliviously: "I wish my mother and father could have heard
> that introduction. My mother would have believed it, and
> my father would have enjoyed it." The audience collapsed
> with laughter. One member said later: "I think D'Amato still
> believes he was a smash."
>
> *(Francis X. Clines and Warren Weaver, Jr.,*
> *"Who Laughs Last")*

COMPETING FOR good opening remarks at constituent events is just one of many ways in which senators from the same state present obstacles to each other in building successful Senate careers. The United States Senate is one of the few legislative institutions in American politics that has two legislators for the same geographic "district."[1] From a representational standpoint, we should expect to see senators from the same state representing similar issue areas and economic interests in their legislative portfolios. From an electoral standpoint, we might also expect to see senators addressing similar issues — if they are perceived to be popular among voters — because they each seek a majority voting coalition in the state. For example, senators from Nebraska, a heavily agricultural state, should both be expected to address farm interests. Senators from the same state should also be expected to respond equally to an overriding policy concern in that state; for exam-

---

[1] There are districts at the state and local level that have elected representatives who overlap, that is, Assembly member and State senator, but there are few existing multimember districts where the members share the same level of power and the same geographic constituency.

ple, both senators from Texas should make immigration a primary focus of their legislative agendas.

However, what we actually observe is that senators from the same state do not build legislative agendas based on similar issues and interests; on the contrary, they build very distinct and separate legislative agendas on which they base much of their reputation as senators, regardless of same- or split-party affiliation. We are therefore faced with the following puzzle: *Why do senators who represent the same state, but who never compete for the same Senate seat, adopt distinct representational agendas?*

The concept of dual representation—two legislators sharing the same geographic constituency—is a vital and underappreciated component of legislative behavior in American politics.[2] From the very first day they enter the Senate, senators face the constraint of having another colleague from the same state who has similar institutional opportunities to represent that state. Each senator's decisions about voting, committee selection, bill sponsorship, amendments, media strategies, political contributions, and campaign behavior are made in the context of sharing the political stage with the other senator from their state. As will be shown throughout this book, senators from the same state join different committees, focus on different policy areas, and address different economic interests through bill and amendment sponsorship. Moreover, senators also adopt contrasting governing styles that are products of their own personal style, the political expectations in their state, and the existing reputation of the other incumbent senator.

The central argument of this work is that the incentive to differentiate within a Senate delegation is a combination of electoral incentives and institutional forces that push senators in contrasting directions. Taking advantage of the particular blend of party, economic interests, and political culture within their state, each public official seeks to develop an identifiable niche, which helps attract media coverage and build the long-term reputation necessary for a successful political career. The behavior of each senator therefore shapes the range of state interests and opinions that are incorporated into federal policy-making. This goes to the heart of democratic decision-making. In assessing how well a senator represents his or her state, we often examine an individual senator's voting record and try to match up that behavior with objective state interests or opinions. Inevitably, we conclude from such a test that there are constituents whose interests and opinions go unheeded by the sena-

---

[2] Adams (1996) explores the effects of having multimember districts at the state level and concludes that such districts produce more heterogeneous parties in a legislature than are found in a single-member electoral system. His study focused on the state of Illinois, which eliminated its multimember system in 1980.

tor. When we do that, though, we are setting up the senator for failure because no legislator can possibly address all the interests and opinions in a single state. Most important of all, a senator is not supposed to represent the majority constituent opinion on every issue because there is another senator who can also provide representation to the state. If we continue to measure Senate representation by examining just one-half of a Senate delegation, we will always produce incomplete results.

As an alternative, this book proposes to assess Senate representation from the perspective of the two senators from each state, each of whom works individually to craft a reputation and seek reelection, but who, when examined as a collective unit, attend to a wide spectrum of interests and opinions in their states. In doing so, this work moves beyond conventional approaches to measurement of representation by demonstrating how senators work within a multidimensional framework. This approach is key for those who believe that partisanship is the clearest signal of accurate representation. If scholars look only through the lens of partisanship, they can construct a "majority" constituent interest in each state when, in fact, no such majority exists. Subsequently, they might mistakenly conclude that constituents from a state where both senators share the same party affiliation would only be represented in the Senate if they shared that party affiliation.

In reality, Senate representation is multidimensional: constituents have a range of interests and political opinions, based on their partisan views, economic status, and geographic location, which may overlap on one dimension but rarely overlap consistently on all three at any given time. Senators react to the varied structure of constituent interests by constructing legislative agendas that appeal to a cross-section of the state, and which go well beyond partisanship. Senators from the same state do not oppose each other directly in an election, but they nevertheless perceive the need to establish contrasting reputations to secure reelection and therefore have a strong incentive to rest the foundation of their support on different combinations of constituent interests. To do that, senators have to take concrete steps, both in the state and in the Senate, to adopt separate portfolios. A theory of representation that takes this behavior into account by incorporating the multidimensionality of constituent interests, and the unique character of the two-member structure of Senate delegations, can provide a more comprehensive understanding of democratic representation in American politics.

Additionally, studying the Senate in this way can yield fruitful comparisons to the behavior of legislators in other political systems that have multimember districts. Even though there are some important differences, namely, that senators do not compete directly in a simultaneous election as legislators in other systems do, there are potential similarities in the way that candidates and legislators shape their portfolios. We would expect parties that run a number of candidates in a given district to differentiate those candidates along some dimension of representation — either ideology or governing style or issue selection.[3] Applying the work of comparative politics scholars to explain behavior in the U.S. Senate can shed light on how and why legislators who share the same geographic constituency make starkly different choices in issue selection, governing style, and ideology, as candidates and as elected officials.

In many respects, representation in the Senate is stronger than often thought. In the world of contemporary politics, enormous public cynicism about representative democracy dominates political discourse; ordinary citizens believe that public officials are out for themselves and not representing voter interests. Although public discontent can be attributed to a number of sources, part of citizen unhappiness may be a function of academic studies that show weaker levels of representation than actually exist. If we redefine the notion of representation to include dual representation, we find that senators are doing a much better job representing voters than is commonly believed.

The remainder of this book sets out to demonstrate key features of this argument. Chapter 1 reviews the origins of dual representation. Going back to the founding period of American history, I discuss how the dynamics of competition and cooperation between same-state senators are an unintended consequence of compromises made at the Constitutional Convention. For all their foresight, the framers underestimated the extent to which state legislatures might use the Senate as a means of ensuring that the maximum number of state interests would be represented at the national level. By sending senators with contrasting economic and political viewpoints to the Senate, states could achieve a broader scope of representation at the national level than if they had chosen to treat their Senate delegation as a single entity. The Senate behavior that we witness today, when we have direct Senate elections, mirrors the ancestral behavior of state legislatures in this regard. Senators from the same state, both in campaigns and in the Senate, now do what state legislatures used to do in differentiating themselves in order to build distinct reputations among constituents.

Chapter 2 examines how senators build their reputations and shape their careers in the Senate. Every day, senators make decisions that affect the way they represent their states as well as their overall reputation

---

[3] Gary Cox (1997), Mathew McCubbins and Frances Rosenbluth (1995), and Jay Dow (1998) provide evidence of this type of behavior in Japan and Chile.

among their colleagues and constituents. At different points throughout a congressional session, a senator's decisions may take on more or less importance, depending on the issue at hand and the legislative arena in which he is operating. A senator casts a roll-call vote, which may or may not accord with the party's or state's interests, in committee and on the Senate floor. At the same time, a senator may be deciding whether to sponsor major legislation, or to cosponsor bills introduced by colleagues. Likewise, a senator may decide to offer an amendment to a chair's mark in committee, or to a bill once it reaches the Senate floor. Every senator makes these decisions within a context that incorporates the decisions that his state colleague makes about the very same potential universe of issues and concerns.

To measure the extent of overlap in legislative areas between two senators from the same state, an index of similarity is constructed as a function of the diversity of state interests, seniority, same- or split-party affiliation, and prior competition in state elections. In general, senators from larger states, which tend to have a more diverse set of interests, will overlap less than senators from small states do because the wider spectrum of state interests makes it easier for them to construct different legislative portfolios. As chapter 2 also shows, senators who share the same party affiliation face greater electoral and institutional incentives to differentiate in these areas of legislative behavior than senators who have opposite party affiliations. Given that senators from the same party and the same state will look very similar on their roll-call voting records, they take great pains to contrast themselves in all the other legislative arenas in which they operate.

Chapter 3 is an in-depth content analysis of local media coverage of senators from the same state. In this chapter, I argue that because the average senator is unlikely to attract a lot of national press attention, it is a more productive and efficient strategy to gear his efforts toward the local media. Unlike most House members, individual senators are likely to receive some minimum level of coverage for their legislative actions in particular issue areas. However, because two senators from the same state share the same media audience, they face constant competition in their efforts to attract individualized media coverage. This competition for visibility provides same-state senators with a strong incentive to develop contrasting and distinct representational agendas, and it pushes them in more divergent directions than we might expect of two legislators who represent the same geographic constituency.

The results support the argument that the need for publicity to build visible reputations in the state drives senators from the same state to diversify their legislative portfolios. In general, the amount and content of local media coverage of a senator reflect choices of committee assignments, issue specialization, geographic ties, and general governing style. There is a direct and strong correlation between committee assignment and media coverage across almost all issue areas. Therefore, the decisions that a senator makes to join a different set of committees from that chosen by a state colleague pays off in terms of individualized media coverage. Moreover, patterns of media coverage discourage encroachment into the other senator's territory because when one senator receives publicity in an issue area, the other senator is less likely to be covered in that same issue area. Lastly, a senator's effort to differ stylistically from his state colleague among the press also reaps rewards because the impressions that the elite media develop are filtered down into everyday newspaper coverage.

In Chapter 4 the main focus is on how senators use reputations to cultivate their home-state audiences. Because the general level of familiarity with elected officials is so low, and party affiliation as a predictor of vote choice has declined, senators face greater uncertainty about potential support among constituents than they did thirty-five years ago. This electoral uncertainty exerts pressure on senators to establish broad reputations, based on party, legislative portfolios, and governing styles, as a means of marketing themselves to their constituents. Given the sheer difficulty of penetrating the many layers of information available to most voters, senators and their staff consider even the vaguest impression among constituents to be a sufficient return for the cost of the resources that are devoted to building a reputation.

Chapter 4 uses both local media coverage and public opinion to test for constituent recognition of senators' legislative portfolios, and to test for awareness of differences between two senators from the same state. To this end, the results provide support for senatorial differentiation in two ways. First, senators' choices about legislative work are reflected in local media coverage about them, which means that senators' reputations are based on reasonably accurate information. Second, differentiation among senators from the same state is recognized by constituents and reflected in their specific reasons for liking and disliking their senators. In sum, the efforts by senators from the same state to use their *legislative* work to establish unique reputations in their states, controlling for their partisan and ideological affiliation, appear to succeed.

Chapter 5 explores the extent to which senators' efforts to differentiate succeed in attracting distinct sets of constituents; in particular, it provides an overview of the geographic and demographic patterns of electoral support for senators from the same state. This chapter includes a model of geographic representation, which shows how senators start from a particular region in their state and build their core group of support by expanding to other parts of the state. When two senators expand their bases into each other's home territory, they come into direct competition with each other for the support of constituents in that region. Such support is not mutually exclusive, but county-level electoral returns indicate that senators from the same state, and the same party, do not attract equal levels of support in the same counties, controlling for the quality of the challenger. In addition, building on existing demographic analysis, this chapter reveals that senators from the same state attract votes from voters in different ethnic and economic class groups, even when they are from the same party.[4]

Chapter 6 examines the patterns of support from economic interests in the state. Constituents' economic interests can be delineated by their profession, for example, doctor or farmer, or they can be employees of a major industry in the state; in either case they are usually represented by organized groups or political action committees (PACs). Senators try to address the economic interests of their constituents in their legislative portfolios. Because the benefits that senators secure for these economic interests are often narrowly concentrated and easily identifiable, this strategy can be a highly efficient means of attracting both electoral and financial support in the state. Electoral support for a senator that stems from targeted economic benefits may overlap with the senator's partisan or geographic coalition, but in some cases, voters who might not be otherwise disposed favorably toward the senator choose to weigh his efforts to help the state's economic interests more heavily than party affiliation or geographic association. Financial support will come from those who benefit from the senator's efforts, either individually or as part of an industry, in the form of sizable campaign contributions to the reelection effort. In this way, the economic dimension of representation, depending on the diversity of the state's economy, can serve to expand the range of interests for senators to choose from when constructing their legislative portfolios.

Chapter 6 also combines work on how two senators court economic interests in their state with current findings on the determinants and effects of campaign contributions on legislative behavior. First, I construct an alternative measure of "demand behavior" by using legislative activities other than roll-call voting as indicators of senators' attentiveness to state interests. Second, I use patterns of campaign contributions by state-based PACs as a test of whether state economic groups distinguish between two senators from the same state. If senators are succeeding in distinguishing themselves in the area of state economic interests, then we should see state-based PACs contributing more to one senator than the other, depending in large part on which senator appears more

---

[4] See also Jung, Kenny, and Lott (1994).

willing to address their specific interest. The results indicate that state-based PACs do not uniformly contribute the same amount of money to each senator from the state, and some PACs only contribute to one senator and exclude the other. Furthermore, PACs clearly appear to be investing in one senator over the other, but not investing based on party affiliation. Rather, a PAC's contribution decision appears to vary with a senator's institutional position and willingness to address its specific economic interest.

Chapter 7 argues for expanding the framework within which we study Senate representation to incorporate the effects of two-person Senate delegations. The comprehensive model of Senate representation presented here leads to a richer and more accurate understanding of individual Senate behavior. This chapter also suggests that the U.S. Senate has more in common with legislatures in other countries than previously believed. Scholars rarely draw parallels between U.S. legislatures and legislative systems with multimember districts, but viewing the Senate as a multimember-district institution makes it possible to do so. In one way, then, this book may add to the growing body of work that bridges the divide between the study of comparative politics and American legislative institutions.

RESEARCH DESIGN AND METHODS

This book relies on qualitative and quantitative data sets that are drawn from a number of sources. The sample of senators that is used includes all senators who held office during the years 1987–1992, with additional references to senators who held office in subsequent years. Because this study explores the multiple facets of Senate representation, data were collected to measure legislative behavior, media coverage, public opinion, and campaign contributions, using the senator as the unit of analysis. Indicators of legislative behavior include committee assignments and positions, roll-call votes, bill and amendment sponsorship, and bill and amendment cosponsorship. (The names of the Senate committees used here conform to the names used during the time period 1987–1992.) Patterns of media coverage are measured by the number and content of newspaper articles about senators taken from local newspapers in a sample of ten states. Public opinion of senators is taken directly from the open-ended like and dislike questions in the 1988-1990-1992 pooled Senate Election Study. The data on campaign contributions were taken from Federal Election Commission records for the same time period. A description of each specific data set is included in the chapter in which it is used, and the definition of the variables that are used in the quantitative analysis is included in appendix A.

The qualitative data used in this book come primarily from personal interviews with Senate staff members on legislative agenda formation. The interviews were conducted over the course of August 1991 to January 1993. To measure elite opinion of senators among members of the media in their states, I sent a mailed survey to newspaper editors and reporters; the bulk of the information from respondents is used in qualitative form, and a copy of the questionnaire is included in appendix B. Lastly, selected newspaper articles were collected as part of case studies to illustrate how specific variables influence dual representation in particular states.[5]

[5] In some cases, the newspaper articles used in case studies were written more recently than 1992.

Chapter 1

A THEORY OF DUAL REPRESENTATION

> The Founding Fathers made a decision that there should be
> two senators from every state. That is not my fault.
> *(Senator Robert Torricelli (D-NJ) on why he and*
> *his senior Democratic colleague, Senator Frank Lautenberg*
> *(D-NJ), compete with each other over issues and publicity)*[1]

FOR THOSE who believe that the framers of the Constitution constructed the Senate as a legislative arena in which states would be represented as units, two senators from the same state should conceivably be more alike than they are different. For example, the two senators from New Jersey, Senator Lautenberg and Senator Torricelli, share the same party affiliation and are therefore likely to draw from the same set of core partisan supporters. As such, the two senators increase the likelihood that they will attract financial support and endorsements from the same set of interest groups in the state. Presumably, the two senators share an equal obligation to serve the same set of state interests so that New Jersey is given its proper voice in the Senate. Therefore, we would expect them to cooperate and function as a team to ensure that New Jersey voters have as much national influence as possible.

One might argue that the degree of similarity between senators from the same state may in fact vary with characteristics of their state. For instance, a state with a competitive partisan distribution of voters may produce two senators from opposing parties, which would result in different roll-call voting records. States that have larger populations are likely to have a greater number of economic interests and a more diverse set of policy opinions than states with smaller populations. Senators from larger states have a larger universe of interests to choose from when they construct their legislative portfolios than their small-state counterparts, which makes it less likely that large state senators will overlap in their legislative choices. However, even taking into account variation in state characteristics, the common expectation would still be that senators from the same state should build legislative portfolios around the same set of issues and concerns.

[1] Dao (1998, A31).

But the reality of Senate representation is that senators from the same state construct individual representational agendas that, for the most part, do not overlap. This pattern of behavior would not come as a surprise if our conception of Senate representation were more comprehensive. The nature of Senate representation is not merely the correlation between the partisan, ideological, or economic preferences of a majority of constituents and a single senator's legislative behavior. Instead, there is a range of preferences over issues, and distinct interests that are held by constituents, who may or may not be part of a majority at any given time. At the same time, there are two senators who are assigned the equal responsibility of serving the state, which in essence establishes a dynamic of competition between them. Senate representation could therefore be more accurately measured if it were viewed as "dual representation" — the product of decisions made by each senator in the context of a two-member delegation.

Throughout this book, I will argue that the differences that we observe between senators from the same state are an outgrowth of electoral and institutional forces that encourage senators to adopt divergent representational agendas. Indeed, the origins of dual representation can be traced back to the institutional designs of the framers of the Constitution. The initial mandate of the United States Senate, as set forth by the framers, was to be a bulwark against the more local, and more populist, tendencies of the House of Representatives. Edmund Randolph, a delegate to the Federal Convention of 1787 from Virginia, stated it this way:

> If he was to give an opinion as to the number of the second branch, he should say that it ought to be much smaller than that of the first; so small as to be exempt from the passionate proceedings to which numerous assemblies are liable. He observed that the general object was to provide a cure for the evils under which the United States labored; that in tracing these evils back to their origin, every man had found it in the turbulence and follies of democracy; that some check therefore was to be sought for, against this tendency of our governments, and that a good Senate seemed more likely to answer the purpose.[2]

The bulk of the debate about the Senate during the ratification of the Constitution focused on how to structure the Senate to accomplish this goal.

Two elements received the most attention from the convention delegates: the mode of election to the Senate, and the size of the Senate. In the very early stages of the debate on the Senate, the conception of the

---

[2] Edmund Randolph, May 31, 1787, as quoted in Farrand (1966, 51).

senator as representing an entire state had not yet taken shape. The delegates conceived of the Senate more as a counterweight to the House than as an institution that would explicitly preserve states' rights.[3] In discussing the mode of election, then, the delegates emphasized the goal of getting the "best" men who would be least subject to popular passions. If either the House or the Executive chose senators, the ability of the Senate to act as a check in the federal government would be severely limited. If senators were chosen by popular election, then the chamber would look too similar to the House, which would defeat the purpose of its existence. At the end of the debate, the delegates concluded that the best way to insulate the Senate was to have indirect elections by state legislatures; such a system would have the added benefit of awarding states the power over appointments to the Senate, which would give the states a voice in national affairs.

As for the size of the Senate, there were two questions to be answered, one considerably more contentious than the other. The first question was the mode of apportionment in the Senate, as compared to the House of Representatives. The debate over apportionment in the House and Senate has been well documented, and the solution is commonly referred to as the Great Compromise. The Great Compromise allotted seats to the House of Representative based on population size (proportional representation) and gave equal representation to states in the Senate by allotting each state the same number of seats.[4]

Once the question of apportionment between the two chambers was settled, the framers could address the second question about the size of the Senate, which required assigning a precise number of senators for Senate delegations. At this stage of the debate, in July 1787, the actual number of senators that each state would send to the Senate was still undecided. The framers knew they did not want a chamber as large as the House, but they did not want a chamber that was so small that a quorum would be hard to achieve, or worse, that it would be easily corruptible by particular interests.

Remarkably, the delegates spent very little time (a single day) discussing the number of senators that would comprise a Senate delegation.[5] On July 23 Gouverneur Morris, a delegate from Pennsylvania, and Rufus King, a delegate from Massachusetts, proposed that "the representatives of the second branch consist of _____ members from each

---

[3] Ibid., 48–54.

[4] Farrand (1966, 1: 444–558; 2: 1–20) (June 28–July 16, 1787). The three-fifths compromise occurred after the adoption of apportionment by population in the House.

[5] There was a discussion of the number of senators prior to this, but in the context of proportional representation in the Senate.

State, who shall vote per capita" (Farrand 1966, 2:94–95). Morris suggested that there should be three senators from each state, because with two senators the quorum would only be fourteen, which was too small a body to have such institutional power in the federal system. Nathanial Ghorum, a delegate from Massachusetts, argued that two was sufficient for the purpose of deciding "on peace & war &c. which he expected would be vested in the 2nd branch" (ibid.). In addition, he noted that more states would be added to the union, which would steadily increase the size of the Senate. Because the Senate was supposed to be the more deliberative of the two chambers, being too large would interfere with its capacity to function as it should. The motion to approve three senators for every state failed by a vote of 9 to 1, and the motion to approve two senators for every state was then unanimously agreed upon.

There was even less discussion on the assignment of per capita voting rights in the Senate. Only one person, Alexander Martin, a delegate from North Carolina, commented on the fact that per capita voting "depart[ed] from the idea of the States being represented in the 2nd branch," and only one state, Maryland, voted against the measure (ibid., 94). If senators were supposed to represent states as "units," insofar as the smaller states would guard against encroachment by larger states, we would have expected each state delegation to be awarded a single vote. But as the noted historian Gordon Wood (1998, 524–36) points out, there was far from unanimous agreement that the states should be represented as units in the Senate. On the contrary, the Federalists argued that the Senate was a national body in essence, and that it was designed to check the inclinations of the more populist House, not to be a protector of states' rights per se. During subsequent debates, the Federalists incorporated state sovereignty into their campaign for ratification only insofar as they argued that equal apportionment in the Senate protected smaller states from encroachment by larger states (ibid., 553–62). By granting senators their own individual voting powers, the delegates loosened the responsibility of senators to represent their state as a single entity. Senators were still expected to address state interests, but, with individual voting power, each senator could respond to the state and influence national policy as an individual, not as part of a political unit.

Though the framers apparently discounted the effects of the number of senators, so long as it was equal across states, the choice of two Senate seats per state turned out to have a major impact on the selection of senators by state legislatures. In his dissertation on the founding of the Senate, Roy Swanstrom (1988) uses archival evidence to show that when state legislatures elected the first senators to the Senate, they chose individuals who would be beholden to different interests, for example, agricultural versus commercial, in the state.[6] In the case of Maryland and Pennsylvania he writes:

> In choosing their first U.S. Senators, several of the legislatures took particular pains to divide the two Senate seats between major geographical or economic divisions within their States. In Maryland, a resolution of the general assembly provided that one Senator was to be from the east shore and the other from the west. . . . In Pennsylvania, the financier Robert Morris of Philadelphia was balanced by Maclay from the agricultural Harrisburg area. "Every Pennsylvanian," said the Pennsylvania Gazette, "must feel a high satisfaction in this respectable representation of the landed and commercial interests of this State." (Ibid., 31)[7]

> Obviously, Morris and Maclay could not both be speaking for Pennsylvania as a political entity but spoke, rather, for conflicting social and economic elements within their state. (Ibid., 172)

The members of state legislatures clearly had a choice in selecting their senators: they could have treated the delegation as a unit and selected two men who would both be accountable to the same set of majority opinions and interests. Instead, state legislators made use of the fact that they had a pair of senators to send to the Senate as a means of balancing internal divisions—economic and political—within the state.

According to Swanstrom, even with high turnover in the early years of the Senate, both in state legislatures and in the U.S. Senate, divided state delegations persisted. Senators from the same state frequently took opposing sides in Senate debates and split their votes on major issues. Swanstrom notes that in the "4th Congress, five states—Georgia, New Hampshire, New York, South Carolina and Vermont—split their vote on every issue." In addition to economic divisions, he points out that ideological divisions also existed within the first Senate delegations: "John Langdon . . . was an ardent Hamiltonian during his first years in the Senate, but as time went on he became more and more identified with the Republican cause. This put him on the opposite side of the fence from that of Samuel Livermore, his Federalist colleague from New Hampshire, in vote after vote in the Senate. (Ibid.) In sending senators with contrasting economic and political viewpoints to the Senate, states

---

[6] In fact, one of the first fights that state legislatures had over the Senate was how to vote for senators—jointly as one body or separately. This in itself might have produced different candidates for Senate seats. The disputes were such that Congress ultimately enacted a law that required separate voting by the houses of the state legislatures, and joint-session voting if the results were different (Swanstrom 1988, 30).

[7] Swanstrom also provides examples from Georgia, North Carolina, South Carolina, and New York.

could achieve a broader scope of representation at the national level than if they had chosen to treat their Senate delegation as a single entity.

Over time, candidates for the Senate formed alliances with different coalitions in state legislatures to secure their candidacy. Even when state legislatures changed their membership, new coalitions could form around newly placed dividing lines within the legislature, thereby maintaining the incentive for Senate candidates to present themselves as alternatives to the other senator who held office at the time. This way, candidates for the Senate, and members of the state legislature, each responded to the two-person structure of Senate delegations in ways that sustained differences along partisan, geographic, or economic lines.

The original design of the Senate, and the unintended consequences of that design, suggest that a more complex conception of representation should govern the study of Senate behavior. The allotment of two seats to every state, coupled with individual voting rights, was initially proposed to ensure that the Senate is a nationally oriented chamber. It was supposed to be large enough to prevent corruption, removed enough to act against the "popular will," but small enough to discuss and debate the issues that came before the federal government. But this is where the framers and state legislatures diverged in their understanding of the Senate. The framers wanted the Senate to be comprised of the "best men" from each state who would be educated enough, and responsible enough, to act in the best interests of the country. State legislatures wanted to send the "best men" to the Senate not only to govern the nation, but also to represent the diverse interests in the state. Hence, judging the representative goals and performance of senators based on a conception of a single set of state opinions and interests is too simplistic. From the very first session of the Senate, senators from the same state were encouraged to contrast their records, and the two senators, taken as a pair, represented the diverse balance of interests and opinions in the state.

ELECTORAL STRUCTURES AND DIFFERENTIATION

The key thing to remember about the relationship between senators and their state legislatures is that there was no right of recall or other form of punishment for ignoring their wishes. The only enforcement mechanism was reelection to the Senate, and that occurred only every six years. That meant that a senator who was elected by one state legislature could, and usually did, face a very different legislature six years later (Swift 1996). The uncertainty of a senator's future reelection base within the state legislature provided an incentive to move outside the legislature to the general public for support. In a number of states, a practice known as the "public canvass" emerged, which served as a referendum on future Senate choices by state legislators. Incumbent senators, or candidates for the Senate, would accompany candidates for state legislatures on their campaign trails to extract a pledge of support once the state legislators reached office (Riker 1955, 463). The coupling of candidates for the state legislature and the office of senator subsequently limited state legislators' ability to veer from that pledge once elected. Moreover, it opened up a more direct link between the senator and constituents because constituents now had access to information about their senator from campaigns for the state legislature.

As parties became more and more dominant in the mid 1800s, elections for state legislature became increasingly partisan, which in turn made choices for senators partisan as well (Swift 1996). But even in states with single-party dominance, where the majority party would control the legislature and choose two senators from the same party, the incentive to differentiate across the two senators persisted. Partisanship was an important signal to voters, but it was not the only way in which senators acted on behalf of their states. The opposition party could make the case that having two senators from the same party gave no representation to the minority on any dimension, and since the elections for state legislature and Senate were linked, such an argument might erode the majority party's dominance in the legislature. Consequently, to prevent such a challenge, the majority party would choose senators who differed on other dimensions, economic or geographic, to ensure that the state's entire set of various interests were addressed, beyond simply the range of their party constituency. In this way, even same-party Senate delegations contained a minimum level of diversity.

In states with more competitive partisan distributions, it was more likely that party control within the state legislature would be more balanced and thereby produce a split-party Senate delegation (Powell 1990; Herrick and Thomas 1993; Segura and Nicholson 1995; Brunell and Grofman 1998). Senators who served in split-party delegations faced less pressure to contrast themselves directly with their state colleague because their different party affiliations provided an "automatic" contrast. In these states, candidates for Senate from different parties could rely on a strong party organization to produce winning coalitions for them. Nevertheless, each party had to ensure that its senator possessed a distinct identity that was secure enough to withstand a strong challenge from a competitive opposition party candidate. Such an identity depended in part on producing distinct accomplishments that could extend beyond the reach of his party spectrum; in one way, then, senators from opposite parties would have had the incentive to encroach on each other's territory more than senators from the same party.[8]

With the ratification of the Seventeenth amendment in 1913, which provided for direct election of senators, differentiation between senators from the same state became more a function of their individual choices than of the choices of state legislatures. It was always in the interest of Senate candidates to contrast themselves with each other to win election from state legislatures, but that task increased tenfold with popular elections. State legislatures were, by comparison, very small, and those within the chamber had a fairly high awareness of the activity in the national Senate. When senators were accountable to state legislators, they knew their specific actions were subject to close scrutiny, and subsequent punishment or reward. As Senator Elihu Root put it in 1911 (as quoted in Riker 1955, 469):

> The members of the State legislature . . . are familiar with the incidents and difficulties of legislation. . . . When members of this body have to explain to the State legislature the reasons for their action, they meet minds that are competent and trained for the appreciation of their explanation. The people at large have far less understanding upon the subject that I am now speaking of than their legislature. . . . This will cease to be a deliberative body if every Senator has to convince, to explain to the great body of the people of his State every act he performs and every concession he makes.

With direct elections, senators faced the prospect of selling themselves to a much larger audience of people who were less familiar with the Senate and more likely to rely on general impressions or vague knowledge of Senate candidates to make their choice.

Over time, Senate elections have evolved into a referendum on the incumbent senator's job evaluation or, in open seat races, the future promises of job performance. Senate elections now depend on a confluence of factors, with party often being less influential than national economic conditions or individual candidate characteristics (Abramowitz and Segal 1992). On one hand, this gives senators more control over how they use their legislative agendas to build electoral coalitions. On the other hand, the decline of party voting can make it more difficult for senators to secure strong support and increase the extent to which senators from the same state actually compete with each other. Senators from the same state can rely on a core group of party supporters, but

[8] There was a substantial amount of conflict surrounding choices for the Senate in state legislatures, especially in states with competitive parties, but even in states with single-party control. In some cases around the beginning of the twentieth century, Senate seats were left vacant because the legislature could not agree (Haynes 1960).

that core comprises a smaller share of their reelection coalition than in past years. The pressures to expand a reelection coalition beyond party affiliation are therefore greater than before, which increases the likelihood that the reelection coalitions for senators from the same state will overlap with each other, regardless of party. Since the two senators do not run against each other, this may not seem like such a large problem. However, if one senator successfully serves the interests of a coalition of voters, the other senator will find it more difficult to shore up or "deepen" his or her support among those same voters (Jung, Kenny, and Lott 1994). Just as it did in the nineteenth century, this will leave that senator more vulnerable to an opposition candidate who will try to build an alternative majority coalition.[9] Consequently, senators from both same-party and split-party states will try to build distinct electoral coalitions.

Historically, then, the pattern of choices by state legislatures in the first forty years of the Senate — that is, electing senators from different regional, economic, or ideological backgrounds — established a precedent for Senate representation that has not drastically changed since then. States were never really viewed as whole or complete units, and therefore two senators from the same state would hardly be expected to address the same opinions or interests because that was not their job. Clearly, some states may have less diversity than others and thus require less differentiation between the two senators. In all cases, though, senators from the same state are part of a two-member delegation, the consequence of which is the broadest representation possible for the disparate interests of the state.

FOUR DIMENSIONS OF SENATE REPRESENTATION

As Sinclair (1989) has demonstrated, the job of the modern senator has become increasingly complicated in the latter part of the twentieth century. The size of the federal government has grown substantially, thus increasing the number of programs that directly affect states. Accompanying the growth in the federal government, the number of national and state-based interest groups has grown as well. While this provides

[9] The recent Senate race in Massachusetts provides a good illustration of this problem. Senator John Kerry (D) serves with a state colleague, Senator Edward Kennedy (D), who has forged a major reputation in a diverse number of issue areas. Taking advantage of the increased party competitiveness in Massachusetts, Governor William Weld mounted a strong challenge to Senator Kerry by attracting part of the Democratic party base in combination with liberal Republicans. Senator Kerry prevailed in a close election, and most people attributed his victory to presidential coattails rather than his individual strength. See Zuckerman (1997).

senators with a potentially larger source of electoral and campaign support, it also increases the number of issues and political actors to which senators are responsible. In addition, senators are more reliant on media coverage for the necessary publicity to build their reputation; unfortunately for senators, more media coverage can also mean more scrutiny. In short, senators are expected to do more and cover more issue areas and still be focused, effective advocates for their states.

Senators balance the requirements of their office by representing their state in a multidimensional fashion, consisting of four interlinked levels: partisan/ideological, economic, geographic, and stylistic. A senator's portfolio comprises the decisions he makes on each of these dimensions, forming the foundation for a comprehensive "Senate reputation." In forming this reputation, a senator will often balance his actions on one dimension against those on another dimension. For example, one legislative director interviewed for this study described how his senator offset an unpopular policy position by emphasizing his attentiveness to local interests and visiting his state more often:

> Gun control and pro-choice are two issues about which [Senator] Daschle feels very strongly and which are not always popular in his state. The NRA is a very powerful force in certain parts of South Dakota. [Senator] Daschle has to work very hard to counter that influence. He does so by emphasizing constituent service, especially personal visits back to the state. A personal visit can go a long way to countering a bad vote. A guy in rural South Dakota who opposes gun control might vote against Daschle but if Daschle goes to visit his farm, he might be more impressed with his visit and forget about his gun control stance.[10]

As this quote illustrates, successful representation requires a careful balance of the senator's personality and policy positions with the partisan balance, economic interests, and policy positions of the state.

The most easily identifiable element of Senate representation is partisan affiliation, which is intrinsically linked with ideology. As opposed to the other elements, partisan affiliation is completely fixed: a senator is either a Republican or a Democrat upon taking office. The part that fluctuates is ideology: over the course of a six-year term in office, a senator can cast votes in such a way as to qualify his partisan affiliation with a more flexible ideological identification, such as liberal Republican or conservative Democrat. This flexibility enables senators to represent a wider constituency than that defined by party identification alone.

---

[10] Personal interview with staff member. This interview took place before Senator Daschle became Senate minority leader in 1995.

Economic interests are defined as major employers or business concerns in the state, and they can be regionally concentrated or spread throughout the state.[11] The size of the interest or industry is important, but only relative to the overall size of the state's economy. Senators represent these interests by casting votes on favorable national policies, but also by seeking legislated benefits for these interests. For a senator to receive an electoral payoff, the benefits should be sufficiently targeted to the industry. It is in this way that senators most resemble House members in their efforts to appear locally attentive.

The geographical element to Senate representation is similar to that proposed by Fenno (1978) in that the entire state is considered a potential electoral base. In staking out policy positions, a senator not only considers the median voter within his party, but also seeks to expand a partisan base to the more broad geographic base (Fenno 1996). A senator will build on a preexisting regional base (usually the origin of the senator's political career) and appeal to voters in other parts of the state by adopting specific ideological or policy positions, such as being pro-immigration in south Texas, or proposing targeted legislative initiatives that provide concentrated benefits to a county.[12] As such, geographical representation often includes the economic dimension of representation because most economic interests have a statewide impact, through employment and tax revenues.

The fourth element of Senate representation is governing style. In his series of books on individual senators, Fenno provides a glimpse of how senators adopt different governing styles, at home and in Washington (Fenno 1989, 1990, 1991, 1992). Governing style is a function of the interaction between a state's political culture and population size and the senator's prior legislative experience and individual personality. The most common delineation of governing style is "national" versus "constituency." This delineation is misleading insofar as every senator faces the pressure of being both national and constituency oriented. All senators are required to vote on bills that come before the Senate, and their Senate reputations will be built in part on their national policy positions. Depending on the character of the state, senators may emphasize one outlook over the other. In some states, constituents may be concerned primarily with economic interests, such as oil or agriculture; in other states, where economic interests are more diverse and less "land locked," constituents may be more concerned with national policy positions. A senator has a great deal of leeway in forging a stylistic reputa-

---

[11] An economic interest in a state can be a major employer or merely generate large tax revenues as a result of doing business in the state.

[12] For an excellent illustrative example, see Fenno (1996, 293).

tion and can mold it to meet what he perceives to be constituent preferences in governing styles.

INSTITUTIONAL OPPORTUNITIES AND CONSTRAINTS IN SENATE REPRESENTATION

Every senator faces the pressure to distinguish himself within a body of one hundred equals in order to build an independent and easily identifiable reputation; it is this reputation that serves as the core of the senator's reelection efforts (Dexter 1969; Fenno 1996). Senators cannot merely randomly choose issues to address; they are accountable to the voters of their state who are concerned with specific issues and interests. In their first year, freshman senators generally adjust to the Senate as an institution, choosing which issues will be the foundation of their first term, and deciding which legislative tools they will use to formulate their agenda.[13] They seek out open territory — issue areas in which they can build a name for themselves, in and outside the Senate, that have not already been co-opted by another member. In doing so, senators rely most heavily on their prior experience, personal interests, campaign promises, and state concerns as the bases for legislative initiatives. They use these factors as the guidelines for seeking particular committee assignments, introducing bills, and offering amendments (Schiller 1995). The logical strategy for any freshman senator is to transform an existing reputation in the state into a broader reputation as a senator, but it is done in a constrained environment.

The most immediate constraint a freshman senator faces is that there is another equally powerful senator — the state colleague — who is also responsible for representing the state. Because Senate elections are staggered by two, four, or six years, one senator almost always enters the Senate facing a senior colleague who has already begun to build a reputation. The importance of staggered elections depends heavily on the number of years that divide the two senators. If the two senators from the same state are only two or four years apart, then the incentives to differentiate may not be as great. At those early stages of a Senate career, reputations are not yet firmly established, and therefore the costs of encroaching on the senior senator's territory are not as great for the junior senator.

The environmental constraints on all senators, but especially newly elected senators, resemble the same types of limitations posited by Gray and Lowery (1995) about state-based interest groups. Based on biolog-

---

[13] For a general examination of the behavior of freshman senators, see Levy (1996).

ical theories of population ecology, they argue that the number of interest groups will be limited to the amount of resources and available
"space" that exists in an issue area for a particular group in a state.
Those groups that are the most adaptive and competitive survive (ibid.,
9). In the same way, junior senators must try to find a sustainable niche
for themselves, relative to their states, but the number of available issues that will be relevant to their states is finite and limited by the
choices of the more senior senator from that state.

Consequently, if a junior senator faces a senior colleague who has
been in office for more than one term, encroachment into the senior
senator's territory becomes expensive. The senior senator will have been
reelected based, in large part, on a reputation as an effective senator in
specific issue areas. The senior senator will also have built successful
relationships with key local actors, such as reporters, issue activists,
campaign contributors, and interest groups. If the junior senator does
decide to specialize in areas similar to a more senior colleague, based on
preexisting interests or experience, the junior person faces higher costs
of reputation building because of the senior colleague's established visibility in the Senate in those areas. The effects of seniority within a Senate delegation are most obvious in cases where the senior senator has
secured a committee chair or ranking position on a committee. Faced
with that kind of constraint, pursuing similar issue areas is clearly an
inefficient strategy. In making these early choices about the content of
their first-term agendas, senators must therefore pay close heed to
which committee assignments and issue areas are already the property
of the other senator from their state.

A case in point is Senator Jim Jeffords (R-VT), who was elected in
1988. Senator Jeffords had specialized in dairy issues, a crucial interest
for his state, during his career as a member of the House of Representatives. In the House he could distinguish his role in dairy issues because
he was the only member of the House from Vermont. In the Senate all
that changed. When he arrived in the Senate, he found that the issue
had been taken by Senator Leahy (D-VT), who was fourteen years his
senior. As Senator Jeff[ord's legislative director put it:

> Senator Jeffords is considered something of an expert in the dairy industry.
> He was the ranking member on the House Subcommittee on Livestock, Dairy
> and Poultry. He probably knew more about the dairy industry than anyone in
> the House. Also Vermont is dairy and dairy is about it in the state. It has a big
> impact on other industries in the state like tourism. . . . The thing about dairy
> is that with Senator Leahy being Chairman of Agriculture, there is not too
> much mileage to be gained in spending time on that issue.

Because of his more senior state colleague's prominence on dairy issues,
Senator Jeffords, the former House member, had to focus on other is-

sues in order to forge a reputation for himself *as a senator*. It is not the case that Senator Jeffords ignores dairy as an issue, but rather that he cannot afford to make dairy a major part of his legislative portfolio because he will be overshadowed by Senator Leahy. Instead, Senator Jeffords chose to take a seat on the Environment and Public Works Committee, where he has actively addressed environmental issues, which are also important to his state, and the Labor and Human Resources Committee, where he assumed the chairmanship in January 1997.

As Ross Baker (1998) points out, the nature of the constraints on pursuing specific issues and committee assignments that freshman senators face vis-à-vis their state colleague depends on whether the two senators share the same party affiliation. If so, then the two senators will be similar on the partisan/ideological dimension of representation, and the pressure to differentiate will be even greater than it is for senators from opposite parties. Take the extreme example of the two senators from California, Dianne Feinstein (D) and Barbara Boxer (D), who were both elected to the Senate in 1992. Senator Feinstein had been mayor of San Francisco, and Senator Boxer had served in the House of Representatives for ten years. According to her legislative director, when Senator Boxer arrived in the Senate she was careful to adjust her legislative portfolio to her new institutional and electoral position: "The environment and the economy were campaign issues in both Boxer's and Feinstein's campaigns. We had a very unusual situation . . . with two races in the same state. So in the beginning of the year, Boxer and Feinstein agreed that Feinstein would do the desert protection bills (to protect the Mojave desert) and Boxer would do the ocean protection bill." Although such a coordinated division of labor is rare in most Senate delegations, the two senators from California realized that having been elected simultaneously, neither senator would have an opportunity to establish a unique reputation if they both addressed the same exact set of issues. Subsequently, Senator Feinstein, technically considered the senior senator, joined the Judiciary Committee and the Appropriations Committee, while Senator Boxer joined the Budget Committee, the Environment and Public Works Committee, and the Banking Committee.

The institutional structure of the Senate itself also encourages contrast between same-party senators. In both the Democratic and Republican party caucuses, there are rules that prohibit two senators from the same party and the same state from sitting on the same committee together.[14] This institutional practice of awarding senators from the same state different committee assignments predates the existence of parties

---

[14] On committees with narrow jurisdictions, such as the Select Committee on Indian Affairs, this rule may be waived.

in the Senate. Even in the earliest years of the Senate, when standing committees were just emerging, senators from the same state were not assigned to the same committee (Swift 1996, 74). A freshman senator who enters a state delegation with a same-party colleague must therefore adjust his preferences for committee assignments to those not already taken by the senior senator. In most cases of split-party delegations, a newly elected senator is technically free to pursue the same committee assignment(s) as a state colleague because senators from opposite parties can sit on the same committee. The structure of the Senate thereby creates an environment that encourages greater differentiation in legislative work among same-party senators than split-party senators from the same state.

REPUTATIONS AND COALITION BUILDING AMONG THE MEDIA, INTEREST GROUPS, AND CONSTITUENTS

Taken together, staggered elections, which create the junior/senior distinction between senators from the same state, and caucus rules governing committee assignments can explain the initial decisions by senators from the same state to contrast themselves with each other. But these factors do not provide a complete explanation for why differences between same-state senators persist over time. Other factors, including media behavior, constituent recognition, and institutional seniority, can be shown to encourage senators from the same state to preserve their distinct legislative portfolios. Media coverage is often the primary way that senators establish reputations as legislators, nationally and in their home states. Cook (1989) details the efforts expended by legislators to attract media attention: press releases, editorial boards, town meetings, and so on. Hess (1981, 1986) found that reporters seek out senators who are considered experts on an issue via their committee jurisdiction because those senators are viewed as the key policy makers in that issue area. Consequently, senators' success in attracting publicity, nationally and in their state, may depend in large part on their institutional position.

Once the media establishes contact with particular senators in issue areas, the tendency is to return to the same senators over and over again. This media bias toward the usual suspects makes it difficult for a senator to establish a foundation in issue areas normally associated with a state colleague, even if the opportunity arises within the Senate to do so. Moreover, since two senators occupy the same media market, it is inherently difficult for both of them to obtain solo press coverage; that is, any article on Senate votes will mention both senators. Therefore, there is a strong incentive for a senator to distinguish legislative accomplishments in the Senate from those of a state colleague in order to attract individual publicity in the state.

State-based interest groups and campaign contributors also help to sustain existing differences in legislative specialization between senators from the same state. Interest groups are commonly classified as ideological or economic. Ideological interest groups usually base their support decisions on senators' partisan roll-call voting record; in this way, a senator's maximum potential support from an ideological interest group (and affiliated PAC) is conditional on party affiliation. For interest groups that represent economic concerns in the state, and their affiliated PACs, the decision rule is different. State-based economic interest groups are more locally focused; they are likely to seek narrow and concentrated benefits, and they will seek to spend as little as possible on lobbying and campaign contributions to secure desired benefits.

The first logical place for these economic interest groups to turn for help is to their own senators, who have a representational interest, if not obligation, to address their concerns, regardless of the senator's partisan affiliation. Even though there is an equal amount of potential support from economic interest groups in a state for both senators, it is a rational strategy for these groups to support more strongly the senator who is most attentive to their concerns. Consequently, senators from the same state will use their separate committee assignments and institutional positions actively to seek support from different economic interest groups in the state. Over time, senators from the same state will establish themselves in specific and separate issue areas, and these interest groups will allocate their support accordingly. It is in this way that economic diversity in a state interacts with the institutional structure in the Senate to encourage different representational agendas among senators from the same state.

In turn, constituents' evaluations of their senators are often based on what they read in the newspaper or see on television, or learn from educational efforts by interest groups. Sinclair (1990) found that national media coverage increases senators' exposure to their constituents and usually results in more favorable evaluations. Franklin (1993) and Sinclair both demonstrate that the higher a constituent's education and attention to media, the more likely the constituent is able to name specific reasons for liking or disliking his senators. Once both senators have used their legislative agendas to become associated with success in distinct issue areas among the media and constituents, it makes little sense for them to branch out into each other's territory.

Once a senator establishes a reputation among the media, interest groups, and constituents that is grounded in specific issues or economic interests, the price of switching committee assignments rises considerably in terms of seniority and legislative power. A senator invests a certain amount of time and energy specializing, forging working relationships with other senators, and ultimately proving to be an effective legislator in particular issue areas. As a senator becomes more senior on a committee, this investment becomes more and more substantial. Consider a hypothetical example of two senators from Nebraska: Senator A has established himself as an expert in defense and rural transportation issues based on his seats on the Armed Services and Commerce committees, and Senator B has specialized in agriculture issues. Senator B leaves the Senate, leaving the opportunity open for Senator A to move to the Agriculture Committee and begin to forge a new reputation as an agriculture specialist. The calculation that Senator A makes is that the costs of starting over and loss in seniority outweigh any possible benefits from switching committee assignments, despite the fact that agriculture is a major interest in his state. Subsequently, Senator C, who replaced Senator B, takes the seat on the Agriculture Committee and thereby maintains the differentiation within the delegation.

As senators from the same state share office for longer periods of time, one might expect the pressure to build distinct identities to subside. In fact, senators continue to feel constrained by their state colleague, especially if one senator has a lot of seniority over the other one. A case in point is that of Alaska, where senator Ted Stevens (R-AK) is senior to Senator Frank Murkowski (R-AK) by twelve years. Despite the fact that the Senator Murkowski has been in office for eighteen years, he still remains overshadowed by Senator Stevens. One Alaska reporter described their relationship this way:

> For Stevens and Murkowski, the problems between them arise not just because of party, but because of the varying lengths of tenure. Stevens has been around since 1968, Murkowski since 1980. But the Republican turnover has meant that Murkowski has progressed steadily up the seniority chart, culminating in the chairmanship of the Energy and Natural Resources Committee — arguably the most influential panel in the Senate on a federal land state. Still, Alaskans are used . . . to Stevens getting things done for them. . . . Stevens thinks he has the better ideas and the better strategy for accomplish[ing] the state's goals. Murkowski, always looking for ways to climb out from behind Stevens' shadow, tries to strike out on his own only to find that there are subtle roadblocks and sniping coming from his colleague.[15]

[15] Included in a written response to a survey to newspaper editors and reporters conducted by the author.

Simply stated then, senators from the same state continuously take into account the behavior of their state colleague when constructing their Senate agendas.

INCENTIVES TO APPEAR COOPERATIVE WITHIN SENATE DELEGATIONS

Although I have argued that senators from the same state pursue different representational agendas, clearly there will be occasions when the legislative activities of the two senators will overlap. This most often occurs in issue areas in which the state has a strong and direct interest, or when a large industry is particularly affected by legislation. The greater the economic impact of the industry on the state as a whole, the more likely it is that both senators will pay attention to it. Senators from the same state have a choice: they can work together (cooperate) on an issue, or they can each address the issue separately (compete), as part of their individual legislative portfolios. As one might expect, there is a range of cooperation that exists across Senate delegations. For example, in the time period under study here, cosponsorship across Senate delegations ranged from 0 to 65 percent. Cooperation may depend on several variables, including the partisan composition of the delegation, state size, and the number of years both senators have served together.

Most senators choose to cooperate with each other on state interests when the benefits of cooperation exceed those of competition, and the costs are fewer. Cooperation most frequently takes the form of cosponsorship of bills and amendments, cosigned letters to the administration, and, in very rare cases, joint filibusters. In most cases, one senator is viewed as the leader, or champion, of a particular state interest, which discourages the other senator from encroaching on that territory. Presuming the senator is an effective champion, the state will receive benefits targeted specifically toward that interest; but at the same time, the other senator from the state cannot afford to appear completely inattentive to a major state economic interest. Cosponsorship enables the less active member of the Senate delegation to appear attentive to a particular state interest or constituency without having to expend time and energy on the issue itself (Krehbiel 1995; Kessler and Krehbiel 1996). One staff member provided an example of this type of symbolic cooperation:

> What we won't do is a bill by Senator Smith to exempt New Hampshire shipyard workers from Maine income tax because they worked in Maine but

lived in New Hampshire. We told them [shipworkers] that it was an unwinn-
able fight and that we would not do it. Senator Rudman was dragged into
cosponsoring the bill because he is from the state. Senator Smith offered it as
an amendment on the floor and got 22 votes. Senator Rudman would not go
to the floor and speak on it because he knew that it would get slaughtered. He
thought it was a waste of time.

Although Senator Smith was clearly the advocate for the shipbuilders in
this case, by cosponsoring the bill, Senator Rudman helped insulate
himself from charges that he ignored that state industry.

One way, then, that cosponsorship creates a free-rider problem is that
the senator who is less active on behalf of a state interest, or state issues
more generally, can benefit from the more active efforts of the other
senator. There is no formal Senate rule that prohibits a senator from
cosponsoring a bill, so a senator could not prevent a state colleague
from cosponsoring bills. The question then becomes, why not cosponsor all of a state colleague's bills, or at least all bills that address state
concerns? The answer is that joint efforts blur the lines of distinction
between the two senators and thus make independent reputation building more difficult. An excerpt taken from a newspaper article about two
Republican senators from Missouri illustrates the potential downside of
cooperation: "Bond calls Danforth 'a very close friend,' and has been
working with Missouri's senior senator on a range of issues. While that
cooperation has often been productive, some critics contend that Bond
too often relies on Danforth to take the lead. . . . Such criticism of Bond
rankles Rep. Bill Emerson (R-MO) who . . . says that 'I don't see him
taking the lead on national issues. But on issues affecting Missouri,
when I've asked Bond to be there, he's been there' " (Koenig 1989).

If every bill or amendment that one senator sponsors to address state
interests is cosponsored by a state colleague, there is little opportunity
to demonstrate distinct and separate achievements. Even if the governing styles of the senators are opposite — for example, one senator is perceived as the "constituency" senator and the other is a "national" senator — neither one can afford to have a state colleague as a cosponsor on
every bill and amendment. Subsequently, reciprocity, or fear of retalia-
tion, limits the extent to which senators from the same state seek to
cosponsor each other's bills and amendments.

Senators from the same state have an incentive to maintain this reciprocity because it allows each senator to appear attentive to issues that
are important in the state while preserving their independent reputation.
Moreover, such cooperation makes the pair of senators appear more
effective for the state in general and will likely result in positive coverage in the local media. Though senators want to ensure that the ratio of

media coverage is balanced in favor of solo coverage, they also benefit from publicity for joint efforts.

The element of personal relationships should also be considered in explaining the extent of cooperation between senators from the same state. Not surprisingly, a number of Senate delegations consist of senators who have fought for the same Senate seat, in a primary or in a general election. If they have not actually competed for the same Senate seat, senators may have faced each other in elections for other state-based offices. On average, about 40 percent of the Senate has served in the House, and another 30 percent of the Senate has held some other statewide office, such as governor or attorney general. The chances are therefore high that the two senators will have interacted at some point in state politics. Depending on the nature and tone of that interaction, the two senators may be more or less inclined to work together; and as each senator accrues more seniority in the Senate, the effects of those prior interactions on cooperation may diminish over time.

Conclusion

To establish a comprehensive understanding of Senate representation, senators should be studied in the context in which they operate — which, is in fact, as members of a two-person delegation. From the very earliest Senate, incentives existed for senators from the same state to compete with one another to build independent reputations and bases of support in the state. The modern-day implications of such competition are that senators from the same state build distinct electoral coalitions by representing diverse and separate interests in the state.

Importantly, studying the interactions of senators from the same state illustrates how senators represent their states on multiple dimensions. It bears repeating here that casting roll-call votes along party lines is just one of several dimensions on which senators build their careers. Senators also construct individual legislative portfolios that address the geographic and economic interests of their constituents. When senators are choosing which interests to represent, they react to the choices of their state colleague and subsequently choose different areas of issue specialization in order to build unique and easily identifiable reputations.

As I will show in subsequent chapters, these choices are framed by the partisan composition of the Senate delegation. When two senators share the same party affiliation, they tend to differentiate far more in their legislative activity than their split-party counterparts. If we merely measured Senate representation along a single dimension, partisanship, we would mistakenly conclude that senators from the same party attend to, and seek the support from, the same exact interest groups, campaign contributors, and voters. I argue that while there is natural overlap between senators who share the same partisan affiliation, such a conclusion would lead us to underestimate the number of interests and constituents who are represented in a unified Senate delegation. Likewise, we would also underestimate the extent to which senators from opposite parties overlap and cooperate in their legislative work.

More generally, all senators, regardless of shared or split-party affiliation, face the pressure of contrasting themselves with their state colleague. There is a limited and finite amount of political resources in any state, and senators wield different powers to address those interests based on their seniority, committee assignments, and majority or minority status. The logical strategy for any successful Senate career is to differentiate from a state colleague in a number of areas in order to maximize support from specific groups and constituencies in the state. When we assess the "quality" of a senator's efforts to represent a state, we should keep in mind that because there are two Senate seats for every state, a single senator has never been expected to represent all interests and opinions in a state. A more realistic framework to use when studying the Senate is to analyze the individual representational agendas of senators, recognizing that they function, in conflict and cooperation, as a pair.

Chapter 2

CHOOSING DIFFERENT INSTITUTIONAL
CAREER PATHS

FROM 1968 TO 1992, Senator Mark Hatfield (R) and Senator Robert Packwood (R) represented the state of Oregon. Senator Hatfield had been governor of Oregon until his election to the Senate in 1966. Senator Packwood had been in the private sector until his election to the Senate in 1968. As one would expect of two senators from the same party, their voting records over time were quite similar, as one newspaper reporter from Oregon remarked: "They both had moderate Republican voting records. They differed significantly on military/defense/foreign policy issues quite a bit; Packwood was considerably more hawkish . . . but I suspect, that day to day they voted more alike than apart."[1] But on legislative issues, the two senators purposely sought out different areas to form the basis for their legislative portfolios. During their first terms in office, Senator Hatfield joined the Commerce Committee and the Interior Committee; Senator Packwood joined the Labor and Human Resources Committee and the Banking Committee. By the end of their second terms in office, both senators had secured committee assignments that they would keep unchanged for the remainder of their time in the Senate. Senator Hatfield sat on the Appropriations and Energy committees; Senator Packwood, on the Finance and Commerce committees. A newspaper reporter described how each senator used his committee assignments to associate himself with particular legislative accomplishments that differed from those of his state colleague:

> Packwood and Hatfield, over time, carved out niches that rarely met and almost never overlapped. Hatfield was the details guy on Oregon issues; Packwood was more national, focusing on broader issues like taxation matters that almost never had any direct connection to a specific Oregon constituency.
>
> . . . [Hatfield] has brought a number of projects to the state and was the most influential player on natural resource issues and on the fate of the Bonneville Power Administration. Packwood played a big role in the 1986 tax reform bill and was influential as one of the first pro-choice members of the U.S. Senate. He was also a big champion of deregulation on the Commerce Com-

[1] Mail survey response from a local Oregon newspaper reporter.

mittee. . . . He became a big champion of the timber industry . . . and passed out tax benefits to local firms through his position on the Finance Committee. Overall I would say Packwood had fewer accomplishments for Oregon and was more of a lone wolf.[2]

One newspaper article, written when both senators retired from the Senate, offered a similar contrast between the two:

> Mark O. Hatfield's name is plastered all over the state, from the marine research center in Newport to a sewage treatment pond in Bend. Bob Packwood's mark is more diffuse, tucked away in tax codes and tariff agreements. Without question, the two senators, both moderate Republicans, have reached the upper rungs of Beltway politics. With the GOP in the majority, Hatfield at the head of the Appropriations Committee and Packwood . . . leader of the Finance Committee, Oregon has enjoyed an unmatched potential for attention.
>
> . . . Across the state, there are examples of Hatfield's ability to make the cash flow in Oregon's direction. Sewers, airports, roads and research centers are among the projects that Hatfield helped engineer. . . . Packwood also held a senior position on the Commerce Committee. Commerce, together with Finance, with its oversight of U.S. trade tariffs, sanctions and agreements, enhanced Packwood's ability to sway international policies and to help Oregon businesses involved in foreign trade and farm exports. (Hill and Suo 1995, A6)

Even though both senators were perceived to share the same partisan and ideological stances, they succeeded in establishing stark contrasts between themselves in the areas of their legislative specialty and their governing styles:

> Hatfield much more sought the role of the statesman and for many years was popular with his colleagues and remains so with the voters back home. He is a quite an unusual blend of political philosophies (his hero is Herbert Hoover; he's also as much of a pacifist as there is in the Senate) and of old-fashioned political pork barreling. Packwood was much more of the political innovator . . . pioneering the way on direct mail. In many ways, it was like Packwood ran a law firm in Washington that had the contract to represent the state. Their staffs in particular often feuded.[3]

Each senator had separate issues that comprised his legislative portfolio, and their relations with one another were not always cordial (Baker 1998, 7), but as with many other Senate delegations, the two senators came together when issues important to Oregon arose in the Senate:

---

[2] Ibid.
[3] Mail survey response from a local Oregon newspaper editor.

"Generally they seemed to carve out different areas of influence, but I can't think of any gigantic local issues where they fought each other. On occasion, I think they did have some disputes over natural resource issues (such as what areas should become wilderness and how to approach them tactically). . . . They tended to work together on state issues. On national stuff, I think they mostly ran in different circles."[4] The behavior of these senators typifies the strategies that senators from the same party and the same state adopt in building their Senate careers and representing their states. They overcame the inherent obstacle of sharing the same party to establish unique identities as legislators. They did so by choosing alternate committee assignments in the Senate, investing their energies in separate issue areas over time, and diversifying the interests of their state such that they could each claim credit for representing Oregon while simultaneously building strong reputations as effective senators.

In contrast to Senators Hatfield and Packwood, who are from the same party, Florida is currently represented by a split-party delegation consisting of a Democrat, Bob Graham, and a Republican, Connie Mack.[5] Senator Graham, the senior senator, was elected to the Senate in 1986 after serving two terms as governor; and Senator Mack, the junior senator, was elected after serving six years in the U.S. House of Representatives. The facts that they were from opposite parties and each had held prior elected office mitigated the necessity for them to contrast themselves with each other in the way that Senators Hatfield and Packwood did. A 1989 St. Petersburg newspaper article exemplifies the way that the media reinforced the differences between the two senators by detailing their roll-call voting records:

> Florida's two U.S. Senators this year voted the opposite way on nine of 16 key issues identified by Congressional Quarterly Magazine. The disagreements between Sen. Bob Graham, D-Fla., and Senator Connie Mack, R-Fla., usually came on partisan fights. . . . Among the areas of disagreement, Mack voted for Bush's nomination of John Tower as Secretary of Defense, while Graham opposed Tower. . . . The two also disagreed on a pay raise and ethics reform package. Graham was for it, Mack against it. They split on a proposed constitutional amendment banning desecration of the U.S. flag: Graham was against it, Mack was for it. And they went separate ways on an effort by Sen. Jesse

[4] Ibid.

[5] Senator Graham came to the Senate in 1986 directly from the governor's mansion and served for two years with Senator Lawton Chiles (D) before the latter retired in 1988. Because Senator Graham was a strong and popular governor in Florida, he had fewer difficulties in establishing a reputation in the Senate. Moreover, he did not face the prolonged same-party competition with his senior colleague, Chiles, because Chiles announced his intention to retire from the Senate a year after Graham arrived.

Helms, R-NC, to ban use of federal money on "obscene or indecent" art. Graham voted to kill the Helms amendment and Mack voted for it. They also disagreed on what is perhaps the biggest ticket item of the year: the way to borrow $50 billion to bail out the savings and loan industry. Mack favored keeping bailout costs "off-budget," meaning the borrowed money would not be counted toward the government's deficit. Graham voted against the off-budget proposal, saying the maneuver would cost taxpayers even more money. (Dahl, December 17, 1989)

But in other legislative activities, such as committee assignments and bill sponsorship, the two senators overlap far more than the two senators from Oregon did. Although Senator Graham had been a member of the Senate Banking Committee for two years, Senator Mack chose to join the same committee when he arrived in the Senate. The reason is simple: banking is a major economic interest concentrated in the heavily populated city of Miami. But as the above excerpt notes, the two senators *disagreed* on a major provision of the savings-and-loan bailout legislation on ideological grounds. Moreover, each senator belongs to additional committees: in particular, Senator Mack spends much of his legislative time focused on the Foreign Relations Committee, and Senator Graham focuses on the Environment and Public Works Committee. As such, the two senators maintain distinct legislative portfolios but overlap and cooperate in more issue areas than is typical of same-party senators, as the quotes below illustrate:

Off the Senate floor, the two have made a point of publicizing their ability to work together, especially on issues important to Florida. (Ibid.)

Graham and Mack have . . . formed an amiable team. The two . . . senators are sponsoring bills together. They're lobbying other senators and the Bush administration to get more money for Florida's needs. . . . Both of them see the need to work together to help their state. They concede that there's a political reward for putting policy-making over partisanship. . . . Graham and Mack started working together [right after Mack was sworn in]. Mack signed on as a cosponsor to a Graham bill seeking up to $20 million in refugee aid. Graham became a cosponsor of a Mack bill that is intended to help Florida's taxpayers get their "fair share" of the government serves they help finance. They've joined the rest of the Florida congressional delegation in asking for a ban on oil drilling off Florida's coast, and they have jointly written a letter to President Bush asking that refugee aid not be cut.

The senators' staffs also communicate regularly. . . . All this coziness will go only so far, however. Mack . . . says he will remain true to the conservative philosophies that placed him in the far right wing of the U.S. Republican membership. Graham is likely to support the Democratic majority in the Senate on most key votes. (Dahl, April 12, 1989)

In this way, the capacity to differentiate their roll-call voting records based on partisan and ideological grounds provides sufficient flexibility to the Florida senators that they can address some of the same issue areas without fear of losing their individual name recognition.

All four of the senators featured in the cases above—Hatfield, Packwood, Graham, and Mack—faced similar pressures to establish themselves as legislators who effectively represented their states, individually and as a team. These senators made decisions about the fundamental construction of their Senate careers in the context of who their state colleague was, and to what extent they could afford to overlap in their legislative portfolios without obfuscating their individual achievements. Senators from the same party face a greater challenge in this regard and are thus less likely to overlap in their legislative agendas than their split-party counterparts.

COMPONENTS OF LEGISLATIVE AGENDAS

In chapter 1 I argued that senators seek to establish reputations that clearly associate them with specific legislative and political accomplishments. There are a number of legislative tools available to senators to form these reputations, inside and outside the institution, over which they have varying degrees of control. For the purposes of this study, I examine roll-call voting, committee selection, bill sponsorship and cosponsorship, and amendment sponsorship and cosponsorship. I have selected these tools as measures of legislative behavior because they are the activities on which senators spend the majority of their legislative time and resources. Roll-call voting is the means by which senators demonstrate their preferences over a wide range of policy outcomes. Through committee selection senators specialize their individual legislative work, both to serve their state and to establish their reputations (Fenno 1973; Evans 1991; Hall 1996). Bill and amendment sponsorship is a more clearly defined way that senators stake out their individual policy positions and issue territory in the context of efforts to enact legislation (Schiller 1995). Bill and amendment cosponsorship allow a senator to claim credit for collective action by a group of senators to enact legislation (Wilson and Young 1997). Taken as a whole, these activities comprise the basis for senators' representational agendas, and they ultimately serve as the basis for reelection campaign platforms (Sellers 1998).

ROLL-CALL VOTING

The extent to which senators can control these activities varies considerably with the activity itself. Senators cannot look to roll-call voting as a means of identifying themselves with particular issues, or as a specific type of senator, because the roll-call voting agenda is usually determined by forces outside their individual control, namely, party and committee leaders. A senator enters the Senate under a party label, with an ideology that exists concurrently with party and which can range from liberal to conservative, and he is responsive to a perceived electoral coalition with fixed interests. Senators can try to cast votes that shore up their bases and attract new support, but the extent to which they can stray from partisan and ideological identification, and objective state interests, in their voting behavior is minimal (Bullock and Brady 1983; J. Wright 1985; G. Wright 1989; Shapiro et al., 1990; Grofman, Griffin, and Berry 1995).[6] For reputation-building purposes, then, senators are limited by their party identification and ideological disposition on roll-call votes.

Compounding the inflexibility of roll-call voting is the fact that there is another senator from the same state who is casting votes at the same time. The work of Jung, Kenny, and Lott (1994) and Uslaner (1999) each address the voting patterns of senators as members of a two-person delegation. They argue that senators from the same state use roll-call votes to draw contrasts with each other and to shore up distinct electoral coalitions. Using roll-call data from the 98th Congress (1983–1984), Jung, Kenny, and Lott argue that senators purposely differentiate their roll-call voting to attract support from different constituencies in their state. They demonstrate that the differences between the ADA ratings for senators from the same state can be explained by differences in the characteristics of the senators' electoral coalitions. They argue that the balance of competing interests in a state will therefore result in a split-party or same-party delegation, and senators' responsiveness to their electoral coalitions sustains that differentiation. Even in states where one party dominates, senators from the state will seek to attract distinct core electoral constituencies. Uslaner performs a similar analysis, using data from 1977–1978 to demonstrate that senators from the

---

[6] There is considerable debate in the congressional literature on the amount of shirking that occurs in the Senate, where senators vote their own personal ideology as opposed to that of their constituents. Kalt and Zupan (1990) argue that considerable shirking occurs, while Uslaner (1999) argues that shirking does not occur that often. Either way, senators will consistently vote in one direction according to their own preferences or those of their constituents, and therefore their voting record remains constant.

same state and the same party will cast opposite roll-call votes at times according to their ideological disposition. In this way, senators from the same party and the same state can carve distinct niches within their state party constituency.

The drawback of these two analyses is that they afford senators with more flexibility in choosing roll-call vote positions than truly exists. In reality, the partisan affiliation of senators is fixed or exogenous once they are elected to the Senate. Ideology is more flexible, but only within a confined range. Democrats may vote with Republicans some of the time, but if they stray too far from the party line, they will face a primary challenge or, worse, be beaten by the Republican in the general election. In some cases, for example, Senator Richard Shelby (R-AL) and Senator Ben Nighthorse-Campbell (R-CO), Democratic senators have been known to switch party affiliations in mid-term, but those instances are rare. Moreover, Jung, Kenny, and Lott suggest that representation and reputation building is unidimensional, as if the only important component of a senator's reputation is his roll-call voting record.

To test for the amount of flexibility in roll-call voting that senators really have, outside party, ideology, and objective economic interests, I performed a simple regression analysis on Senate roll-call data from 1991–1992. Unlike Jung, Kenny, and Lott and Uslaner, I divided the total number of votes into party votes and nonparty votes. By definition, party votes are those votes on which a majority of one party casts votes against the majority of the other party. In most party-line votes, the divisions between the majority and minority party are well known prior to the time that the vote is taken. In many instances, senators are reminded of these party divisions on the Senate floor by the party leaders and the floor managers of a bill prior to casting their votes.

Because a majority of senators vote according to their partisan affiliation on party-line votes, the opportunity to move outside party boundaries lies mostly in nonparty votes. For senators from the same state and the same party, nonparty votes provide much greater opportunity to contrast themselves than on party votes. Consequently, if senators do use roll-call votes to expand their electoral coalition on other dimensions, we should see this behavior manifest itself on nonparty roll-call votes. Specifically we should see that sharing the same party affiliation exerts a negative effect on the overall unity of Senate delegation voting, but that for senators from different parties, nonparty votes provide the opportunity to cross party lines and vote together.

For the 102nd Congress, 280 of the 550 roll-call votes cast (51 percent) in the Senate were party votes; the remaining 270 votes (49 percent) were nonparty votes, which comprised unanimous, ideological, and distributive votes. In the first analysis of roll-call voting in Senate delegations, I deleted the 55 unanimous votes and looked at a total of 215 *nonparty* roll-call votes cast over the two-year period (table 2.1).[7] I regressed the percent of nonparty votes on which two senators from the same state agreed on combinations of the following variables: shared party affiliation, a dummy variable coded 1 if the senator shared the same party affiliation and 0 if not; difference in ideology, measured by the absolute difference in Americans for Democratic Action ratings for the two senators; state population size, the number of state residents; size of the state's economy, the number of industries in the state generating $500 million or more; reelection, a dummy variable coded 1 if one of the senators was up for reelection in 1991–1992; and shared party

TABLE 2.1
Roll-Call Voting Unity within Senate Delegations, 1991–1992: Nonparty Votes

Variable	Model 1	Model 2	Model 3	Model 4
Intercept	.77***	.86***	.77***	.86***
	(.02)	(.03)	(.03)	(.03)
Shared party affiliation	.07**		.07**	
	(.04)		(.04)	
Ideological difference		−.002**		−.002**
		(.001)		(.000)
State population size	−.001	.000		
	(.002)	(.002)		
Size of state economy			−.0002	−.0000
			(.0007)	(.0006)
Reelection		−.01		.01
		(.03)		(.03)
Shared party/Reelection	−.01		−.01	
	(.04)		(.04)	
Adj. R²	.07	.17	.08	.17
prob > F	.09	.01	.09	.01
N	50	50	50	50

Standard errors in parentheses. ***Statistically significant at .01, one-tailed test. **Statistically significant at .05, one-tailed test. *Statistically significant at .10, one-tailed test.

[7] Sixty-eight percent of these nonparty votes could be defined as distributive votes (e.g., transportation formulas), and the remaining 32 percent as ideological (e.g., death penalty).

affiliation and seeking reelection, an interactive term to measure the effects of running for reelection as a member of a same-party Senate delegation.

Both state size and the size of the state's economy are included as measures of the diversity of a state, on the assumption that senators from more heterogeneous states are more likely to vote differently. But because a good portion of these votes were cast on distributive policies, there is the contrary expectation that senators will vote together to preserve state interests on distributive bills, rather than pushing senators from the same state apart. Voting patterns on distributive legislation should reflect some element of universalistic logrolling (Shepsle 1979; Shepsle and Weingast 1981), thereby producing higher than expected agreement on these types of bills across states. Within states, because senators represent the interest of their state on distributive legislation, delegation unity should be much higher on these types of votes than on party-line votes. In fact, senators from the same state voted in agreement on 81 percent of these votes.

Although the literature is divided on whether senators change their voting behavior in the last year of their reelection cycle (Lott and Reed 1989; Wright and Berkman 1986; Bernstein 1991, 1992), I included the reelection variable to control for reelection effects on Senate delegation behavior. The expectation is that when one senator from a delegation is seeking reelection, he will try to attract the widest potential base of support; in the case of same-party senators, that may mean additional efforts to differentiate. For split-party delegations then, we would expect the opposite effect, in that the senator who is running for reelection is likely to vote more often with his opposite party state colleague.

The results of the regression analysis predicting delegation unity on nonparty roll-call votes indicate that party and ideology exert a significant effect on roll-call voting, even on votes that are not perceived as party votes. Senators from the same state and same party vote together 7 percent more of the time than senators from split-party states. The same is true of ideology: when the difference in ideology is substituted for party affiliation, it also shows that the bigger the gap between senators from the same state in ideology, the less they are likely to vote together. The diversity of a state, measured in population and economic terms, does not appear to influence whether two senators will vote together or not. The latter result is not surprising in that senators from the same state are likely to vote together in the state's objective economic interest as it relates to the way that funds are distributed in the legislation. Therefore, variation in state size across states should not affect the extent of unity within Senate delegations.

When I regressed the percent agreement of all votes cast, party and nonparty, in the 102nd Congress on the same combinations of variables, the results indicated that senators from the same party and the same state vote together 32 percent more than senators from split parties (table 2.2). The analysis also suggests that when one senator from a same-party delegation is up for reelection, he will vote with a state colleague 5 percent less often than at other times. The latter result may be evidence that when senators run for reelection, they shift their voting slightly to attract more widespread support from new interest groups, or regional bases.

Roll-call voting does not afford senators an opportunity to move beyond their party, ideology, or the state's economic interest in cultivating their reputation as a senator. On party-line votes, senators vote according to the stated goals of their party, as we saw in the cases of the senators from Oregon and Florida; on nonparty votes, the bulk of which are on distributive legislation, senators vote their state's eco-

TABLE 2.2
Roll-Call Voting Unity within Senate Delegations, 1991–1992: All Votes

Variable	Model 1	Model 2	Model 3	Model 4
Intercept	.53***	.85***	.53***	.85***
	(.02)	(.03)	(.03)	(.03)
Shared party affiliation	.32***		.32***	
	(.03)		(.03)	
Ideological difference		−.005***		−.005***
		(.000)	(.000)	
State population size	−.001	.0006		
	(.002)	(.0023)		
Size of state economy			−.0003	.0002
			(.0007)	(.0006)
Reelection		−.002		−.002
		(.025)		(.025)
Shared party/Reelection	−.05*		−.05*	
	(.03)		(.03)	
Adj. R^2	.75	.76	.75	.77
prob > F	.0001	.0001	.0001	.0001
N	50	50	50	50

Standard errors in parentheses. ***Statistically significant at .01, one-tailed test. **Statistically significant at .05, one-tailed test. *Statistically significant at .10, one-tailed test.

nomic interest. Votes on highly ideological issues, such as abortion or the death penalty, provide slightly more flexibility to senators to distinguish themselves in ways that are different from their party affiliation. But even with ideological voting, once a senator casts a vote on one side or the other of a contentious issue, he is unlikely to change that position over the course of a term.

Because senators' roll-call behavior is likely to be delineated by partisan, ideological, or state interests, they turn to other legislative instruments, such as committee selection and bill and amendment sponsorship and cosponsorship, over which they have considerably greater control, to establish unique identities. Senators from the same state but opposite parties clearly possess an advantage in staking out contrasts with their state colleagues over senators from the same state and the same party, who face a much greater obstacle in creating separate identities. Consequently, in examining senators' decisions on which committees to join, which issues to address through bill and amendment sponsorship, and, more generally, how to build a unique identity, we would expect to find that same-party senators purposely diverge much more than their split-party colleagues.

INDICATORS OF LEGISLATIVE AGENDA SETTING

Committee Selection

Committee selection is arguably the most important choice for legislators when building a reputation. Senators concentrate the bulk of their time and resources on issues that fall within their committee jurisdictions because that is where they have the most direct control over legislation (Evans 1991; Hall 1996; Deering and Smith 1997). Although senators possess direct access to legislating on the Senate floor, success rates for floor activity are very limited and as such, the floor is the least efficient arena for reputation building (Sinclair 1989, 1990; Smith 1989). In general, committee assignments remain the central foundation of individual agenda setting in the Senate.

There are few formal rules that guide the committee assignment process in the Senate. Most senators receive the assignments that they request based on availability and seniority, with one important exception: senators from the same state and the same party are not seated on the same committees. Although this is not a formal Senate rule, it is a guiding principle in both the Democratic and Republican caucuses in the Senate. As I noted in chapter 1, the practice of separating senators from the same state has been in place since the inception of the committee system in the early nineteenth century (Swift 1996). Then, as now, the reason for such a practice appears to have been grounded in preventing any one state from dominating a committee. This is especially important in those committees that have direct jurisdiction over distributive policy, such as Agriculture or Environment and Public Works. Senators from the same state are likely to agree on basic policies and formulas that benefit their state, and they might therefore skew the balance of the committee in their state's favor. As parties emerged as strong coordination tools in the House and the Senate, party caucuses became the forum for deciding on committee assignments, and thus the practice of splitting up Senate delegations became the purview of the party, rather than the institution as a whole. The result is that senators from the same state and the same party are much less likely to be assigned to the same committee than are senators from the same state and opposite parties.

In the time period under study here, the patterns of committee membership conform to expectations generated by the institutional rules governing the process of committee assignment. I examined the membership patterns of sixty-eight pairs of senators over six years on seventeen standing committees of the Senate.[8] Of the sixty-eight different pairs of senators that held office during this time, only seventeen shared at least one committee assignment; of these, fifteen pairs were from split-party delegations. Table 2.3 lists the senators and their shared committee assignments: of the total number of senators who shared committee assignments, only three pairs did so for the entire six-year period, six pairs did so for four years, and eight pairs did so for just two years.

Moreover, even when senators do share a similar committee assignment, they are rarely from the same party. In this time period, there are only two same-party delegations that share the same committee assignment, and they are on the Select Committee on Indian Affairs, which is not considered a major committee in the Senate. One can conclude, therefore, that there is an effective and operative prohibition on senators from the same state and the same party sitting on the same major committee. Same-state senators who do sit on the same committee are from opposing parties, as in the example of the senators from Florida, and more often than not they adopt opposing policy positions on the same issues. The consistently low frequency of shared committee assignments is solid evidence that most senators from the same state are unwilling to incur the costs of direct competition with their state colleague over specific policy areas.

---

[8] I excluded all select and special committees except for the Select Committee on Indian Affairs.

TABLE 2.3
Shared Committee Assignments within Senate Delegations, 1987–1992

State	Senator	Committee	Years
Arizona	DeConcini (D) McCain (R)	Select Committee on Indian Affairs	6
Colorado	Armstrong (R)	Banking	4
	Wirth (D)	Budget	4
	Wirth (D) Brown (R)	Budget	2
Connecticut	Weicker (R) Dodd (D)	Labor and Human Resources	2
Florida	Graham (D) Mack (R)	Banking	4
Hawaii	Inouye (D) Akaka (D)	Select Committee on Indian Affairs	2
Iowa	Grassley (R)	Appropriations	4
	Harkin (D)	Agriculture	2
Kentucky	Ford (D)	Energy	4
	McConnell (R)	Rules	4
Maine	Cohen (R) Mitchell (D)	Government Affairs	2
Minnesota	Durenberger (R) Wellstone (D)	Labor and Human Resources	2
Montana	Baucus (D) Burns (R)	Small Business	4
New Mexico	Domenici (R) Bingaman (D)	Energy	6
North Carolina	Helms (R) Sanford (D)	Foreign Relations	6
North Dakota	Burdick (D) Conrad (D)	Select Committee on Indian Affairs	4
Washington	Evans (R) Adams (D)	Foreign Relations	2
	Adams (D) Gorton (R)	Appropriations	2
Wisconsin	Proxmire (D) Kasten (R)	Appropriations	2

Source: Congressional Quarterly Almanac (Washington, DC: Congressional Quarterly Press, 1987–1992); Michael Barone and Grant Ujifusa, *Almanac of American Politics* (Washington, DC: National Journal, 1988, 1990, 1992).

To explore more rigorously the determinants of committee selection within a Senate delegation, I constructed a simple logistic regression model. I used a dichotomous dependent variable (shared committee assignment or not) and regressed it on whether the senators had the same or opposite party affiliations, the number of years separating the two senators, the population size of the senators' state, and the number of years that the senators shared federal office together, for example, the junior senator was a member of the House of Representatives prior to being elected senator.

Each pair of senators is treated independently for the three congresses, for two reasons. First, there was a shift in the actual membership in eighteen delegations during this period, and second, committee assignments are reevaluated at the outset of a new Congress. In this study, twenty-seven senators (from twenty-three states) either switched or added a committee assignment between the 100th and 101st Congress, and eighteen senators (from sixteen states) did so between the 101st and 102nd congresses. Because senators can shift committee assignments every two years, there is constant opportunity to join a new committee. As I noted in chapter 1, there are costs and benefits to switching committee assignments. On the one hand, over time, senators accrue seniority and expertise in their committee jurisdictions, which serve as important tools for building a reputation as an effective lawmaker in those issue areas. On the other hand, some committees are more important and powerful than others — either generally (such as Finance) or with respect to a major state interest (such as Energy). A senator has to weigh the costs of giving up an established reputation in one committee against the potential future benefits of another committee. Part of that calculation, I argue, is whether the senator's state colleague sits on the committee, and whether the costs of encroaching on a state colleague's territory are worth bearing.

Sharing a party affiliation, because of informal Senate rules, is expected to exert a negative influence over whether senators from the same state share the same committee assignments. The number of years separating the two senators might also influence committee assignment, in the following way. Senators seek different committee assignments in order to establish distinct reputations among their constituents. A senator who has been reelected at least once has presumably succeeded in this regard and is likely to be identified with his or her committee issues. The fact that the sitting incumbent senator is well established relieves some of the pressure on the junior colleague to draw distinctions between the two senators, so he or she may calculate that joining the same committee will not impede their efforts to build a reputation. Overall, it still remains an inefficient strategy for a freshman senator to join the same committee as his or her more senior colleague, but the number of years separating the two senators may have a mitigating effect.

The population size of the state may also provide expanded opportunities for a junior senator to pursue different issue areas within the same committee jurisdiction as a more senior colleague because larger states are more likely to benefit from a wider range of federal policies. In addition, in delegations where the two senators have worked together before — for example, congressman and senator, or governor and senator — there may be less inclination on the part of the junior senator to encroach on the senior senator's existing committee jurisdictions. Recall the example of Jeffords and Leahy from Vermont: Senator Jeffords sat on the Agriculture Committee in the House but did not join it in the Senate because Senator Leahy was already chairman. Presumably, then, House members who are elected to the Senate will seek committee assignments that build on their preexisting reputations, but not if their state colleague already occupies a seat on such committees.

The sample mean probability of senators from the same state sitting on the same committee, all else being equal, is 21 percent, or one in five (table 2.4). The results of the analysis indicate that sharing the same party affiliation decreases the probability of sharing a committee assign-

TABLE 2.4
Shared Committee Assignment within Senate Delegations, 1987–1992
(logistic regression)

Variable	Coefficient	Change in Probability
Difference in years served	−.08** (.04)	+1%
Shared party affiliation	3.56*** (.75)	−69%
State population size	.09** (.05)	−1%
Number of years as congressional team	−.01 (.06)	NA
Number of cases correctly predicted	85.1%	
−2 Log L	43.540	
prob > χ^2	.0001	
N	150	

Standard errors in parentheses. ***Statistically significant at .01, one-tailed test. **Statistically significant at .05, one-tailed test. *Statistically significant at .10, one-tailed test.

ment by 69 percent; essentially, then, sharing the same party affiliation and the same committee is highly unlikely.

Controlling for same- or split-party affiliation, the number of years in seniority that separate the two senators does allow for some leeway in joining the same committee, albeit very small. For every year that separates the two senators, the chances that they will sit on the same committee increase by 1 percent. But in real terms, even for senators from the same state who are two terms apart (twelve years) but share the same party affiliation, the chances of sitting on the same committee are still very low. State size, as measured by population, exerts a small negative effect on sharing the same committee assignment: for every increase in one million people, the chances of two senators sitting on the same committee decrease by 1 percent. Sharing federal office together does not seem to influence committee selection in any direction; the coefficient is substantively and significantly insignificant.

In the preceding analysis, I counted the Appropriations Committee as a single committee assignment, but one could argue that the power of subcommittees in the Senate Appropriations Committee warrants examination of the subcommittee assignments therein.[9] For those states that have a senator on the Appropriations Committee, there is still potential for overlap between the jurisdictions of the senator's Appropriations Committee subcommittees and the issues that fall under the jurisdiction of the other senator's authorizing committees.[9] For example, one senator from a "farm" state may join the Agriculture Committee, while his colleague may join the Appropriations Subcommittee on Agriculture. The two senators technically sit on different committees, but they can both use their committee assignments to address the same relevant state issue. In other words, senators on the Appropriations Committee might use their subcommittee jurisdictions to encroach on the territory of their state colleague. If there is such overlap, I expect to find that the causality is unidirectional, measured as the Appropriations member's response to the jurisdictions of the state colleague's committees, not the other way around. Indeed, given all the factors that go into committee selection, it is hard to imagine that a senator would choose committee assignments, the anchor of a legislative program, based on the subcommittee assignments of a state colleague who sits on the Appropriations Committee.

Furthermore, there are strong reasons to believe that senators view the opportunities presented by the Appropriations Committee quite dif-

---

[9] Technically, all appropriated money is "authorized to be appropriated," but I am using the distinction as the power of the Appropriations Committee to set the actual amount of money that can be spent for a federal program as opposed to all other committees that do not possess the same direct control over discretionary federal outlays.

ferently from those presented by authorizing committees when building their reputations as legislators. If a senator wants to make a name as a legislator in a particular policy area, he will seek membership on the authorizing committee that oversees that area (Deering and Smith 1997; Schiller 1995). If a senator wants to make a name by securing federal funds for the state, he will seek membership on the Appropriations Committee. It is the nature of committee work in the Appropriations Committee that distinguishes itself from work in authorizing committees. One legislative director depicted a senator's work on the committee this way: "We don't introduce bills in the Appropriations Committee. We work on New Hampshire projects and fight some legislative battles. . . . the work of the Appropriations Committee is straightforward—basically dollar amounts. That is easier to deal with than writing legislation—language to design a program." Another legislative director emphasized the importance of the Appropriations Committee for achieving recognition in the state: "For reelection what usually counts is his work on the Appropriations Committee—that is where you get stuff that's important to the state. At the end of the Appropriations process, we have a huge list of things that we get for the state. The Appropriations Committee is a double-edged sword between wasting taxpayer money or helping the state. You need to get your story out about what you did." For many senators, then, a seat on the Senate Appropriations Committee is an instrument to show constituents they are effectively serving the state by securing federal funds.

Moreover, there is little evidence to show that senators use their Appropriations sub-committee assignments to establish an identity as a policymaker in a specific issue area. In fact, senators often seek membership on a subcommittee that covers the same jurisdictions as the authorizing committees that they sit on in an effort to hold a monopoly over both the funding of a program and the policy content of the program (Evans 1991, 142). Senator Hatfield pursued such a strategy when he joined the Appropriations Committee by seeking a seat on the Energy Subcommittee, to correspond to his seat on the Senate Energy Committee. Of the five subcommittee assignments Senator Hatfield received, only one overlapped with Senator Packwood's authorizing committee jurisdiction. In that case, Senator Hatfield sat on the Appropriations Committee's Subcommittee on Commerce, State, and Justice, which partly overlapped with Senator Packwood's jurisdictions in the Senate Commerce Committee.

In an effort to gauge the amount of committee overlap between senators from the same state for those states where at least one member sat on the Appropriations Committee, I compared the subcommittee jurisdictions of senators who sat on the Appropriations Committee with the committee assignments of their state colleagues. There are two important caveats to this test. One is that the subcommittee assignment process in the Appropriations Committee is not well documented, so it is difficult to attribute clear, purposeful behavior to subcommittee assignments therein. Seniority and subcommittee availability may be very important in this regard, which reduces a senator's personal control over subcommittee placements. Second, most senators on the Appropriations Committee had an average of five, out of a possible thirteen, subcommittee assignments. Often these subcommittees have jurisdictions that cross the boundaries of several authorizing committees. Therefore, without any purposeful behavior at all, it may be the case that a senator's subcommittee territories will overlap with those of his state colleague.

During the time period of this study, 1987–1992, there were twenty-nine seats on the Senate Appropriations Committee (that number has since been reduced to twenty-eight). The potential for overlap between Appropriations Committee work and authorizing committee work existed for thirty-three pairs of senators (n = 58) from the same states. I divided up the sample of senators into two groups: (1) senators who chose their Appropriations subcommittee assignments after their state colleague had chosen his committee assignments, and (2) senators who chose their authorizing committee assignments after their state colleague had chosen his Appropriations subcommittee assignments.

Table 2.5 lists those junior senators who joined the Appropriations Committee after their more senior colleague had chosen authorizing committee assignments. The extent of overlap is measured from the initial choices senators make about their subcommittee assignments on the Appropriations Committee. The measure itself is the percent of total subcommittee assignments that coincides with the state colleague's authorizing committee jurisdictions, and an additional value of 1 is computed for senators from the same state who both sit on the Appropriations Committee. On average, senators on the Appropriations Committee overlap very little with their state colleagues' committee jurisdictions (.30 out of a possible 2.0). Moreover, the extent to which senators on the Appropriations Committee choose subcommittees to overlap with their other committee assignments is greater in comparison (.21 out of 1.0 or, for comparison, .42 out of 2.0).

Senators who obtain a seat on the Appropriations Committee do not use their subcommittee assignments to build reputations as policymakers per se, or to encroach on the territory of their state colleagues. Therefore, it is unlikely that the reverse causality exists, whereby senators choose their authorizing committee assignments in response to the choices of their state colleagues who sit on Appropriations. Table 2.6

TABLE 2.5
Overlap between Appropriations Subcommittee Assignments and Authorizing
Committees for Senators from Same State[a]

State	Appropriation Member[b]	State Colleague[c]	Overlap[d]	Monopoly[e]
South Carolina	Hollings	Thurmond	.60	.20
New York	D'Amato	Moynihan	.00	.33
Oklahoma	Nickles	Boren	.00	.00
New Jersey	Lautenberg	Bradley	.00	.25
New Mexico	Domenici	Bingaman	.38	.13
Iowa	Harkin (1985)	Grassley	.00	.50
Iowa	Grassley (1987)	Harkin	1.25	.00
Maryland	Mikulski	Sarbanes	.70	.10
Georgia	Fowler	Nunn	.50	.25
Missouri	Bond	Danforth	.00	.50
Nebraska	Kerrey	Exon	.00	.20
Nevada	Reid	Hecht	.25	.00
New Hampshire	Rudman	Humphrey	.25	.40
Texas	Gramm	Bentsen	.25	.00
Vermont	Leahy	Stafford	.00	.20
Wisconsin	Kasten	Proxmire	1.25	.00
Pennsylvania	Specter	Heinz	.10	.00
Utah	Garn	Hatch	.00	.15
Average			.30	.21

[a]Italics denotes split-party delegations.

[b]Senator who went on Appropriations after senior colleague had chosen committee assignments.

[c]Senator who had chosen committee assignments before state colleague chose Appropriations subcommittee assignments.

[d]Ranges between .00 and 2.00; the extent of overlap between the senator's subcommittee assignments and the authorizing committees of state colleague.

[e]Ranges between .00 and 1.00; the extent of overlap between the senator's subcommittee assignments and authorizing committee assignments.

lists those senators who chose their authorizing committee assignments after their state colleague had chosen Appropriations subcommittee assignments. There is minimal overlap between the authorizing committee jurisdictions of senators and the subcommittee jurisdictions of their state colleagues who sit on the Appropriations Committee (.27 out of a possible 2.00). Overall, for both groups of senators, there appears to be little support for the hypothesis that encroachment occurs among Senate delegations between authorizing and appropriating jurisdictions.

In sum, it is clear that senators respond to both institutional rules and individual incentives in seeking out their committee assignments, which

TABLE 2.6
Overlap between Authorizing Committees and Appropriations Subcommittee
Assignments for Senators from Same State[a]

State	State Colleague[b]	Appropriations Member[c]	Overlap[d]	Monopoly[e]
Oregon	Packwood	Hatfield	.20	.00
Arkansas	Pryor	Bumpers	.50	.00
Alaska	Murkowski	Stevens	.33	.00
Tennessee	Gore	Sasser	.20	.00
West Virginia	Rockefeller	Byrd	.25	.00
Arizona	*McCain*	*DeConcini*	.20	.00
Louisiana	Breaux	Johnston	.00	.33
Connecticut	*Dodd*	*Weicker*	.60	.20
Florida	Graham	Chiles	.20	.00
Idaho	Symms	McClure	.00	.25
Mississippi	Lott	Cochran	.20	.40
Nevada	Bryan (1989)	Reid	.00	.00
New Hampshire	Smith (1991)	Rudman	.20	.00
Washington	*Gorton (1989)*	*Adams*	.66	.00
Wisconsin	*Kohl (1989)*	*Kasten*	.20	.20
North Dakota	Conrad	Burdick	.50	.25
Average			.27	.11

[a]Italics denotes split-party delegations.

[b]Senator who chose committee assignments after state colleague had chosen Appropriations subcommittee assignments.

[c]Senator who was on Appropriations Committee when state colleague chose committee assignments.

[d]Ranges between .00 and 2.00; the extent of overlap between the senator's committee assignments and the Appropriations subcommittee assignments of state colleague.

[e]Ranges between .00 and 1.00; the extent of overlap between the senator's Appropriations subcommittee assignments and authorizing committee assignments. This measure presumes an alternative measure of causality in that I am testing to see if senators respond to the Appropriations subcommittee assignments of their state colleagues when choosing their committee assignments.

are a crucial component of their reputations as legislators. A major determinant of a senator's choice of committee assignments is the set of committees to which a state colleague belongs. Not only are senators from the same state and the same party prohibited from sitting on the same committee, even senators from different parties usually choose to join separate committees. When given the chance to alter their committee portfolios by switching or adding committees, senators from the same state persist in maintaining distinct committee assignments.

Bill Sponsorship

Building on committee assignments, there are other indicators of over-lap between two senators from the same state that can serve as mea-sures of the extent to which the two senators pursue the same issue areas. The most visible of these are the number and content of bills that senators sponsor and cosponsor. Bill sponsorship is an important instru-ment that senators use to establish independent reputations as legisla-tors. Senators will use bill sponsorship in several different ways: to stake out issue territory, to enact policy change, and to appear attentive to constituent interests and concerns. The number of bills that senators introduce is a function of the heterogeneity of their state, their com-mittee assignments, their committee positions, and whether they are running for reelection (Schiller 1995). The content of their bills is closely related to their committee jurisdictions and their personal policy interests.

Because bill sponsorship is very strongly determined by committee assignment, and we know that senators from the same state do not generally choose to sit on the same committees, we should not expect to see any considerable overlap in the subject matter of the bills that they sponsor. Still, senators from the same state do represent the same *poten-tial* universe of state economic and geographical interests, and, depend-ing on the number of interests in the state, both senators could use bill sponsorship to address the same important state interests, even symbol-ically. A legislative director provided one such example involving the two senators from Colorado: "The [Rocky Flats Bill] was about the employees at the Rocky Flats nuclear plant. Senator Wirth had a similar bill so the Armed Services Committee took both bills and wrote a new version and included it as part of the FY 1993 DoD Authorization so that is how it got enacted."[10] In this case, Senator Wirth, a Democrat, was a member of the Armed Services Committee, but Senator Brown, a Republican, was not a member. By introducing a similar bill, Senator Brown could also claim credit for acting on an important local interest. In a different instance, the two senators actually compromised between themselves on an acceptable version of a bill that protected Colorado land: "We will re-introduce the Colorado Wilderness bill. Last session we struck a late night compromise with Senator Wirth . . . and it passed the Senate but it did not pass the House. Land exchange is one issue that is generally important to Western states and important locally."[11]

---

[10] Personal interview with legislative staff member.
[11] Ibid.

But the above examples are the exception, not the rule. In the end, encroachment remains an inefficient strategy in the Senate, where compromise is key to passing legislation. Ultimately, even when senators from the same state encroach on each other's territory, the final result is that they receive credit for cooperating in the interest of the state, rather than garnering credit for individual achievement (Obmascik 1991, 1-A).

To compute a simple indicator of encroachment, I divided the number of bills that both senators from the state introduced in the same issue area (which were not cosponsored by the state colleague) by the total number of bills introduced by the two senators.[12] The result indicates that in general there is little overlap between senators from the same state in the content of the bills they introduce; on average, only 5 percent of all bills introduced by senators from the same state addressed similar issue areas.

To explore the systematic determinants of encroachment through bill sponsorship, I regressed the encroachment indicator on variables that explain other forms of overlap within Senate delegation: state size, difference in seniority, shared party affiliation, number of shared committee assignments, and reelection. It was necessary to run two models because two independent variables, shared party affiliation and shared committee assignment, are too highly correlated to be included in the same model.

I found that sharing the same party decreases overlap in bill sponsorship by 5 percent, which is equal to the average amount of overlap in bill sponsorship among all pairs of senators from the same state. In essence, then, there is little or no overlap between senators from the same state and the same party. This result makes sense in light of the fact that senators from the same state and the same party will rarely, if ever, share the same committee assignments, thus the contents of their bills are unlikely to overlap. States where one senator is seeking reelection have more overlap (3 percent) than states without a reelection campaign; and state size exerts a slight positive effect on overlap (.004 percent). When the number of shared committee assignments is substituted into the regression for shared party affiliation, it shows that for each committee assignment that senators from the same state share, the overlap in bill sponsorship increases by 3 percent (table 2.7).

The results in Table 2.7 reinforce two findings about Senate delegations. First, they reiterate the strong role that the party composition of the delegation plays in determining the amount of legislative differentiation within the delegation. Senators from the same state and the same party do not choose to address the same issue areas; senators from the

---

[12] I performed this analysis on all bills introduced in the 101st Congress (1989–1990).

Table 2.7
Bill Sponsorship Overlap within Senate Delegations, 1989–1990

Variable	Model 1	Model 2
Intercept	.04**	.006
	(.02)	(.02)
Difference in years served	−.0002	−.0006
	(.0009)	(.0010)
Shared party affiliation	−.05***	
	(.01)	
Shared committee assignment		.03***
		(.00)
State population size	.004**	.004**
	(.002)	(.002)
Reelection	.03*	.03*
	(.02)	(.02)
Adj. R^2	.24	.14
prob > F	.003	.003
N	50	50

Standard errors in parentheses. ***Statistically significant at .01, one-tailed test. **Statistically significant at .05, one-tailed test. *Statistically significant at .10, one-tailed test.

same state but different parties do encroach on their state colleagues, but even then, the amount of encroachment is very minimal. In general, then, it is reasonable to conclude that when senators construct their bill sponsorship agendas, they do not cross paths with their state colleagues, despite the fact that they both share the same potential universe of state interests.

Cosponsorship

The extent of legislative overlap between two senators from the same state can also be measured by the number of each other's bills and amendments that they cosponsor. As several scholars have noted (Wilson and Young 1997; Krehbiel 1995; Kessler and Krehbiel 1996), the incentives and costs and benefits of cosponsorship differ from individual sponsorship. Senators do not rest the foundation of their legislative record on cosponsored legislation, but they do use it as a means of extending their legislative portfolio without expending a lot of resources on an issue. In the context of Senate delegations, cosponsorship rewards both senators from a state because they can each receive credit for addressing a state issue by supporting one bill, and in some cases for acting as a "team" on behalf of the state. But cosponsorship may reduce the amount of contrast that exists between the two senators and can thus impede senators' efforts to build individual reputations. Therefore, there is a strong incentive for both senators to refrain from cosponsoring the majority of each other's bills.[13]

The extent of cosponsorship between senators from the same state may be a function of the same set of variables that explains overlap in other legislative activity. On average, 26 percent of total number of bills introduced by senators from the same state are cosponsored by both senators. I regressed the percent of cosponsored bills within a Senate delegation on shared party affiliation, difference in seniority, state population size, years as a congressional team, and reelection. If we assume that senators from the same state will cosponsor primarily state-specific bills, then we should find no effect for the shared-party variable. However, senators from the same party and the same state may face greater pressure to cosponsor their colleague's policy-based bills to appear attentive to party goals, as well as state interests. Prior working relationships might also increase cosponsorship for the simple reason that the two senators are likely to have supported initiatives in the past, for example, introducing companion bills in the House and the Senate, which would make them more likely to continue some cooperation in the Senate.

The results of the analysis bear out these expected directions of influence. Sharing the same party affiliation increases cosponsorship within a Senate delegation by 7 percent. Having prior experience in Congress together also increases cosponsorship, but by a smaller amount (.005 percent). State size decreases cosponsorship by .005, which is as we might expect; senators from larger states have a wider range of interests to address through legislation and will therefore have less incentive to cosponsor their state colleague's bills (table 2.8).[14]

---

[13] Whether senators cosponsor each other's bills because they genuinely want to work together to accomplish a goal for the state or because one senator does not want to appear inattentive to a particular interest is impossible to discern from the outside. Either way, the percentage of bills cosponsored within a Senate delegation can be used as an overall indicator of the overlap between senators from the same state.

[14] Interestingly enough, there is a slight twist to the results when the bills that were cosponsored by only the two senators from the state (team bills) are sifted out of the total sample of bills. These team bills represent specific targeted efforts by the two senators to address a local state interest. It appears that there is a moderate and negative correlation ($-.17$) between sharing the same party and the percent of all cosponsored bills that are team bills. A simple regression model predicting the percent of cosponsored bills that were team bills as a function of state size and shared party affiliation indicates that senators

TABLE 2.8
Bill Cosponsorship within Senate Delegations, 1987–1992

Variable	Percent of Bills Cosponsored
Intercept	.23***
	(.03)
Difference in years served	−.0017
	(.0015)
Shared party affiliation	.07***
	(.02)
State population size	−.005***
	(.002)
Number of years as congressional team	.0053**
	(.0026)
One senator running for reelection	.02
	(.02)
Adj. R²	.12
prob > F	.0002
N	150

Standard errors in parentheses. ***Statistically significant at .01, one-tailed test. **Statistically significant at .05, one-tailed test. *Statistically significant at .10, one-tailed test.

The dynamics of amendment cosponsorship are substantively different from bill cosponsorship in several important ways that all might reduce the frequency of cosponsored amendments in Senate delegations. Unlike bills, which can be used proactively to set the legislative agenda for both the sponsor and Senate colleagues, amendments are offered in response to legislation that has come to the Senate floor, usually by way of committees. The legislative history of an amendment is therefore often shorter than a bill, which means the political ramifications and potential support are less frequently known in advance. Moreover, when a senator cosponsors a bill, he can legitimately disavow the bill once it reaches the Senate floor because of the changes it has undergone in committee (Krehbiel 1995). But amendments do not go through com-

from the same party sponsor 6 percent fewer bills as a team than do senators from opposite parties. In other words, senators from the same state but different parties are slightly more likely to work together in sponsoring state-specific bills than senators from the same party.

mittee, and thus it is much more difficult to oppose an amendment on these grounds; therefore, when a senator cosponsors an amendment, he is more committed to vote for it. Considering that the success rate of amendments is only about 30 percent (Smith 1989), the potential costs-to-benefit ratio is much higher on amendments than it is for cosponsored bills. It is not surprising, then, that the overall rate of amendment cosponsorship in Senate delegations is only .10, compared with .26 for the overall rate of bill cosponsorship.

However, there is a link that exists between amendment cosponsorship and bill cosponsorship, and it stems from the relationship between bills and amendments. On average, about 40 percent of senators' amendments are based on the bills they introduce (Schiller 1994). It follows, then, that senators from the same state who cosponsor each other's bills are likely to cosponsor amendments that are based on those bills. Controlling for differences in seniority and reelection, the effects of bill cosponsorship on amendment cosponsorship are considerable. For every percent increase in the rate of bill cosponsorship among Senate delegations, the rate of amendment cosponsorship increases by 19 percent (table 2.9).

Each measure of overlap—shared committee assignments, the percent of cosponsored bills, and the percent of cosponsored amendments—

TABLE 2.9
Amendment Cosponsorship within Senate Delegations, 1987–1992

Variable	Percent of Amendments Cosponsored
Intercept	.12***
	(.02)
Difference in years served	−.0007
	(.0009)
Percent cosponsorship	.19***
	(.05)
One senator running for reelection	.023*
	(.014)
Adj. R^2	.10
prob > F	.0003
N	150

Standard errors in parentheses. ***Statistically significant at .01, one-tailed test. **Statistically significant at .05, one-tailed test. *Statistically significant at .10, one-tailed test.

taps a related but distinct element of legislative representation. As such, these measures can be added up into a summary indicator of the extent to which senators from the same state address the same issue areas, ranging from 0 to 2.44, with an average of .59. Tables 2.10, 2.11, and 2.12 list the Senate delegations, by Congress, with the values of their summary indicator. When the values of the similarity indicator are compared, it is clear that senators in divided party delegations have a great deal more overlap in legislative activity than their unified party counterparts.

The effect of split-party or same-party delegations on legislative similarity is even more pronounced when we look at those delegations whose party composition changed during the period 1987–1992. In general, there is a large shift in legislative overlap when the delegation

TABLE 2.10

Scale of Legislative Similarity within Unified Party Senate Delegations (range of scale .00–2.44)[a]

State	1987–1988	1989–1990	1991–1992
Alabama	.58	.59	.28
Alaska	.46	.35	.54
Arkansas	.34	.41	.44
Georgia	.16	.16	.09
Hawaii	.49	.32	1.67[b]
Idaho	.28	.64	.70[b]
Illinois	.49	.39	.20
Indiana	.17	.19[b]	.35
Kansas	.20	.41	.36
Louisiana	.24	.32	.28
Maryland	.52	.70	.47
Massachusetts	.36	.29	.45
Michigan	.37	.24	.35
Missouri	.73	.48	.67
New Hampshire	.04	.31	.52[b]
New Jersey	.71	.59	.59
Ohio	.30	.14	.16
North Dakota	.31	1.51	1.41[b]
Oregon	.23	.32	.39
Tennessee	.32	.32	.41
Utah	.36	.29	.29
West Virginia	.00	.57	.09
Wyoming	.11	.62	.33

[a]Constructed from the number of same-committee assignments, percent of cosponsored bills, and percent of cosponsored amendments.

[b]Membership of delegation changed, but party composition remained the same.

TABLE 2.11
Scale of Legislative Similarity within Divided Party Senate Delegations (range of scale .00–2.44)[a]

State	1987–1988	1989–1990	1991–1992
Colorado	2.44	1.23	1.26
Kentucky	.02	2.23	2.30
Arizona	1.59	1.22	1.14
Iowa	1.19	1.24	1.19
Maine	1.48	.69	.21
New Mexico	1.86	1.62	1.48
North Carolina	1.11	1.08	1.10
Washington	1.62	.74[b]	1.46
Wisconsin	1.02	.31[b]	.21
California	.27	.21	.18[b]
New York	.27	.31	.30
Oklahoma	.30	.47	.40
Rhode Island	.24	.20	.19
South Carolina	.30	.15	.22
South Dakota	.38	.30	.22
Texas	.10	.30	.15
Vermont	.25	.31[b]	.52
Delaware	.00	.06	.06

[a]Constructed from the number of same-committee assignments, percent of cosponsored bills, and percent of cosponsored amendments.

[b]Membership of delegation changed, but party composition stayed the same.

changes party composition. For example, the similarity rating for Connecticut decreased when the delegation changed from split-party to same-party. In contrast, the similarity rating for Florida increased when its delegation changed from same-party to split-party.

Variation in this composite measure of overlap can be more rigorously explained by the same set of variables that explain individual measures of overlap. Table 2.13 displays the results of the regression analysis predicting the similarity rating for a state as a function of differences in seniority, shared party affiliation, state population size, and the number of years spent as a congressional team. Sharing the same party reduces overall legislative similarity by .40, which is the opposite result from the analysis that predicts roll-call voting behavior for senators from the same state. Given that senators from the same party and the same state will look very similar on their roll-call voting records, they take great pains to contrast themselves in all the other legislative arenas in which they operate. Moreover, senators from larger states with a more diverse set of state interests have an advantage in this regard: for every increase in one million residents in the state, legislative

TABLE 2.12
Scale of Legislative Similarity within Senate Delegations that Changed
Composition (range of scale .00–2.44)[a]

State	From Unified to Divided Party		
	1987–1988	1989–1990	1991–1992
Pennsylvania	.32	.16	.20[b]
Virginia	.55	.57[b]	.57
Florida	.47	1.63[c]	1.61
Minnesota	.29	.16	1.11[b]
Montana	.20	1.33[b]	1.43

	From Divided to Unified Party		
Connecticut	1.53	.34[b]	.53
Mississippi	1.35	.61[b]	.49
Nebraska	.27	.85[b]	.57
Nevada	.77	.66[h]	.57

[a]Constructed from the number of same-committee assignments, percent of cosponsored bills, and percent of cosponsored amendments.
[b]Time period when composition of delegation changed.

TABLE 2.13
Similarity in Legislative Behavior within Senate Delegations, 1987–1992

Variable	Similarity Index
Intercept	.78***
	(.10)
Difference in years served	.004
	(.005)
Shared party affiliation	−.40***
	(.08)
State population size	−.020***
	(.007)
Number of years as congressional team	.004
	(.009)
One senator running for reelection	.09
	(.08)
Adj. R^2	.15
prob > F	.0001
N	150

Standard errors in parentheses. ***Statistically significant at .01, one-tailed test. **Statistically significant at .05, one-tailed test. *Statistically significant at .10, one-tailed test.

similarity between the senators decreases by .02. The greater the choice of state interests, the more likely it is that two senators from the same state will address distinct state interests, controlling for the partisan distribution in the state.

CONCLUSION

Although they do not run directly against each other, senators from the same state do compete with each other to be considered the effective champion for state interests and concerns. Rather than pursuing the identical legislative portfolios, senators from the same state work hard to address markedly different issues and interests to ensure that they will have readily identifiable *individual* achievements on which to base their records. To this end, they purposely join different committees, sponsor legislation in separate issue areas, and limit the bills and amendments they cosponsor together to those directly address state issues. In general, senators from the same state refrain from encroaching on each other's areas of legislative expertise.

Overall, senators who share the same party affiliation face greater electoral and institutional incentives to differentiate in these areas of legislative behavior than senators who have opposite party affiliations do. This chapter began by describing the efforts of senators from Oregon and Florida to build reputations and address the needs of their states — efforts that extended far beyond the votes they cast on the Senate floor. In Oregon, the two senators shared the same party affiliation but pursued different issue areas, adopted contrasting governing styles, and emphasized distinct local or national perspectives in their roles as senators. In Florida, the two senators were from opposing parties and constructed contrasting legislative portfolios, but, with the luxury of starkly different roll-call voting records, they could overlap in more areas, and work together more frequently than the senators from Oregon.

The contribution of the findings presented in this chapter is that they broaden the horizons for evaluating Senate representation. If we confine our assessment of Senate representation merely to the actions taken by a single senator on behalf of his state, then we fail to measure accurately the extent to which senators from the same state branch out legislatively to focus on different issues. The effect of this narrow view of Senate behavior is that it largely underestimates the range of state interests and opinions that are represented through the separate and collective efforts of the two senators from each state. Senate representation has been, and continues to be, a more comprehensive endeavor than that.

Chapter 3

DIVERSIFICATION AND MEDIA
RECOGNITION

> Having spent the third year of his first Senate term on the
> presidential campaign trail, [Senator] Simon acknowledged
> that he needs to devote his full attention to the Senate and
> getting re-elected. . . . If there was a weekend radio or
> television public affairs show he did not tape, it wasn't for
> lack of demand or effort by his staff. *In fact, his chief rival
> for media attention seemed to be his colleague and
> Downstate neighbor, Democratic Sen. Alan Dixon, who
> doesn't face re-election until 1992.* . . . Members of Simon's
> Washington staff have taken to bombarding the press room
> [at the Tribune] with phone calls and press releases about
> Simon's activities, including "fact sheets" about "Simon
> related provisions" in various bills moving through
> Congress.[1]

MEDIA COVERAGE is the primary conduit of information to
constituents about their senators, and it is the most important way that senators establish reputations as legislators,
nationally and in their home states. The impression of their senators
that constituents form is often based on what they read in the newspaper or see on television. Even if constituents themselves do not see a
newspaper article or hear a news story, they may learn about it from
others who do, such as friends, family, and colleagues. As some have
pointed out (Hibbing and Brandes 1983; Hibbing and Alford 1990; Lee
and Oppenheimer 1997), the larger size of most states prevents senators
from having the kind of personal contact (meeting, letter, etc.) with constituents that facilitates home style in the way that House members can.
Consequently, senators rely more on the media to convey information
to constituents about themselves and their legislative records than House
members do. The extent to which constituents can hold their senators

---

[1] Neal (1988) (emphasis added). For a description of a similar rivalry in New Jersey, see
Jones (1997).

accountable therefore depends in part on the quality and quantity of the media coverage devoted to their senators.

The most comprehensive work on how members of Congress seek out press coverage is actually about House members (Cook 1989), but much of it also applies to the Senate. Legislators seek out publicity in a number of important ways: they issue press releases, tape satellite feeds for television, and regularly meet with reporters in Washington as well as in their home states. In addition to that, senators often meet with the editorial boards of local newspapers to discuss a wide range of issues. In their efforts to attract press attention, senators and their staff make a clear distinction between national and local media coverage. They view national media coverage as more effective for running for president and influencing other senators on issues, and they view the state media as clearly more effective for building a reputation at home. As one legislative director noted, "Whether the senator pays more attention to national over local media often depends on his plans and aspirations. It usually runs from all local to 50/50 local/national."[2] An aide to Senator Exon (D-NE) claimed that for legislation important to his state, "we issue a press release, blanket the state media, do radio and television satellite feed [but] we don't send information about the bill to inside the beltway media."[3] Even if senators receive national media coverage, they do not assume that their constituents will read or hear it. The typical constituent in a state is more likely to read a local newspaper, or watch a local television newscast, than to read the *New York Times* or watch a network newscast (Goodwin 1997). The average senator, then, relies more on local media than on national media to establish a reputation among home-state constituents.

A complicating factor for senators in attracting local media coverage is that there is another senator who is simultaneously seeking attention in the same local media market. In one sense, senators from the same state are equals in the eyes of the local press insofar as they each hold an office of comparable political power at the federal level, a unique structural arrangement in American politics. Any news article that focuses on major legislation considered in Congress, such as taxes or defense, or that focuses on Senate roll-call votes more generally, is likely to report the actions of both senators. The potential for "solo" news coverage in the state is thereby limited by the very existence of another senator. Given that most constituents probably find it hard to distinguish between their senators on any level, senators from the same state

---

[2] Personal interview with staff member.
[3] Personal interview with staff member.

face the challenge of attracting individualized local coverage in order to demonstrate separate legislative achievements to their constituents.

Senators from the same state meet this challenge by behaving in a counterintuitive way: they construct markedly different legislative agendas. The pressure to establish an independent reputation in order to garner sufficient publicity in the state encourages senators to contrast themselves legislatively, and stylistically. Senators from split-party delegations face a somewhat easier task here because they will usually vote differently. But even still, partisanship is only one dimension of Senate representation, and all senators, regardless of same- or split-party affiliations, perceive the need to forge distinct personas. As such, senators from the same state join different committees and specialize in different issue areas in order to maximize the likelihood that constituents will recognize their separate accomplishments. The greater the differences between the two senators that are portrayed in the local media, the more easily constituents will distinguish between them and identify them as effective legislators. In this way, the quest for media coverage directly influences the choices that senators make about their legislative portfolios and, more broadly, the ways in which they represent their states.

media as incentive to differentiate

RESEARCH DESIGN

Scholars have studied patterns of national media coverage for senators and found that state size, committee position, and seniority all influence the amount of national press attention a senator receives (Weaver and Wilhoit 1980; Hess 1986; Squire 1988). For those senators who do not hold committee chairs, or who are not senior, the likelihood of getting national press attention is small (Tidmarch and Pitney 1985). The studies cited above found that committee leadership positions and state size all increased national news coverage of senators, but seniority and specific committee assignment had little to no effect.

To explore the determinants of local media coverage of senators, I selected the ten major newspapers for which electronic access was available to articles written in the years 1987–1992.[4] In many ways, this

---

[4] Ultimately, the larger purpose of this study is to determine whether senators' strategies for differentiation in issue areas pay off in terms of media coverage and constituent opinion. Therefore, I chose a time period for which survey data are available on constituent knowledge of their senators. I rely on the Senate Election Study, which covers the 100th–102nd congresses (1987–1992) for this type of survey data; the analysis of constituent evaluations of senators is included in chapter 4.

study parallels the work of Douglas Arnold (1999), who analyzes newspaper coverage of House members in twenty-five districts across the country. His work is a comprehensive effort to measure the degree to which local media coverage enables constituents to hold representatives accountable for their individual and collective legislative behavior.

The ten newspapers are in states that vary by region, population size, partisan distribution, and the partisan composition of the Senate delegation; the sample includes six states where the composition of the delegation remained constant and four states where one Senate seat changed hands. The senators included in the sample vary in their seniority, party affiliation, committee assignments, and committee positions. The states, names of newspapers, circulation, and senators who held office during 1987–1992 are listed in table 3.1. The data were organized and coded

TABLE 3.1
Sample of State Newspapers

State	Newspaper	Circulation	Senator	Length of Term
California	*Los Angeles Times*	1,054,123	Alan Cranston (D) Pete Wilson (R) John Seymour (R)	1968–1992 1982–1990 1990–1992[a]
Florida	*St. Petersburg Times*	257,105	Lawton Chiles (D) Bob Graham (D) Connie Mack (R) 1988–	1970–1988 1986–
Georgia	*Atlanta Constitution*	469,071	Sam Nunn (D) Wyche Fowler (D)	1972–1996 1986–1992
Illinois	*Chicago Tribune*	762,842	Alan Dixon (D) Paul Simon (D)	1980–1992 1984–1996
Kentucky	*Courier-Journal*	170,699	Wendell Ford (D) Mitch McConnell (R)	1974–1998 1984–
Massachusetts	*Boston Globe*	509,464	Edward Kennedy (D) John Kerry (D)	1962– 1984–
Minnesota	*Minneapolis Star-Tribune*	381,808	David Durenberger (R) Rudy Boschwitz (R) Paul Wellstone (D)	1976–1994 1978–1990 1990–
Nebraska	*Omaha World-Tribune*	221,023	Jim Exon (D) David Karnes (R) Robert Kerrey (D)	1978–1996 1987–1988[b] 1988–
New York	*Newsday*	555,757	Daniel Patrick Moynihan (D) Alfonse D'Amato (R)	1976– 1980–1998
Texas	*Houston Chronicle*	439,044	Lloyd Bentsen (D) Phil Gramm (R)	1970–1992 1984–

[a]Appointed to office; both senators sought election to a full term.

in the following way. I searched each newspaper for articles that mentioned the name of the senator(s) from the state and downloaded the list of all articles by their headlines for each year from 1987 to 1992. I divided the search into three categories: articles that included the senior senator but not the junior senator, articles that included the junior but not the senior senator, and articles that mentioned both senators.

Using a combination of headlines and the full text of articles, I coded the content of the articles using fourteen categories: foreign policy/defense, judiciary, education, environment/energy, infrastructure, health, welfare/labor, agriculture, budget/tax/trade, banking/housing, state politics/issues, pork, presidential politics, and other. The vast majority of the newspaper articles were coded as a single mention in a single category; less than 1 percent of the total number of articles about a senator included more than one subject category. In the rare instances where a newspaper article mentioned two subject categories in association with a senator, the article was counted twice, as a mention in each category. Articles that mentioned a senator's reelection campaign but had no specific issue content were placed in the state politics category. In general, about 75 percent of the articles could be coded without the full text of the article, and 25 percent had to be checked against the full text. As a check for accuracy in coding, I selected one newspaper, the *Chicago Tribune*, coded all the headlines, and compared them with the full text of articles; overall the inaccuracy rate was less than 3 percent.

The data collected for this study were selected to measure how certain variables influence local media coverage of senators, across and within states. Across states, factors such as state size or number of congressional districts can limit or enhance prospects for newspaper coverage. For example, we might expect senators from small states to garner more media attention than senators from larger states simply due to less competition from other elected officials, notably other members of the state delegation. Within states, the media coverage of a senator should vary according to a senator's institutional positions, individual media strategy, and the prominence of the other sitting senator from the state. If senators from the same state do indeed compete for local press attention, does one senator consistently overshadow the other? I have argued that senators from the same state construct different legislative portfolios in order to attract individualized press coverage. Are senators from the same state covered on different issues? Examining patterns of newspaper coverage of senators in their home states in this way can yield findings about the role that the media play in publicizing senatorial behavior.

STUDIES OF LOCAL NEWSPAPER COVERAGE OF SENATORS

To study the dynamics of media coverage of senators, I use the data in two primary ways. First, I place them in context by presenting case studies of the media coverage of the senators in four out of the ten states. These case studies are designed to illustrate how variables such as committee assignment or reelection might actually explain variation in coverage across senators. Second, I construct a quantitative model to estimate the precise effects of these variables on the number and content of local newspaper articles about senators.

Georgia and Massachusetts: The Power of Institutional Positions

In Georgia and Massachusetts, the delegations were same-party (Democrat), and in each case one senator had a great advantage in media coverage over the other, due either to institutional power or to a specific committee assignment. From 1987 to 1992, Georgia was represented by Sam Nunn, who had held office since 1972, and Wyche Fowler, who was elected from the House of Representatives in 1986. Figure 3.1 tracks the local newspaper coverage for both senators during this time; as we can see, Senator Nunn overshadows Senator Fowler in every year except 1992, when Senator Fowler sought reelection. On average, Senator Nunn was mentioned in 671 newspaper articles per session as compared to 407 articles that mentioned Senator Fowler; the two senators were mentioned together in an average of 240 articles per session.

The institutional power of Senator Nunn, who was chairman of the Armed Services Committee, garnered him tremendous media attention and left his junior colleague, Wyche Fowler, struggling to emerge from his shadow by focusing on an entirely different issue area. As a columnist for the *Atlanta Constitution* put it, "Sen. Sam Nunn has made himself consistent with Georgia thinking in matters such as defense, foreign policy and the budget deficit. Mr. Fowler [is] more of a behind the scenes player . . . his support for peanut subsidies [is] balanced out by his minority farmers' rights act" (Williams 1992). Table 3.2 shows the distribution of newspaper articles about the two senators by issue category.[5] Senator Nunn was mentioned in an average of 340 articles per session on defense issues, which fell under his committee jurisdiction, while Senator Fowler was mentioned in just 14 articles on defense dur-

---

[5] Data for four states — Georgia, Massachusetts, Illinois, and Kentucky — are displayed in the chapter as part of case studies of media coverage in those states. The data for the remaining six states are displayed in appendix C.

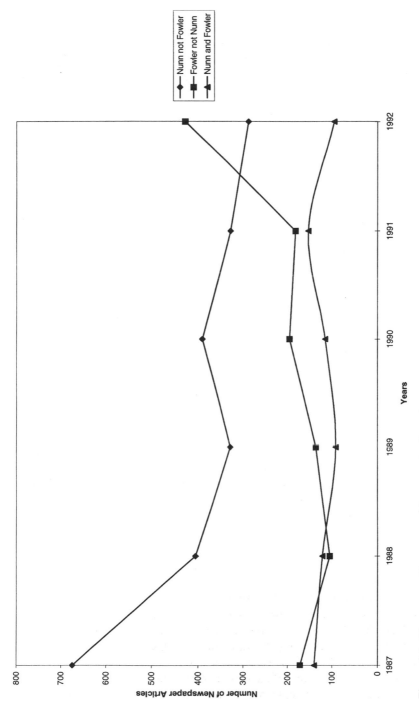

Figure 3.1. Newspaper Coverage of Senators in Georgia

TABLE 3.2
Content of Newspaper Coverage: Georgia

Subject Matter	1987–1988		1989–1990		1991–1992	
	Nunn	Fowler	Nunn	Fowler	Nunn	Fowler
Foreign policy/defense[a]	438*	15	303*	14	280*	13
Judiciary	45	25	66	24	34	37
Education	16	4	26	10	19	13
Environment/energy	6	11	19	29	5	23
Infrastructure	5	7	3	6	2	3
Health	3	4	3	8	19	13
Welfare/labor	3	1	3	3	6	3
Agriculture[a]	0	24*	1	30*	2	23*
Budget/tax/trade[a]	17	9*	30	23*	17	16*
Banking/housing	1	6	2	11	5	7
State politics/issues[b]	76	71	89*	95	44	331*
Presidential[c]	402*	43	68	12	123	38
Pork	0	1	6	2	6	10
Other	69	56	91	68	56	79
Total	1,079	277	719	334	618	611

Source: *Atlanta Constitution*, Dow Jones News Retrieval Service.

[a]Numbers followed by asterisk indicate that the senator sat on the Senate committee whose jurisdiction includes the issue category.

[b]Asterisk indicates that a senator was in a reelection cycle.

[c]Asterisk indicates that the senator was considered for or ran for president during the time period.

ing the same time period. Alternatively, Senator Fowler was featured in an average of 26 articles per session on agriculture issues, which fell under his committee jurisdiction, as compared with only 1 article mentioning Senator Nunn on agricultural issues.

Unfortunately for Senator Fowler, being behind the scenes was not the best strategy for establishing a reputation as a senator from Georgia, especially when contrasted with Senator Nunn. Senator Fowler was overshadowed in the press for most of his career by Senator Nunn, until his last two years (1991–1992), when he sought reelection; Senator Fowler lost his bid for reelection to a second term, and he attributed his loss, in part, to a lack of sufficient media coverage. In Fenno (1996, 225) Senator Fowler is quoted as saying, "Our biggest problem . . . was with the media. All things being equal, I should have won. If the media had done their job . . . I would have won." Of course, his loss can be explained by a number of factors, but an examination of media coverage suggests that at least one factor was his limited visibility in the press. It appears that Senator Fowler was correct in his assessment of media coverage—he never managed to get the press to recognize his work as a senator. Without adequate press coverage, he had little opportunity to establish a reputation among constituents and was thereby left vulnerable to a successful challenge by the Republican candidate, Paul Coverdell, who ultimately beat Fowler in a runoff election.

In Massachusetts there was a substantial disparity between the attention afforded to Senator Kennedy, the senior senator, and that given to his junior colleague, Senator Kerry. On average, Senator Kennedy was mentioned in 914 articles per session as compared with 410 for Senator Kerry; the two senators were mentioned together in 137 articles per session (fig. 3.2). As in the case of Georgia, there were great differences in seniority and institutional position between the two senators: Senator Kennedy had been in office twenty-three years when Senator Kerry was elected. Senator Kennedy is most dominant in education, health, and welfare and labor issues, all part of the Labor and Human Resources Committee, which he chaired during this time. On average, Senator Kennedy was mentioned in 108 articles in these issue areas per congressional session while Senator Kerry was mentioned in only 15 articles (table 3.3).

A typical description of the differences between the two senators appeared in a recent article about Senator Kerry: "Among the state's 10 Democratic lawmakers in the House, the majority say that if they want to get something done for the Commonwealth, such as funding for the Central artery project, they turn to Senator Edward M. Kennedy. Kerry, they said, is not always interested or helpful, or he overstudies issues without taking action. . . . While Kerry has always attracted national attention, he has struggled to find his own place in the Senate, apart from Kennedy" (Zuckerman 1997). The striking thing here is that this article was written in 1997, after Senator Kerry had won his second reelection bid; despite his victory, the local press continued to question his effectiveness as a senator. Although Senator Kerry did not suffer the same fate as Senator Fowler, who lost his seat, they both faced similar constraints in attempting to overcome the shadow of a more senior, more powerful colleague from the same party.

Illinois: Committee Assignment and Individual Media Strategy

As the quote that begins this chapter illustrates, Illinois is a state where the two senators also competed for press attention. During the years 1985–1992, Illinois was represented by two Democratic senators: Alan Dixon, who was elected in 1980, and Paul Simon, who was elected four years later. Unlike Georgia, the senior senator from Illinois (Senator

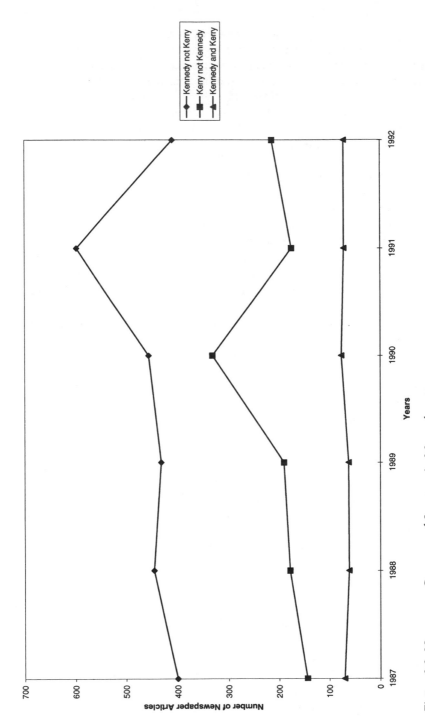

Figure 3.2. Newspaper Coverage of Senators in Massachusetts

TABLE 3.3
Content of Newspaper Coverage: Massachusetts

Subject Matter	1987–1988		1989–1990		1991–1992	
	Kennedy	Kerry	Kennedy	Kerry	Kennedy	Kerry
Foreign policy/ Defense[a]	53	66*	106	39*	75	101*
Judiciary[a]	127*	71	92*	62	97*	31
Education[a]	18*	2	16*	2	41*	7
Environment/ energy	36	13	17	41	7	10
Infrastructure	6	2	5	5	4	3
Health[a]	49*	8	43*	4	66*	2
Welfare/labor	34	3	27	7	31	9
Agriculture	0	0	0	0	0	0
Budget/tax/trade	8	10	13	24	22	14
Banking/housing[a]	4	8*	25	16*	4	51*
State politics/ issues[b]	208*	52	283	195*	273	73
Presidential	141	36	84	26	87	31
Pork	11	0	29	2	12	1
Other	151	50	147	99	289	54
Total	846	322	888	522	1,008	387

Source: Boston Globe, Dow Jones News Retrieval Service.

[a]Numbers followed by asterisk indicate that the senator sat on the Senate committee whose jurisdiction includes the issue category.

[b]Asterisk indicates that a senator was in a reelection cycle.

Dixon) did not overshadow his more junior colleague (Senator Simon). In fact, Senator Simon consistently received much more media coverage than Senator Dixon did. On average, Senator Simon was mentioned in 618 articles per session and Senator Dixon was mentioned in 240 articles per session; both senators were mentioned together in an average of 167 articles. When articles about Senator Simon's 1988 presidential bid are deleted from the tally, he was still mentioned in an average of 450 articles, far more than his colleague (fig. 3.3).

The variation in news coverage for the two senators cannot be explained by differences in seniority or committee position because there was only a four-year difference between the senators, and neither senator held a committee chairmanship. Instead, Senator Simon's media preeminence may be explained as a function of his specific committee assignments, for example, the Judiciary Committee, which enabled him to associate himself with highly salient issues, as well as his considerable

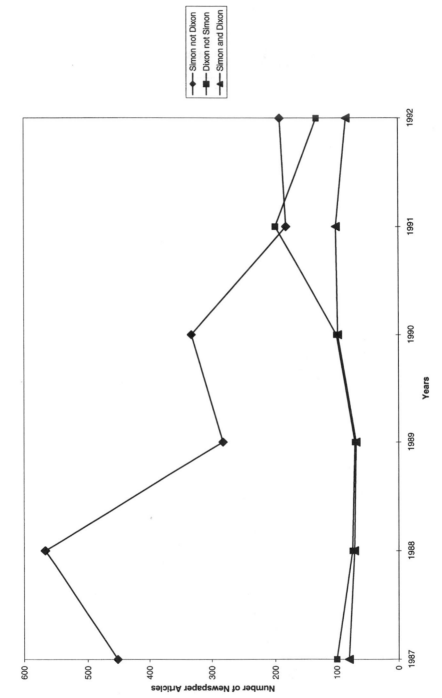

Figure 3.3. Newspaper Coverage of Senators in Illinois

efforts to attract publicity. As one Judiciary Committee staff member remarked: "This Committee deals with many high profile issues: crime, the constitution, judicial nominations including the Supreme Court. . . . If a senator wants to get his name in the paper, this committee will let him do that with very controversial things—not things like the senator brings home the bacon again."[6] Indeed, the highest percentage of articles mentioning Senator Simon focused on judiciary, welfare, and labor issues, while the highest percentage of articles mentioning Senator Dixon focused on defense, banking, and housing issues, each corresponding with the senator's committee assignments (table 3.4).

In some ways, Illinois presents the greatest puzzle because Senator Dixon had been in state government for thirty years before entering the Senate, and he prided himself on serving the interests of Illinois as opposed to focusing on national issues. Although Senator Dixon's strategy of portraying himself as a champion of local interests was successful, it

TABLE 3.4
Content of Newspaper Coverage: Illinois

	1987–1988		1989–1990		1991–1992	
Subject Matter	Dixon	Simon	Dixon	Simon	Dixon	Simon
Foreign policy/defense[a]	29*	35*	37*	47*	26*	27*
Judiciary[a]	24	68*	11	90*	11	77*
Education[a]	1	4*	1	24*	6	18*
Environment/energy	3	3	5	16	2	7
Infrastructure	3	13	4	6	9	6
Health[a]	9	3*	4	31*	4	7*
Welfare/labor	4	23	2	15	4	10
Agriculture	6	4	2	3	2	3
Budge/tax/trade	17	11	11	22	13	21
Banking/housing[a]	14*	10	32*	13	17*	3
State politics/issues[b]	28	115	27	154*	130*	87
Presidential[c]	11	641*	0	6	5	26
Pork	13	3	2	6	10	1
Other	14	69	23	62	91	74
Total	174	1,019	216	463	332	374

Source: Chicago Tribune, Dow Jones News Retrieval Service.
[a]Numbers followed by asterisk indicate that the senator sat on the Senate committee whose jurisdiction includes the issue category.
[b]Asterisk indicates that a senator was in a reelection cycle.
[c]Asterisk indicates that the senator was considered for or ran for president during the time period.

[6] Personal interview with committee staff member.

left him vulnerable to being overshadowed by the national stature of Senator Simon. Senator Dixon lost his bid for reelection in a three-way primary challenge in March 1992, which ended a forty-two year career in public service in Illinois.

Kentucky: Different Party Affiliations

During the years 1985–1992, Kentucky was represented by a split-party delegation. The senior senator, Wendell Ford, was a Democrat, and the junior senator, Mitch McConnell, was a Republican. In this case, the junior senator also devised a media strategy to take advantage of party differences and overcome the obstacle to media coverage presented by a more senior state colleague. On average, over the two congressional sessions for which data are available, Senator McConnell was mentioned in 434 newspaper articles compared with an average of 321 for Senator Ford. Both senators were mentioned in an average of 115 newspaper articles (fig. 3.4). In specific issue areas, Senator McConnell was mentioned more often than Senator Ford in most categories, with the biggest differences in the areas of foreign relations and agriculture. Senator Ford, on the other hand, was mentioned more in the economy/ finance category, which includes articles about commerce. The variation in issue coverage corresponds to differences in committee assignments: Senator McConnell sat on the Foreign Relations Committee and the Agriculture Committee, and Senator Ford sat on the Commerce Committee (table 3.5).

Furthermore, both senators received about equal coverage in the energy and environment area, and both sat on the Energy Committee, though Senator Ford had far greater seniority on the committee than did Senator McConnell. Kentucky is the only state in this sample where the junior and senior senators shared two committee assignments. In 1989, after four years in the Senate, Senator McConnell joined both the Rules Committee and the Energy Committee, a move that Senator Ford clearly viewed as encroachment. Senator McConnell sought the seat on the Rules Committee to advance his role as the "lead Republican senator" on campaign finance reform and a seat on the Energy Committee because of "his interest in coal and uranium enrichment" (Brown 1990).

Despite the fact that both senators sat on the same committee, they staked out different positions on state-based interests, as the following excerpt from an article on acid-rain legislation demonstrates:

Kentucky's U.S. senators disagree on whether Congress will pass acid-rain legislation before adjourning next year. "The days when you could hope there will be no bill at all are over," Sen. Mitch McConnell told a coal industry

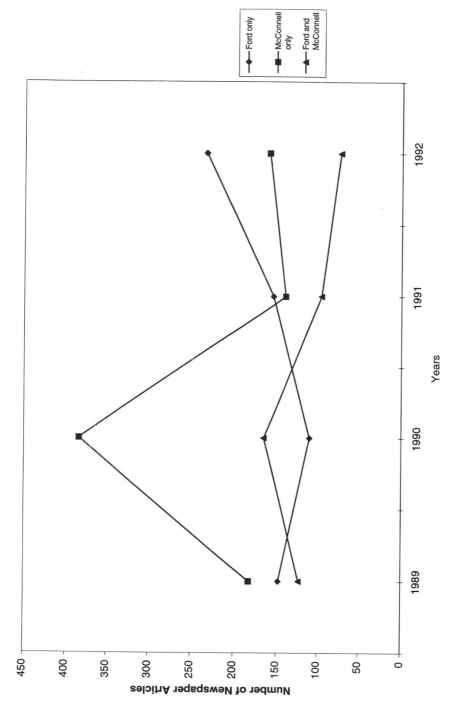

Figure 3.4. Newspaper Coverage of Senators in Kentucky

TABLE 3.5
Content of Newspaper Coverage: Kentucky

Subject Matter	1987–1988		1989–1990		1991–1992	
	Ford	McConnell	Ford	McConnell	Ford	McConnell
Foreign/ defense[a]	NA	NA	15	34*	15	21*
Judiciary	NA	NA	9	39	13	30
Education	NA	NA	13	5	6	5
Environment/ energy[a]	NA	NA	22*	40*	40*	13*
Infrastructure	NA	NA	5	1	3	1
Health	NA	NA	0	7	4	12
Welfare/labor	NA	NA	3	5	12	2
Agriculture[a]	NA	NA	7	28*	5	7*
Budget/tax/ trade[a]	NA	NA	25*	12	24*	14
Banking/ housing	NA	NA	4	9	4	2
State politics/ issues[b]	NA	NA	86	355*	154*	81
Presidential	NA	NA	3	11	37	43
Pork	NA	NA	6	22	3	17
Other	NA	NA	58	98	66	52
Total	NA	NA	256	567	388	300

Source: Courier-Journal, Dow Jones News Retrieval Service.
[a]Numbers followed by asterisk indicate that the senator sat on the Senate committee whose jurisdiction includes the issue category.
[b]Asterisk indicates that a senator was in a reelection cycle.

group. . . . But Sen. Wendell Ford . . . said in an interview yesterday that acid-rain controls are not inevitable in this Congress. Ford said the issue may be too complex and involve too many interests, such as state commissions that set rates for coal-burning electric utilities, to produce a consensus in the next two years. "We could have a bill if we could find something that we could agree on," said Ford, who has been more involved in coal issues than McConnell. . . . McConnell recently gained a seat on the Senate Energy and Natural Resources Committee, of which Ford in a longtime member. . . . McConnell . . . said that there is a disagreement in the administration about the issue, and that he hopes to work on the bill with Bush advisors before it is introduced. (Cross 1989)

Kentucky is an example where two senators seem to converge on similar issues over time, while at the same time maintaining partisan distinctions. Moreover, despite Senator McConnell's attempt to encroach, he did not manage to establish himself on a par with his more senior colleague in environmental issues.

More recently, in May 1998, the two senators from Kentucky found themselves on the opposite side of an issue equally important to Kentucky — tobacco. Senator Ford, as a member of the Commerce Committee, voted to support a major bill that would impose penalties on tobacco companies and discourage teenage smoking. Kentucky, a major tobacco-growing state, was relying on a provision sponsored by Senator Ford and others that could continue crop-support payments for tobacco farmers. Senator McConnell, a member of the Agriculture Committee, proposed eliminating the crop-support program in favor of limited lump sum payments. A May 18, 1998, *Courier-Journal* article described the conflict this way:

> Republican Sen. Mitch McConnell, joined by Sen. Richard Lugar of Indiana, yesterday proposed abolishing the tobacco price-support program. McConnell's action, a surprising break with Kentucky's Sen. Wendell Ford — a Democrat and consistent champion for tobacco farmers — marks the first crack in a 60 year wall of unanimity on tobacco issues by Kentucky's congressional delegation.
>
> McConnell and Lugar . . . proposed an $18 billion plan to buy out farmers and help tobacco dependent communities adjust to new political and economic realities. . . . McConnell's proposal differs sharply with a plan offered by Ford, Kentucky's senior senator. . . . Ford would keep the tobacco price support program, provide $28 billion over 10 years in payments to tobacco farmers who opt out of the program. . . .
>
> "This is not personal," McConnell said later of his differences with Ford on the price support program. "We both looked at the facts and reached different conclusions."
>
> "This shows exactly how excruciating all this is," said Tim Cansler, director of national affairs for the Kentucky Farm Bureau. "When in history have two senators from a tobacco state disagreed on tobacco policy?" (Carroll 1998).

Once again, the two senators converged on a single important issue to their state, but in doing so, they adopted strikingly different policy positions, differences that were emphasized in the local media coverage of the issue.

The examples of Georgia, Massachusetts, Illinois, and Kentucky are meant to illustrate the ways in which same-state senators use their institutional positions, such as committee assignments, and their prior experience, in the context of the size and diversity of their states, to attract publicity in their home media market and to emphasize clear distinctions between one another. The amount and type of media coverage a senator receives throughout a term clearly contributes to overall visibility in the state. The more visible the senator, the less likely it is that a strong candidate will provide a reelection challenge. Intrinsic to a senator's media strategy is an awareness of the activity of the state colleague, especially where that colleague is more senior and of the same party. Constructing a legislative portfolio that focuses on different substantive issue areas is one important way that senators from the same state overcome the direct competition they face from the senator who shares the same media market.

PATTERNS OF COVERAGE IN LOCAL NEWSPAPERS

To further support the connections between senators' legislative portfolios and local media coverage, I performed a quantitative analysis on the data collected from the ten newspapers in my sample. Model 1 (table 3.6) predicts the amount and subject matter of media coverage of senators in each two-year congressional session, and the amount of coverage for each senator is treated independently for each time period.[7] Variation in the amount of coverage is treated as a function of the following variables: state population size, committee assignment, committee position, prior experience as a House member or governor, running for president, seniority within the delegation, shared party affiliation, bills introduced, and the amount of coverage allotted to the other sitting senator.

The results of model 1 indicate that state size has little impact on the amount of media the average senator receives; the coefficient is both statistically and substantively insignificant. Of the major Senate committees, the only ones that showed any effects on total coverage were the Judiciary Committee and the Foreign Relations Committee. Senators who sat on the Judiciary Committee receive substantially higher

[7] Some scholars might object to pooling the data for senators across three time periods because the observations may be correlated. In other words, if we assume that senators' legislative behavior, publicity-seeking behavior, and the news media's issue priorities all stay constant across congressional sessions, it would create imprecision in our estimators to pool the data in this way. However, I argue that these factors do not stay constant over time, and that senators' behavior, their institutional positions, the Senate's agenda, as well as that of the news media all vary across congressional sessions sufficiently that it warrants treating a senator's media coverage in each congressional session as an independent observation.

TABLE 3.6
Selected Determinants of State Newspaper Coverage of Senators, 1987–1992

Intercept	524.4***
	(157.2)
State population size	−8.3
	(5.5)
Senior senator	−464.5***
	(105.3)
Chairman	151.9*
	(94.0)
Reelection	182.1***
	(66.7)
Presidential candidate	794.8***
	(126.7)
Shared party affiliation	−67.0
	(81.9)
Former member of House	−255.0***
	(81.5)
Former governor	88.8
	(93.4)
Judiciary Committee	270.5**
	(126.7)
Foreign Relations Committee	−368.2***
	(90.5)
State colleague's media	.26**
	(.11)
Number of bills sponsored	5.5**
	(2.5)
Adj. R^2	.55
prob > F	.0001
N	58

Source: Dow Jones News Retrieval Service, 1987–1992.
 Standard errors in parentheses. ***Statistically significant at .01, one-tailed test. **Statistically significant at .05, one-tailed test. *Statistically significant at .10, one-tailed test.

media coverage, all else being equal, while sitting on the Foreign Relations Committee decreases coverage. This is not a surprising result in the context of local media coverage because the Judiciary Committee's jurisdiction is likely to be more salient to the local reader than that of the Foreign Relations Committee. Being a committee chair increases local media coverage, a pattern that is consistent with trends in national media coverage of senators. Introducing a bill, which may be considered a proxy for overall legislative activism, also exerts a statistically significant effect on media coverage; for every bill introduced, the senator receives mention in five additional articles. Running for reelection and running for president substantially increased media coverage for senators in their own states.

The effects of holding prior office on media coverage are mixed. Being a former member of Congress decreases coverage by a large amount, while the coefficient for being a former governor is positive but statistically insignificant. Clearly the small size of this sample warrants a cautious interpretation of these results, but the difference in the effect of prior experience may be due to the localized nature of congressional districts. A House member may have established contact with only the newspaper(s) in his or her district, while a governor would have had extensive experience dealing with major newspapers throughout a state (Arnold 1999). Since I only sampled one major newspaper in the state, the difference between the two could be exaggerated. Still, the results do suggest that coming to the Senate from a statewide office provides new senators with a comparative advantage in building reputations and may reduce the extent to which they are overshadowed by their more senior state colleague in the Senate.

Model 1 also includes three variables designed to test the dynamics of having a two-member delegation. Surprisingly, being the senior senator within the delegation has a large and significant negative effect on media coverage, controlling for other variables. In terms of sheer numbers of newspaper articles, then, being the senior senator is no guarantee of high visibility. The direct effect of one senator's media coverage on the amount of coverage allotted to the other senator appears to be positive but small.[8] Sharing the same party with a state colleague decreases media coverage, but the parameter estimate is not statistically significant. Therefore, although the statistical results provide limited support, there

---

[8] The inclusion of media coverage for one senator as an independent variable to predict media coverage of the other senator might be thought to be a problem because of the potential correlation between the disturbance terms. However, a comparison of the residuals from regressions using total media coverage for one senator as an independent variable to predict total media coverage for the other yields no significant correlation.

are indications from the data that senators from the same state compete for general visibility in their local press.

Moreover, if senators purposely pursue different issue portfolios, the effects of one senator's behavior would be more likely to emerge in specific issue areas, rather than in the total amount of media coverage. Senators construct a legislative agenda — a portfolio — that serves as evidence of the issues and problems they try to address as senators. If there is a correlation between the content of that agenda and the content of media coverage, then senators have achieved a level of success in publicizing their activities. Furthermore, the issue content of media coverage provides constituents with information about what their senators actually do in the Senate, and around the state, to represent them. After all, the total number of articles may measure the extent of a senator's potential visibility, but it is the subject matter of the articles that really provides constituents with information to monitor their senators.

To test more systematically for patterns of local media coverage of senators' legislative activity, I constructed model 2 (table 3.7) to predict coverage in six issue areas: judiciary, labor/health/education, energy/environment, finance/budget, agriculture, and defense/foreign affairs, using seniority, reelection, prior experience, committee assignment, and the amount of coverage in that issue area afforded to the other sitting senator as independent variables. Because senators focus most of their legislative behavior on issues that fall under their committee jurisdiction (Schiller 1995), I used committee assignment as a proxy for legislative activity in specific issue areas. Model 2 also differs in that it measures seniority by the number of terms in office, rather than seniority within the state delegation (senior or junior senator). This substitution occurs because this model is seeking to test the effects of issue specialization over time on visibility in specific issue areas. One would not expect that seniority within the delegation per se would provide any advantage in a particular issue area, whereas seniority within the institution would enable senators to develop expertise in issue areas and thereby become identified with them in their local media.

As Table 3.7 reveals, sitting on the Judiciary, Labor, Finance, or Armed Services committees significantly increases the number of local newspaper articles about a senator in those issue areas. Interestingly, sitting on the Foreign Relations Committee has no effect on state media coverage in that issue area. It may be that the local nature of the defense industry enables senators to make much better use of a seat on Armed Services than on Foreign Relations for the purposes of attracting state media coverage. Sitting on the Agriculture Committee also increases media coverage, but the impact of the coefficient is minimal. Having been a former governor substantively and significantly increases media

TABLE 3.7
Determinants of State Media Coverage of Senators in Specific Issue Areas,
1987–1992

Variable	Judiciary	Labor	Energy/EPW
Intercept	40.9***	25.0**	17.5*
	(10.4)	(12.7)	(11.8)
Seniority	−5.8**	5.4**	−1.9
	(2.9)	(3.2)	(2.8)
Reelection	1.8	5.7	18.1***
	(6.6)	(7.5)	(6.6)
Former member of House	−17.3**	−6.1	−2.05
	(8.2)	(9.0)	(8.3)
Former governor	10.1	23.0**	51.3***
	(9.1)	(10.3)	(9.6)
Judiciary Committee	72.3***		
	(11.5)		
State colleague media	−.02	−.20**	.10
	(.11)	(.12)	(.12)
Labor Committee		24.7**	
		(11.3)	
Energy/EPW Committee			−6.0
			(8.3)
Adj. R^2	.38	.30	.41
prob > F	.0001	.001	.0001
N	58	58	58

Variable	Finance/Budget	Agriculture	Defense/Foreign
Intercept	−1.2	.29**	53.2**
	(8.7)	(.14)	(29.4)
Seniority	4.6**	−.07**	8.0
	(2.3)	(.04)	(7.3)
Reelection	6.6	.01	−3.7
	(5.7)	(.09)	(17.0)
Former member of House	24.4***	−.10	−44.6**
	(8.3)	(.10)	(21.2)

TABLE 3.7 (*continued*)

Variable	Finance/Budget	Agriculture	Defense/Foreign
Former governor	24.1*** (7.9)	−.19* (.13)	−27.0 (24.6)
Finance Committee	27.2*** (7.7)		
State colleague media	.07 (.12)	−.005*** (.002)	−.02 (.12)
Agriculture Committee		.014*** (.002)	
Foreign Relations Committee			−3.9 (19.8)
Armed Services Committee			64.5*** (21.7)
Adj. R^2	.34	.47	.35
prob > F	.0004	.0001	.0003
N	58	58	58

Source: Dow Jones News Retrieval Service, 1987–1992.

Standard errors in parentheses. ***Statistically significant at .01, one-tailed test. **Statistically significant at .05, one-tailed test. *Statistically significant at .10, one-tailed test.

coverage in the subject areas of labor and welfare, environment, and the budget; this may be an indication that the advantages of prior statewide office are more concentrated in traditionally domestic issue areas. For former members of the House, the effect is negative and statistically significant in judiciary and defense issue areas; budgetary issues were the only subject area where the parameter estimate is positive and significant.

The impact of media coverage for one senator on media coverage for the other senator from the state is statistically significant in the areas of labor and agriculture issues, where the coverage for one senator suppresses coverage for the other. In two other areas, defense/foreign relations and judiciary, the effect is also negative, but the parameter estimates are insignificant. These results give stronger indications that same-state senators' decisions to differentiate their issue portfolios reap rewards in the local media.

Senators from the same state choose different committee assignments and concentrate their legislative work in those committee areas in an effort to attract distinct and individual media coverage. The combined results of model 1 and model 2 provide support for such a strategy because they establish a concrete connection between committee assignment and media coverage in specific issue areas. Furthermore, the models indicate that senators from the same state do have an impact on each other's visibility, although these results are not consistent across all issue areas.

CONCLUSION

Media coverage is an important vehicle through which senators establish reputations among their constituents, and the need for publicity serves as one major determinant of a senator's institutional behavior. In this chapter I have argued that because two senators from the same state share the same media audience, they face constant competition in their efforts to attract individualized media coverage. This competition for visibility provides same-state senators with a strong incentive to develop contrasting and distinct representational agendas, and it pushes them in more divergent directions than we might expect of two legislators who represent the same geographic constituency.

In general, the amount and content of local media coverage of a senator reflects his choices of committee assignments, issue specialization, geographic ties, and general governing style. There is a direct and strong correlation between committee assignment and media coverage across almost all issue areas. Therefore, the decisions that senators make to join different committees from their state colleague pays off in terms of individualized media coverage. Moreover, patterns of media coverage discourage encroachment into the other senator's territory because when one senator receives publicity in an issue area, the other senator from the state is less likely to be covered in that same issue area.

Notably, the competition between senators for media attention is sustained over time. One might assume that the senior senator from the state would always maintain an advantage over a junior colleague in visibility and media contacts. But seniority within a Senate delegation is not consistently sufficient to overshadow the other senator from the state. If a junior senator targets alternative issue areas, he may not only reach parity with a senior colleague, but also overtake him in terms of visibility in the press.

In sum, this study of local media coverage of senators from the same state demonstrates the ways in which the press serves to keep senators accountable. For the most part, local media coverage accurately details senators' efforts in the institution, and the ways that they present themselves at home. The existence of the local press plays an important role in enabling senators to build reputations; the combination of having two elected officials of the same stature, with equal power, automatically sets senators up for competition. Because there are two senators from each state, neither is ever guaranteed individualized publicity on an issue. Therefore, to maximize individual publicity in their state and reduce competition, senators from the same state diversify their representational agendas.

Chapter 4

REPUTATION AND
CONSTITUENT EVALUATION

THROUGHOUT this book, I have argued that securing an independent reputation is the most powerful incentive for senators from the same state to contrast their representational portfolios. Defining senatorial reputation requires identifying a senator's audience. Every member of Congress has two primary audiences: the "inside the Beltway" audience and the "folks back home" audience (Fiorina 1977; Fenno 1978). The main focus of this chapter is on how senators use reputations to cultivate their home-state audiences. The underlying goal in exploring this process is to assess the strength of the connection between senators' legislative work and reputation formation among constituents, all in the context of a two-member Senate delegation.

Although the voters are the ultimate audience because they are the ones who decide a senator's electoral fate, there are intermediaries who stand between the senator and the "folks back home." As early as 1963, Miller and Stokes described the multiple layers separating legislators from their constituents:

> The relation of Congressman to voter is not a simple bilateral one but is complicated by the presence of all manner of intermediaries: the local party, economic interests, the news media, racial and national organizations, and so forth. . . . Very often the Representative reaches the mass public through these mediating agencies, and the information about himself and his record may be considerably transformed as it diffuses out to the electorate in two or more states. As a result, the public—or parts of it—may get positive or negative cues about the Congressman, which were provoked by legislative action but which no longer have a recognizable issue content. (55)

The information that is gathered from these intermediaries can be refiltered through elite commentators (pundits) as well as more proximate influences, such as family, friends, and co-workers (Popkin 1991, 41).

In the past, the party label was the most influential intermediary because it was the most easily accessible piece of information about senators and guaranteed the senator a certain percentage of support in his state. However, with the decline of straight party voting and the emergence of more independent voters, the percentage of guaranteed support from party-line voters has diminished, with increasing emphasis being placed on candidate-specific qualities (Abramowitz and Segal 1992; Wattenberg 1996). Moderate partisans and independents often use other criteria to judge their senators, above and beyond party and ideology. As Samuel Popkin (1991, 61) writes:

> Voters care about the competence of the candidate, not just the candidate's issue positions, because they do not follow most government activity and because they care about what the candidate can deliver from government. . . . [T]hey worry about the character of the candidate, about his or her sincerity, because they cannot easily read "true" preferences and because they care about uncertain future situations. . . . In reality, voters sometimes care less about candidates' issue positions than they do about which candidate can deliver the most on these issues, and which candidate can do a better job simply managing and running the government. In short, they care about competence.

For those voters who do not have strong partisan preferences and those voters who do not pay sufficient attention to the party's positions on issues, overall competence may be the most important criterion for judging their senators.

Ironically, it may be harder for the average constituent to judge a senator's competence today than it was when Miller and Stokes wrote about representation because there are more sources of information from which constituents can learn about their senators. In addition to national and local news media, there are cable news outlets, C-span and the Internet. The sheer wealth of information about legislators that is now within the reach of the average constituent can cause greater confusion and make it harder for constituents to identify their senators, much less award them credit for specific accomplishments (Sinclair 1990; Arnold 1990; Franklin 1993).

Senators and their staff understand how little specific information ultimately filters down to most voters, and in many of the interviews they readily acknowledged the inherent difficulty in cultivating familiarity among constituents. As one legislative director put it:

> What constituents know varies considerably. It is the senator's responsibility to educate his constituents about his bills — they all attempt to do that. A lot of this education process is selective, i.e., they won't tell senior citizens about a bill to cut Social Security but they will tell urban residents about a tax credit for sewers. The constituents themselves do not go out of their way to learn about what a senator is doing in terms of bills. Senators do not believe that constituents will educate themselves. They know they have to go out and educate them.[1]

[1] Personal interview with staff member.

Another legislative director, when asked about publicizing a senator's bill sponsorship activity, said that "Constituents have an idea that he's helping, maybe they know about a bill but it's more likely that they have an impression he is doing something on an issue." A third staff member put it more bluntly, "You do your best to let people know about your bills — you publicize them. You need to repeat it a million times for it to get through."[2] Consequently, the average constituent is unlikely to know specific details about a senator's record by the time the information has been disseminated from the senator, through the intermediaries, to the constituent.

Reputation Building in a Two-Member "District"

Compounding the challenge of becoming known among voters is the fact that there are two senators in every state trying to establish themselves as effective legislators. It is difficult enough for any elected official to attract publicity, but in no other circumstance are there two elected officials who hold the same level office, with the same range of potential powers, and who represent the same geographic constituency. Even if a constituent is aware of a bill, or a federal grant that is awarded to the state, and knows that one of the senators from the state accomplished the feat (as opposed to a House member), the constituent still may not be able to identify which senator should receive credit. Consequently, senators from the same state need to work hard to make a sufficiently unique and distinctive impression such that they will stand apart from each other in an easily identifiable way.

A senator's success at attracting the attention of the local media, interest groups, and constituents rests in part on the capacity to establish a contrast to the other senator from the state. For this reason, senators from the same state choose to join different committees, specialize in different issue areas, and adopt different governing styles. Importantly these choices are designed to set the two senators apart from each other enough so that the average constituent does not confuse them. By choosing alternative representational agendas, senators attempt to increase the probability that constituents in their state will come to know them as separate and effective legislators. In sum, the effect of the two-member structure of a Senate delegation is to create an incentive to establish a concrete reputation among constituents, as filtered by media coverage and interest groups, that is distinct from that of the other senator from the state.

[2] Personal interview with staff member.

The pressure to form a unique identity among constituents is greater among two senators who share the same party affiliation than among their split-party colleagues. Party affiliation may not be the only predictor of electoral choice, but it is still a sufficiently powerful informational cue that senators can be defined by it. Sharing the same party presents a double-edged sword in reputation building for senators. On the one hand, it is inherently more difficult for the average voter to distinguish between same-party senators in the same state. In this context, forging an independent reputation therefore requires creating some distance from the party. However, if the party is popular in the state, or nationally, then the two senators each benefit from the party affiliation and will not want to take strong steps to disassociate from the party.[3]

For split-party senators, however, party affiliation exerts a different effect on their capacity and inclination to establish separate identities. Constituents are more likely to be able to tell the difference between their senators if they have opposing partisan affiliations, and they may be more aware of partisan differences between their senators than about legislative or stylistic differences between their senators. Thus senators in split-party states have an advantage from the outset in building individual reputations. However, states with split-party delegations usually have a competitive two-party structure, so neither senator can be assured of majority support in the state. At any given time, one party could be more popular nationally or statewide than another, and its senator may not be viewed as favorably by constituents as a result. The logical response to shifting tides of partisan support is to develop a broader reputation, one that builds on party affiliation (which essentially serves as a constant) and ideological leanings by presenting a legislative record that can be used as a measure of competence.

Indeed, it can be argued that legislative portfolios are the primary means by which senators demonstrate their competence *as legislators*. To provide a range of criteria on which to judge them, senators construct their legislative agendas with an eye to advertising concrete accomplishments in specific issue areas and areas of concern to their states. One legislative director put it quite clearly: "People make the connection between bills passing and something getting done. A much used charge in campaigns is that the senator could not pass a bill with his name on it; people feel that is the business of the Senate."[4] Fenno (1996) has described this process of reputation building as twofold: the governing stage, when senators actually engage in legislating, and the

[3] This idea is owed in part to discussions with Eric Uslaner, Sarah Binder, and Forrest Maltzman.
[4] Personal interview with staff member.

reelection stage, when senators sell their records of accomplishment. During the governing stage, senators and their staff select specific issue areas to address, and they engage in a continuous struggle to publicize their efforts in order to appear productive and attentive to voters' concerns. One legislative director described how her senator fought on behalf of a major state interest to attract favorable publicity and get noticed by constituents: "When you wage a fight, you can break through [constituents'] fog. Last session, we fought to protect retirement benefits of coal miners and we threw our heart and soul into it and won. You have to make your fights worth it."[5]

Senators target their efforts with an eye toward publicity by trying to make their legislative feats as clear as possible. Although these efforts may not register with voters immediately, local media and interest groups pay closer attention during the governing phase. If these intermediaries come to associate senators with particular issues and accomplishments, they will provide publicity and campaign support and thus help the senator generate a reputation as an effective legislator.[6] A strong reputation and high enough familiarity with constituents may help convince potential challengers that the costs of mounting a campaign against the senator are prohibitive. In this way, a senator's efforts to educate and serve intermediaries during the governing stage can go a long way to diminishing the possibility of a strong challenger in the next reelection campaign.

In contrast, if senators scatter their efforts too far and too wide, they may have greater difficulty associating themselves with particular accomplishments to attentive audiences, such as interest groups or the local media. Such was the case of Senator Paul Wellstone (D-MN) in his first two years in the Senate. A legislative director related the story of how Senator Wellstone instructed the 1993 incoming freshman class of senators not to do what he had done: "[He] went to the freshman orientation meeting and told them all not to do what he did in his first two years. He used to go to the floor all the time to speak on everything when he did not know what he was talking about and he didn't have anything to contribute. He said he realized that he was wasting his time and pissing people off."[7]

If a senator's agenda is not sufficiently focused, interest groups and the local media will not award the senator credit for specific accomplishments, which makes it even more unlikely that the average voter will be able to do so. A senator with an unfocused agenda thus assumes

[5] Personal interview with staff member.
[6] See chapter 6 for an extended discussion of interest-group support of senators from the same state.
[7] Personal interview with staff member.

the risk of becoming known for being ineffective and inattentive. It may be a reputation, but it is certainly not the reputation that senators desire.

Reelection campaigns are the last stage of a reputation-building process, and, as such, they often serve as summaries of senators' portfolios and reflect the set of choices that senators made about committee assignment and bill and amendment sponsorship and cosponsorship over the previous five years. As one staff member declared, "you can't go out and say that you are doing something without physical evidence."[8] One way in which legislative work is emphasized on the campaign trail is typified by the following quote from Senator Mitch McConnell (R-KY): "Why in the world would Graves County want to trade a senator with rising seniority on the Agriculture Committee for a fellow who wouldn't know which end of a cow to milk? I think that's the sale pitch here" (Cross 1989).

Even with a strong legislative record, senators still believe in infinite repetition during a campaign as a means of reminding the inattentive public of what the senator has accomplished:

> In order to remind people what the senator has done, we put a lot of money in advertising. We use early media to say what was done before the opponent even begins the campaign. In the last campaign, we spent $200,000 in Nebraska in February for four or five weeks for five-minute spots. [This is] all done as an insurance policy. We consider the campaign a failure if a constituent can't list two or three things the senator has done for the state at the end of the campaign. The campaign is designed to narrow things down and repeat specific things over and over again.[9]

It is not merely a perception on the part of senators and their staff that a solid legislative record translates into greater electoral success. A recent *New York Times* article pointed out the importance of campaigning on an established legislative record:

> An examination of hundreds of commercials broadcast by Democrats and Republicans alike shows that a striking proportion of contenders are cramming their advertisements with bland, but they hope, convincing pitches that include insider attributes like "experience" and "record" and "proven." Sen. Christopher Bond, R-Mo., this week unveiled a commercial with this tag line: "So much experience. So much he's done." . . . Many advertisements this year could be best described as 30-second, televised resumes. One after another, they feature newspaper headlines telling of candidates' accomplishments or bills they proposed. (Berke 1998)

[8] Personal interview with staff member.
[9] Personal interview with staff member.

More systematic evidence of the importance of a legislative record to a reelection campaign can be found in Patrick Sellers' (1998) study of the 1988 Senate races. Sellers demonstrates that successful candidates for the Senate build their campaigns around their legislative records and emphasize issues that align closely with constituent interests. Moreover, candidates who tried to market themselves as legislators in specific issue areas but in reality had no record to back up their claims fared worse then candidates who adhered to a valid record of accomplishment throughout their campaign.

However, there is no set guarantee that constituents who previously paid little attention to the Senate are going to transform into attentive publics during reelection campaigns; it often depends on the amount of publicity the campaign receives. As Benjamin Page and Robert Shapiro (1992, 393) have demonstrated, voters display less familiarity and knowledge about their government when the overall amount of available information is limited. They write that "for reasons of chance or design; the public may have no way (no helpful cue givers, no free information on TV) to know what is going on." Consequently, the extent to which Senate campaigns can be effective devices for informing constituents depends on whether the campaign is high intensity or low intensity (Westlye 1991). High-intensity races involve strong candidates (or challengers), focus on salient issues, and receive a lot of local media coverage, so there is a great deal of information available to constituents to form impressions of the candidates. Interest groups also play a greater role in high-intensity races, more now than ever, not just through campaign contributions, but in disseminating information through paid "issue" advertising (West and Loomis 1998). In contrast, low-intensity races are characterized by weak challengers and little news coverage and are therefore highly inefficient means of informing voters.

In the case of incumbent senators, a low-intensity race is evidence that the senator has probably become established prior to the reelection campaign, because no strong candidate emerged as a challenger. One of the risks of a low-intensity campaign is that voters will not be mobilized by the campaign and will fail to turn out at the polls; one result of low voter turnout is that the race can be influenced by factors external to the candidate. A high-intensity race, on the other hand, may be an indication that the senator did not succeed in establishing a strong reputation prior to reelection and thus invited a strong challenge. Ironically, the conditions under which a campaign will be most informative about a senator's record are also the conditions that might reflect inherent vulnerabilities for the incumbent. If a reelection campaign turns into a high-intensity race, the incumbent senator has already lost the opportunity to set the agenda of the campaign by running on an established record. Instead, the senator will be forced to respond to a challenger's attacks, on issues determined jointly by the challenger, interest groups, and the media. The bottom line is that senators cannot afford to wait until the beginning of a campaign cycle to try to establish a reputation among constituents.

Patterns of Constituent Recognition of Senators

To this point, the emphasis has been on senators' perceptions of their constituents, and how those perceptions influence legislative agenda setting. The remainder of this chapter explores the nature and content of the opinions that constituents actually exhibit about their senators, and what relationship, if any, exists between senators' legislative work and constituent evaluations.

Although there is a large body of literature on the extent to which voters know anything about their elected officials and public policy in general, there is no consensus in the literature on the extent and content of constituent knowledge of senators, individually, or in comparison with their state colleagues.[10] However, scholars have analyzed public opinion data about senators in an effort to identify which constituents appear to be familiar with their senators, and why. For example, population size has been shown to facilitate or hamper reputation building: the smaller the state, for example, the easier it is for senators to establish contact with residents in person, or by mail (Hibbing and Brandes 1983; Hibbing and Alford 1990; Oppenheimer 1996). Sinclair (1990) showed that senators who received national media attention were more familiar to, and viewed more favorably by, constituents than senators who did not receive such coverage. Others, such as Franklin (1993), have tried to analyze relative levels of constituent familiarity with their senators using the 1988 and 1990 Senate Election Study like and dislike mentions data. Franklin found that 59 percent of respondents could name a like or dislike about their senators, and the degree of recognition of senators was a combination of state size, reelection campaigns, seniority, and educational levels among constituents.

As an alternative to using like and dislike mentions as a measure of familiarity with senators, Binder, Maltzman, and Sigelman (1998) use a data set on approval ratings of senators compiled from a 1996 Mason-Dixon poll. They argue that a senator's individual approval rating is influenced by ideological proximity to constituents, as well as state size

---

[10] The major works on this subject include Berelson, Lazarsfeld, and McPhee (1954); Campbell et al. (1960); Converse (1964); Nie, Verba, and Petrocik (1976); Bartels (1988); Carmines and Stimson (1989); Zaller (1992); and Erikson, Wright, and McIver (1993).

and diversity, but that attentiveness to state interests by a senator does not exert an impact on approval ratings. As such, their work confirms that when constituents are familiar with their senators' ideology, it appears to be the strongest predictor of whether or not they approve of the senator. However, their model does not include any comprehensive measure of legislative activity other than membership on the Appropriations Committee, and therefore they were unable to test for correlations between legislative activity in specific issue areas and constituent awareness of their senators.

Two other scholars have more directly addressed the question of constituent approval of both members of a Senate delegation. Born (1997) examined the patterns of recognition and approval among constituents of their two senators and members of the House delegation from their state. Using a combination of measures, including Senate Election Study thermometer ratings, he found that "most of the time, satisfaction with one public official has no impact on the popularity of the second," with the exception of the 1990 Senate elections (198). In the 1990 Senate elections, Born found that favorable evaluations of the senator who was seeking reelection were correlated with favorable evaluations of the other incumbent senator. He argues that the effect is due to high or low saliency of the Senate at a given point in time. When one senator attracts a lot of media attention to a reelection campaign, constituents are more likely to focus their attention on the Senate and are therefore likely to have an impression of the other senator.

Bernstein (1992) more specifically focuses on the relationship between approval ratings for senators from the same state. Using thermometer approval ratings from the 1988 Senate elections, he tests for the influence of ideological disparity on constituent ratings for both senators. Bernstein hypothesizes that the farther apart two senators are along the ideological spectrum, the greater the distance should be in constituent approval ratings for the two senators. Using differences in seniority, national media coverage, constituency service, and ideology, he predicted differences in constituent approval ratings. His results run contrary to those of Binder, Maltzman, and Sigelman in that ideological disparity did not influence constituent evaluations of both senators as much as differences in perceived attentiveness and governing style. From these results, Bernstein concludes that constituents can perceive both senators to be adequately representing them despite the fact that the senators are separated by major differences in ideology and/or partisanship.

Taken in combination, these works are suggestive as to what might serve to facilitate reputation building among constituents. Clearly, state size, heterogeneity, and partisanship will all play a role in whether or not a senator is viewed favorably by residents of the state. Taking into account the partisan or ideological distribution in a state, senators will face a larger or smaller potential support base depending on where they lie on the ideological spectrum.[11] Bernstein's work suggests that legislative efforts can reduce the distance between approval ratings for two opposite-party senators from the same state. By constructing a popular legislative portfolio, with sufficient attention to state interests and concerns, senators can overcome a partisan disadvantage. For senators from split-party states, a strong legislative record can compensate for lower approval ratings; for senators from same-party states, legislative records can establish tangible differences between them and, in doing so, attract individual and partisan support. In either case, all senators benefit from constructing an independent and easily identifiable representational agenda.

LEGISLATIVE WORK AND REPUTATIONS: EMPIRICAL EVIDENCE

This work differs from the works noted above in that it delves deeper into the nature of constituent opinions about senators by analyzing the content of like and dislike mentions from the 1988–1992 Pooled Senate Election Study. The purpose of this analysis is to test for the effects of a senator's institutional choices on his overall reputation across the state. In this case, therefore, it is appropriate to use a summary measure of all like and dislike responses about a senator as the dependent variable, rather than trying to predict individual constituent responses. To this end, I rely heavily on the argument set forth by Page and Shapiro (1992) that collective public opinion is a better barometer of the relationship between elected officials and voters than individual public opinion.[12] They state their case succinctly in the concluding chapter of *The Rational Public* :

---

[11] Binder, Maltzman, and Sigelman (1998) suggest that senators from a split-party delegation face a greater electoral challenge more generally, and hence they may have to work harder to shore up their bases than senators from a single-party state. Despite the fact that it is easier to distinguish between split-party senators from the same state, it is no guarantee of favorable approval ratings. Senators from the same party have the opposite problem in that their electoral coalition is naturally larger in a state where they share the majority party, and it leads to somewhat higher approval ratings, all else being equal, but their capacity to distinguish themselves on other legislative dimensions is diminished.

[12] Bartels (1991) makes a similar point in analyzing the relationship between collective public opinion and congressional action on defense spending.

The apparent paradox that collective opinion is solid and meaningful, while the measured opinions of many or most individuals seem to be shaky or non-existent, can probably be explained by a combination of three factors. First, random measurement errors cancel out across large numbers of respondents, so that surveys yield much more accurate information about the collectively than about any particular individual. Second, temporary opinion changes by different individuals occur in offsetting directions, so that they, too, cancel out and allow collective measurements to reflect the more enduring tendencies of opinion. Third, processes of collective deliberation, and reliance upon trusted cue givers, enable people to arrive at reasonable policy preferences without an extensive informational base. (384-85)

By analyzing the sum of like and dislike mentions about senators over the course of six years, I am essentially constructing a measure of the collective public opinion of senators in their home states. The issues that respondents associate with their senators, as well as the more intangible measures of trust and confidence, are essentially treated as proxies for senators' reputations.

Although the design of the Senate Election Study relies on relatively small sample sizes, it is still among the best available data because it provides access to unstructured constituent knowledge of their senators. There are approximately 800 possible responses from constituents in this data set that can be classified in two categories: issue and nonissue. Examples of issue responses include specific reference to "poverty, education, crime, drugs, nuclear policy, abortion, social security, wages, veterans, military, central America, etc." Examples of nonissue responses include more personal references to character or activity, such as "honest, young, energetic, experienced, represent views of the district, helps district economy." If constituents are aware of senators' legislative work, it is more likely to be directly reflected in issue mentions, and it is less likely to be reflected in nonissue mentions. In contrast, awareness of governing style is more likely to emerge in nonissue responses and less likely to be displayed in issue mentions.

The Senate Election Study like and dislike responses can be used to study senators' reputations in several ways. First, as both Sinclair and Franklin have argued, the total number of like and dislike mentions is a good measure of overall constituent familiarity with their senators. Second, the six-year time period offers the opportunity to judge a senator's reputation over the course of an entire term and, just as important, offers the opportunity to study constituent opinion of senators from the same state over time. The extended time period also allows for a study of changes in constituent opinion of a senator when a state colleague is replaced. Third, the wide-ranging content of the like and dislike responses can be used to assess constituent evaluations on a number of dimensions, from issues to personal character to governing competence. Moreover, these evaluations can be tested for correlations to a senator's actual legislative record, as well as the content of local media coverage, to see if senators' efforts to publicize their activities yield dividends among constituents. If senators do pursue particular strategies to cultivate a reputation by choosing specific committee assignments or courting members of the local press, then it is important to test for correlations between that activity and the overall visibility of senators, as measured by the total number of like and dislike mentions about them.

FINDINGS

The first model is designed to determine how factors like state size, local media coverage, committee assignments, reelection campaigns, and sharing the same party as a state colleague influence a senator's ability to become well known among constituents. The sample used in this chapter includes data on twenty-four senators from ten states; the states vary by region, population size, and partisan distribution, and the senators under study vary in their seniority, party affiliation, committee assignments, and committee positions. As explained in chapter 3, one of the goals of this book is to determine whether a connection exists among senators' legislative work, local media coverage of that work, and constituents' opinions of their senators, all in the context of a two-member delegation. One of the limits of the quantitative analysis is that it must be performed on the sample of states for which all three types of data are available. In this case, electronic access to *local* newspaper coverage of senators during the years 1987–1992 is available for only ten states, and detailed public opinion data from the Senate Election Study is also available only for this same set of years. Despite the limitations on the size of the data set, as a whole it contains sufficient variation across states and senators over time to make it an appropriate and valid means of exploring the dynamics of Senate representation.

Media coverage exerts a substantive and significant effect on the total number of like and dislike mentions for senators; for every additional twenty-five newspaper articles in which a senator is mentioned, respondents named one additional mention about the senator (table 4.1). However, few of the institutional variables exert a statistically significant impact on overall visibility. The only committee assignment to exert an effect on like and dislike mentions was the Judiciary Committee; being a member of the Finance Committee or the Appropriations Committee, two highly distributive committees, did not register a significant

TABLE 4.1
Selected Determinants of the Number of Constituent Mentions about Senators

Intercept	33.0**
	(14.3)
State population size	−.79**
	(.46)
Senior senator	1.6
	(8.9)
Chairman	4.2
	(9.1)
Reelection	11.1*
	(6.7)
Presidential candidate	−27.0**
	(13.7)
Shared party affiliation	3.5
	(7.4)
Number of committee assignments	1.5
	(3.8)
Finance Committee	3.9
	(10.5)
Appropriations Committee	5.9
	(10.0)
Judiciary Committee	21.6**
	(10.2)
State media coverage	.04***
	(.01)
Adj. R^2	.32
Prob > F	.004
N	55

Source: Dow Jones News Retrieval Service, 1987–1992; Pooled Senate Election Study 1987–1992.

Standard errors in parentheses. ***Statistically significant at .01, one-tailed test. **Statistically significant at .05, one-tailed test. *Statistically significant at .10, one-tailed test.

effect on overall constituent recognition. Not surprisingly, and as Franklin (1993) also found, running for reelection exerts a positive effect on constituent like and dislike responses, while state size exerts a negative effect.

It is more likely that the strong connections between institutional behavior and constituent recognition, as filtered by media coverage, are found in specific issue areas. To test for such effects, I subsampled like and dislike mentions that dealt with particular issue areas.[13] Although the actual percentage of respondents who can name specific issues as reasons for liking or disliking their senator is relatively low (ranging from 15 to 20 percent), at the same time, these are the respondents who probably represent the better informed among a senator's constituents. If these respondents can identify issues that are included in a senator's legislative portfolio and associate different issues with each senator, then senators' efforts to differentiate do yield an informational payoff. In addition, other constituents, who comprise the "inattentive" public, are likely to pick up on signals or clues sent from the attentive public about their senators.

In the second model, I group specific-issue like or dislike mentions for each senator in six major issue areas, namely, judiciary, labor and human resources, energy/environment and public works, finance/budget, agriculture, and defense/foreign relations, that correspond to the jurisdictions of major Senate committees. For each issue area, I predict the number of like or dislike mentions as a function of seniority, reelection, prior elective office, shared party affiliation, media coverage in the issue area, and the state colleague's media coverage in the issue area. Because local media coverage of senators in specific issue areas is highly dependent on holding a committee seat in that issue area (see chapter 3), I exclude committee assignment from the model.[14] I omit state size from the model because it is a strong predictor of media coverage, and because there is no logical expectation that state size should affect constituent recognition of a senator in a specific issue area the way state size affects overall constituent familiarity.

The results of model 2 indicate that constituents respond to information contained in local media coverage in specific issue areas when naming likes and dislikes about the senators from their state. In five out of six issue areas—judiciary, labor and human resources, finance/budget, agriculture, and defense/foreign affairs—media coverage increased constituent like or dislike responses about the senator (table 4.2). This

[13] These are the like and dislike responses that are coded from 900 to 1199.

[14] The correlations between committee assignment and state media coverage in committee jurisdiction areas are as follows: Foreign Relations = −.14, Armed Services = .48**, Finance = .43**, Labor and Human Resources = .36, Judiciary = .58**, Energy/EPW = .02, and Agriculture = .62**.

TABLE 4.2
Effects of State Media Coverage on Constituent Recognition of Senators in
Issue Areas

Variable	Judiciary	Labor	Energy/EPW
Intercept	.39	−.28	−.31
	(.81)	(.63)	(.41)
Seniority	−.34**	−.09	−.08
	(.19)	(.16)	(.10)
Reelection	.87**	.24	.85***
	(.49)	(.40)	(.28)
Presidential candidate	−1.5**	−.77	−.43
	(.84)	(.68)	(.43)
Former member of House	.23	−.07	−.16
	(.54)	(.44)	(.28)
Former governor	.90	.33	.94**
	(.63)	(.53)	(.44)
Judiciary media	.03***		
	(.01)		
State colleague judiciary issues	.10		
	(.14)		
Labor media		.02**	
		(.01)	
State colleague labor issues		−.001	
		(.149)	
Energy/EPW media			−.002
			(.005)
State colleague energy/ EPW issues			.36***
			(.13)
Shared party affiliation	−.48	.99**	.43
	(.65)	(.48)	(.29)
Adj. R^2	.31	.25	.29
prob > F	.002	.009	.004
N	52	52	52

Variable	Finance/Budget	Agriculture	Defense/Foreign
Intercept	1.14**	−.19	.002
	(.68)	(.40)	(.806)

TABLE 4.2 *(continued)*

Variable	Finance/Budget	Agriculture	Defense/Foreign
Seniority	−.14 (.16)	.15 (.09)	−.03 (.21)
Reelection	1.03** (.40)	.43** (.22)	.69* (.48)
Former member of House	−.19 (.51)	.10 (.24)	.90* (.60)
Former governor	−.83* (.56)	−.01 (.30)	−.41 (.66)
Finance/budget media	.003 (.009)		
State colleague finance/ budget issues	.40*** (.14)		
Agriculture media		.011** (.005)	
State colleague agriculture issues		.33** (.14)	
Defense/foreign media			.012*** (.004)
State colleague defense/ foreign issues			−.08 (.14)
Shared party affiliation	.06 (.46)	−.09 (.24)	.17 (.58)
Adj. R^2	.19	.23	.16
prob $>$ F	.03	.01	.05
N	52	52	52

Source: Dow Jones News Retrieval Service, 1987–1992; Senate Election Studies, issue mentions, 1987–1992.

Standard errors in parentheses. ***Statistically significant at .01, one-tailed test. **Statistically significant at .05, one-tailed test. *Statistically significant at .10, one-tailed test.

result, combined with the results from chapter 3 that showed that media coverage accurately reflects legislative work, suggests that the media does appear to serve as an informational intermediary between senators and their constituents.

On average, there was approximately 20 percent overlap in specific issues that were mentioned for senators from the same state, suggesting that there is some degree of correlation between issue mentions among same-state senators. However, the fact that the remaining 80 percent of issue mentions for senators from the same state did not overlap is a stronger indication that constituents associate different accomplishments with each of their senators. The effects of the issue mentions for one senator on the issue mentions for the other senator vary across issue areas. In three out of six issue areas—finance/budget, agriculture, and energy/environment—there is a statistically significant and positive correlation between issue mentions for one senator and issue mentions for the other senator from the state. But in the other three issue areas—judiciary, labor and human resources, and defense/foreign relations—there is no significant correlation between the two senators.

The contrasting results for each set of issue areas may have something to do with the nature of the issues and their importance to the state. Issues such as agriculture may be locally concentrated in a state, such that even if one senator from the state does not actively address the issue, constituents may simply assume that the senator is attentive because the interest is so important to the state. For more ideological issue areas, such as judiciary and labor and human resources, it may be easier for senators from the same state to stake out clear positions, or adopt distinctly different portfolios, because these issues are less directly connected to concrete state concerns.

It is important not to overestimate the findings of models 1 and 2; they do not suggest that constituents are fully aware of the distinctions between their two senators on every dimension. Rather, this work examines the types of information that constituents possess about their senators, and whether there is a discernible influence from the two-member structure of Senate delegations on constituent impressions of their senators. To this end, these quantitative results provide support for the anecdotal data presented earlier, in two ways. First, senators' choices about legislative work are reflected in local media coverage about them, which means that senators' reputations are based on reasonably accurate information. Second, differentiation among senators from the same state, as covered in the local media, is recognized by constituents and reflected in their specific reasons for liking and disliking their senators. In sum, the efforts by senators from the same state to use their *legislative* work to establish unique reputations in their states, controlling for their partisan and ideological affiliation, appear to succeed.

Reputation as a Reflection of Home Style

The other major component of senatorial reputation consists of personal characteristics typically associated with a senator, such as personality, trust, honesty, integrity, and competence. These types of responses reflect less tangible aspects of reputations than concrete legislative accomplishments do, but they are often the by-product of senators' legislative work. In the case of the New York senators, Moynihan and D'Amato, constituent like and dislike suggest that they were successful in establishing distinct governing styles. Respondents said they liked Moynihan for such reasons as his "intelligence, he is well known, his speaking ability, he is liberal, his government experience, his honesty, and his role as a statesman." In contrast, constituents said they liked D'Amato because he "helps people on a personal level, he gets more done, he represents the views of the district, he brought money to the district economy, he is a Republican, and he favors 'people like me.' "

Respondents also gave different reasons for disliking the two senators. For Moynihan, respondents said, "he hasn't done anything, does not represent the views of the district, can't talk to the common man, too old, and isn't accessible to constituents." For D'Amato, respondents said that he is "undependable, dishonest, unintelligent, runs a dishonest government, and was involved in a scandal." Granted, these responses are not as unique as the issues associated with both senators, but the very fact that, even within the vaguest measure of reputation, these two senators are assigned markedly different characteristics indicates that their particular governing styles are noted by constituents.

It bears examining these stylistic references about senators from the same state to amass a more accurate picture of the impressionistic knowledge that constituents possess about their senators. Unlike issue mentions, which can be categorized according to specific areas that correspond with committee jurisdictions, the amorphous character and style references are more difficult to group together and analyze in a systematic way. For this reason, these responses were analyzed qualitatively and will be used in a more descriptive fashion to highlight the stylistic impressions that constituents form about each of their senators. Because nonissue mentions tend to be less specific in general, we would expect to see more overlap between senators from the same state in constituents' responses in this category. Yet there was only an average of 33 percent overlap in nonissue mentions for senators from the same state, only 13 percent greater than for issue-based mentions. The fact that 67 percent of nonissue mentions did not overlap for pairs of senators is a strong indication that nonissue mentions can be used to measure differences in how constituents assess the two senators from their state on the basis of performance and character.

Throughout this book, certain independent variables, including partisan affiliation, ideology, seniority, committee assignment, and committee positions, have been shown to influence senators' strategies to differentiate themselves. These variables shape the incentive and the opportunity for senators to establish separate reputations among constituents. If the typical informational flow is from senator to local media and interest groups to constituents, then we may see signs of recognition of these variables in constituents' nonissue or "stylistic" responses about their individual senators.

For example, the partisan composition of a delegation strongly influences how much overlap exists between senators' legislative portfolios, but there appears to be little difference in the extent of overlap of constituent like and dislike mentions (table 4.3). However, there was a ten-

TABLE 4.3
Overlap in Like and Dislike Mentions for Senators from Same State (in selected states)

State[a]	Senators	Same Party	Issue (percent)	Nonissue (percent)	Total (percent)
Nebraska	Exon (D) Karnes (R)	N	17	30	23
	Exon (D) Kerrey (D)	Y	30	40	35
Texas	Bentsen (D) Gramm (R)	N	33	41	37
New York	Moynihan (D) D'Amato (R)	N	24	30	27
Illinois	Dixon (D) Simon (D)	Y	19	31	20
Georgia	Nunn (D) Fowler (D)	Y	18	42	30
California	Cranston (D) Wilson (R)	N	10	32	21
Florida	Graham (D) Mack (D)	N	21	25	23
Minnesota	Durenberger (R) Boschwitz (R)	Y	19	36	27
	Durenberger (R) Wellstone (D)	N	14	21	17
Kentucky	Ford (D) McConnell (R)	N	17	41	29

Source: Pooled Senate Election Study, 1987–1992.

[a]The sample of states for which local newspaper coverage data are available (see chapter 3 for details).

dency in *same-party* states for constituents to name party or ideology as a reason for liking or disliking one senator from the state, but not the other. In Massachusetts, Georgia, Nebraska, and Illinois, constituents identified party or ideology as a like or dislike of one senator but not the other. In Massachusetts Senator Kerry was a Democrat and too liberal, but no such complaint was made about Senator Kennedy, who was certainly one of the more liberal members of the Senate. In Georgia being a Democrat was a problem for Senator Nunn, but his junior Democratic colleague, Senator Fowler, was accused of being too liberal. In the case of Nebraska, being a Democrat and a liberal were seen as negative attributes for Senator Kerrey, but his Democratic colleague, Senator Exon, received no such criticism. In Illinois constituents assigned the wrong party affiliation to Senator Dixon, a Democrat, who was praised for being a Republican. The confusion may have been in part based on the fact that Senator Dixon's roll-call voting record was to the right of that of his Democratic colleague, Senator Simon. These sorts of distinctions provide support for the more general behavior pointed out by Eric Uslaner (1999), who makes the argument that in same-party states, one senator will adopt a more extreme partisan position than the other. Even if same-party senators are not that far apart ideologically, constituents may come to perceive them as farther apart than they are as a result of their more general efforts to draw contrasts with one another.

In split-party states there were clearer and more accurate demarcations between the two senators in both like and dislike mentions. For example, in California respondents correctly described Senator Wilson as a Republican and conservative, while Senator Cranston was labeled a Democrat and liberal. In Florida Senator Mack was aptly described as Republican and conservative, as compared with his colleague Senator Graham, who was labeled a liberal. In Kentucky Senator Ford was duly noted for being a Democrat and liberal, while Senator McConnell was noted for being Republican and conservative. In Texas constituents clearly identified the fact that their two senators were from different parties: Senator Bentsen was a moderate Democrat and Senator Gramm was a flexible Republican. Once again, though, it bears repeating that partisan distinctions were not the only types of distinctions made about these senators, and senators do not rely solely on their partisan affiliation in a competitive two-party state as the foundation for their reputations. Still, it is apparent that the task of differentiating within the same state is made easier when senators are from opposing parties.

It is also interesting to note what happens to impressions of senators when the occupant of the other Senate seat changes. In Nebraska, when it was represented by split-party senators, respondents correctly identified Senator Karnes as a Republican and Senator Exon as a Democrat. When Senator Kerrey replaced Senator Karnes, respondents did not name Senator Exon's party as a reason for liking or disliking him, but they did name being a Democrat and liberal as reasons for disliking Senator Kerrey. In Minnesota, when Senator Durenberger was paired with the more conservative Senator Boschwitz, who shared his party affiliation, Senator Durenberger was viewed as a moderate and improperly labeled a Democrat. When Minnesota changed from a same-party delegation to a split-party delegation with the election of Senator Wellstone in 1990, Senator Durenberger was noted for being conservative, while Senator Wellstone was correctly identified as liberal and a Democrat. Interestingly, with the election of a clearly more liberal and opposite-party state colleague, Senator Durenberger looked more conservative in comparison.

Another factor in distinguishing between senators is the recognition of seniority by using the labels "junior" and "senior" to delineate which senator was elected first. Senators and their staff acknowledge that perceptions change when a senator moves from junior to senior senator, as the legislative director to Senator Hank Brown (R-CO) pointed out:

> What has changed is public expectation in our state. People will say things like—now he's the senior senator from the state. Even House members and our new Democratic Senator, before they make their decisions they will ask what he will do—how he will react. He has more visibility in our state . . . if you do something together [the Democratic senator and Brown] and you agree that both senators are going to do it, he will take the lead on the bill because he is senior.[15]

A comparison of the specific like mentions for senators from the same state that do not overlap reveals that constituents tend to associate seniority and government experience with the senior senator in the delegation and not with the junior member. For example, in the case of Massachusetts, respondents said they liked the senior senator, Senator Kennedy, because of his "experience and seniority," and they liked the junior senator, Senator Kerry, because he was "young, flexible and energetic." In Georgia the senior senator, Senator Nunn, was described as "decisive, a leader, and had government experience" while the junior senator, Senator Fowler, was lauded for "talking to the common man, being efficient, and supporting equality." In Texas the senior senator, Senator Bentsen, was described as "mature, experienced, and a leader" while the junior senator, Senator Gramm, was described as "flexible, and someone who listened to people." In California respondents described the senior senator, Senator Cranston, as "experienced, a leader, and senior" while they described the junior senator, Senator Wilson, as

---

[15] Personal interview with staff member.

"decisive, honest, and young." While these individual examples are not conclusive, the very fact that these *different reasons* for liking (and disliking) senators were offered suggests that constituents' impressions reflect actual differences in seniority status between two senators from the same state.

Unlike issue-based responses, there were few substantive mentions in the nonissue category that could be construed as related to senators' committee positions or committee assignments. At best there were only scattered references for some senators that coincided with their campaign platforms or committee assignments. For example, Senator Nunn, who was chairman of the Armed Services Committee during the time of the survey, was described as a "military man." Senator Kerry and Senator Kerrey were both cited for being "military men, and proveterans," but neither of these men sat on the Armed Services Committee. Senator Kerry did sit on the Foreign Relations Committee, he was a Vietnam War veteran, and he used his position to investigate missing POWs, so his constituents may have associated military issues with his prior experience and his work. Senator Kerrey did not sit on a relevant military committee but was well known for losing his leg in battle in the Vietnam War; in his case, his preexisting individual reputation as a Vietnam veteran also may have carried over into constituent evaluations of him as a senator.[16] Despite these few examples, there were no consistent patterns among nonissue-based responses that reflected senators' legislative agendas.

It also appears that constituents come to perceive one senator from the state as more attentive or more helpful to constituents than the other, as in the case of the two senators from New York. In Nebraska, Florida, California, Illinois, New York, and Kentucky, one senator was praised for "representing district views" or "helping the district economy," while the other was not associated with such district- (state-) level activity. Being seen as inattentive to the district can also hurt senators, as in the case of Texas, Florida, New York, and Georgia, where constituents disliked one of the senators for "not helping the district" or "not representing the views of the district."

But these differences in judgments about senators' attention to their states do not appear to correlate strongly with senators' legislative portfolios. In other words, typical state-directed behavior, such as joining the Appropriations or Agriculture Committee, did not explain which senators were perceived as more helpful than their state colleagues were. In the case of Senator D'Amato of New York, whose entire legis-

---

[16] Both Senator Exon and Senator Kerrey received like issue mentions for their work in defense and military issues.

lative portfolio consisted of securing funds for his state, the connection is obvious. But for other senators, such as Senator Simon, who has been described as a policy wonk at times, respondents' descriptions of his helping the district were not directly linked to his legislative agenda. It may be the case that one senator emphasizes service to the state far more than the other, based on institutional opportunities within the Senate, but that all senators try to secure targeted benefits for their state at some time during their six-year term. Even if the information that constituents possess about a senator's activity is limited to a single benefit, such as helping someone get a passport more quickly, or securing an earmarked grant for a local college, the senator can be generally perceived as attentive to individual or state needs as a result.

In sum, although there was more overlap between same-state senators in the nonissue category than in the issue category (33 percent to 20 percent), the responses that were offered about one senator were markedly different than those offered about the other senator from the state. Partisanship, ideology, seniority, honesty, and attentiveness to the state were all offered as reasons to like or dislike a senator, but these responses were not offered to the same degree in assessing each of the senators. For example, in a state with two Democratic senators, only one would be lauded or criticized for party affiliation, while the other might be lauded or criticized for being young or old, inexperienced or experienced. Even in split-party states, constituents appeared to use different criteria in their judgments of each senator. Overall, constituents correctly associated different traits and characteristics with the two senators from their state, which is an indication that senators appear to be moderately successful at distinguishing themselves from each other on measures of competence and sincerity.

Conclusion

In this chapter, I have argued that senators seek to develop broad reputations, based on party affiliation, ideology, legislative specialization, and governing style, in order to create a favorable impression among voters. To this end, senators and their staffs spend six years constructing a legislative portfolio that will set them apart from all other senators, but most importantly from their state colleague, who competes for attention and approval in the same geographic area. Forming a broad reputation requires targeting legislative work and publicity, and, depending on the partisan composition of their states, senators will emphasize one or all of the components of their reputation to varying degrees. Successful reputation building occurs when the informational intermediaries between a senator and constituents—party, local media, and interest groups—each reinforce the senator's reputation by transmitting favorable impressions to the general public.

Analysis of public opinion data reveals that the amount of effort and resources that senators expend trying to get through to their constituents yields dividends. In general, the legislative specialization that occurs among senators from the same state is successfully translated by the media; when the media allots coverage to senators in specific issue areas, based on their legislative record, constituents reflect that coverage in their like and dislike responses about senators. Distinctions between same-state senators even show up in nonissue or stylistic opinions offered by constituents, albeit not clearly along the traditional "national" versus "state" dichotomy. Instead, constituents associate particular and personal characteristics, for example, a war record or seniority, with one senator but not the other senator. As a collective public, constituents are able to associate different accomplishments with each of their incumbent senators, even with limited amounts of information.

It is the apparent gap between senators' perceptions of the importance of reputations and constituent knowledge that presents the puzzle for students of representation. Clearly senators get a return for their reputation-building efforts, but it is in no way an equal return, and it is not always profitable because strong reputations do not always guarantee reelection. However, because senators are risk-averse legislators, they construct legislative portfolios that are designed to establish the appearance of responsiveness to pertinent state interests and constituent opinions. It is the very perception that senators need to build independent reputations in their home states that ensures at least a minimum level of service from senators.

For those who wish to assess the quality and nature of Senate representation and accountability, the two-person structure of a Senate delegation is the key component that should be examined. The very existence of another senator who represents the same state guarantees that senators will be attentive to state interests and opinions because there is always another senator to whom constituents can look in comparison. If one senator takes a stand against an important state interest, the other senator is there to present a contrasting position, which automatically limits the extent that senators will ignore or undermine their own constituents. One could make the argument that no senator, being risk-averse, would contradict the interests of the state, but there are a number of issues and interests on which senators can act that constituents might never learn about. The same potential electoral forces, which prospectively hold senators accountable, are magnified by the presence of a state colleague of equal position.

In much the same way that V. O. Key (1949) argued for the importance of a competitive two-party system, a similar case can be made for a two-person district. The very same need to establish solid electoral bases among constituents, which encourages two parties to be more responsive, also encourages senators from the same state to be more responsive as well. That responsiveness is embodied in the fact that senators from the same state, regardless of shared or split-party affiliation, incorporate different issues and interests into their agendas, in order to court a distinct set of home state voters. If there were only one senator per state, senators might represent only elite economic interests, or residents in the most populous region, or voters in one party, because there would be no implicit or explicit competition from another senator. But with two senators, there is always competition for credit, publicity, visibility, and the ultimate goal of being an effective senator for the state — thus the very structure of a Senate delegation sustains the incentive for two senators to diversify their representational agendas.

Chapter 5

EXPANDING THE BOUNDARIES OF
ELECTORAL COALITIONS

A S I ASSERTED in the beginning of this work, Senate representation is multidimensional: partisan, economic, geographic, and-
stylistic. Senators use the legislative tools at their disposal to
address the "interests" of their state on these four levels. But identifying
and defining the "interests" of a state is a complex task for both the
senator and the political scientist. Average voters, who make up the
senator's ultimate audience, can have preferences across several dimensions. For example, a voter might be a Republican, Democrat, or Independent; that same voter might be employed in a steel mill or be a
corporate lawyer; that same voter might live in a city or in a small
town; and that same voter might prefer a "statesman" senator over a
"pork-barreler." These divisions among constituencies are not mutually
exclusive; voters who live in geographic regions may have identifiable
economic interests associated with living in those regions, and voters in
demographic groups may have partisan or ideological views that are
associated with being a member of a group. Explaining how senators
perceive their states in terms of geographic regions and constituent
groups therefore becomes an important element in defining Senate representation.

Because constituent interests can take on several forms—for example,
as individual interest, a larger economic interest, or part of an organized
interest group—senators can use different legislative tools to formulate
various types of appeals to voters. Ideally, all senators want to maximize their reelection prospects and attract as many votes as possible.
Theoretically, one could argue that the entire state is open to such vote-
seeking efforts by a senator because he is elected statewide. But in reality, such strong, widespread support is difficult to achieve due to the
limited time and resources afforded to any individual senator. Additionally, the existence of two senators from the same state creates implicit competition between the two senators when they try to serve the
same constituents.

One way that senators from the same state can meet the challenge of
limited resources and being part of a two-person delegation is to select
different subsets of constituent interests and opinions to address in their

respective legislative agendas. In doing so, senators try to build clearly identifiable and separate reputations as senators that will form the basis for electoral support among voters. If same-state senators are successful in using their agendas to attract support among distinctive sets of voters, then voting trends in the state should reflect their efforts.

In this chapter and the next, I discuss the ways in which senators perceive the interests of their state in terms of geography, demography, and economics. This chapter explores the ways that same-state senators target geographic areas and related demographic groups in order to increase electoral support. Chapter 6 illustrates the differences between same-state senators in terms of the economic interests they represent, and it shows how the patterns of campaign contributions by state economic interest groups reflect senators' efforts to build distinctive coalitions.

GEOGRAPHY AND COALITION BUILDING

Geography plays an important role in shaping the political landscape of individual states, and navigating that landscape is a key element to winning a statewide election. When a candidate for the Senate first decides to seek office, he relies heavily on a home base. Clearly the easiest base from which to pursue a Senate seat is a previously elected office, which can range from a statewide jurisdiction, such as governor, to a local jurisdiction, such as mayor (Fenno 1996). Senate candidates who are former governors have a large advantage in that they had to build a winning coalition across the state in order to get elected governor in the first place. Members of the House, however, face a more difficult task depending on the size of their state. In small states, such as North Dakota, holding a congressional seat is tantamount to holding a statewide seat and therefore brings with it all the associated advantages (Fenno 1990). But in medium- to large-population states, the challenge of expanding an electoral coalition is much greater, notably because the task of becoming well known to voters across the entire state is more difficult (Hibbing and Alford 1990; Oppenheimer 1996).

Insofar as they can, Senate candidates want to secure a majority vote in areas that are solidly and strongly partisan in their favor. Based on the past history of partisan voting trends, Senate candidates will devote greater or fewer resources to particular regions in their state. For example, if a region has voted solidly Republican for fifty years, a Republican Senate candidate is not likely to devote a lot of campaign resources to that region except to ensure high turnout. Instead, the candidate would be more likely to devote resources to more competitive partisan regions, or regions with many independent voters.

The benefits of being regionally based are that the strength in that region is likely to be deep and enduring; that is, the senator is perceived as a "favorite son." For example, one newspaper editor surveyed for this study pointed out how the two Republican senators from his state, Pennsylvania, were perceived as representing different regions of the state: "Heinz was considered . . . to be the senator from western Pennsylvania, while Specter was the senator from eastern Pennsylvania." [1] Perhaps most striking about this remark is that it reflects the same divisions in the Pennsylvania Senate delegation that existed almost two hundred years earlier, in the very first Congress.

In becoming associated with a particular region in the state, the senator acquires a reputation of being responsive to those needs. For example, another newspaper editor offered this remark about the two Democratic senators from Montana: "Max [Baucus] was more typically an eastern senator. John [Melcher] was more typically an ag state senator who represented Montana's rural issues well." [2] The potential cost associated with basing support regionally is that constituents in other parts of the state may be less likely to perceive the senator as responsive to their needs, especially if their needs, for example, urban versus rural, differ from those of the senator's home base (see also Baker 1998, 11–12).

STATE COLLEAGUES AS IMPEDIMENTS TO COALITION BUILDING

The existence of another sitting senator compounds the numerous other challenges of forging a solid, enduring, and winning electoral coalition in a state. If two senators share the same party affiliation, they will present greater obstacles to each other in attracting constituent support than do two senators who have opposite party affiliations. Senators from the same party and the same state essentially rely on the same core party constituency to serve as one base of reelection support. Because these two senators will look similar on the partisan dimension, it is more important for them to differentiate on other dimensions in order to establish separate identities. In contrast, senators from opposite parties can rely on the stark contrast of their partisanship to establish distinct identities. Senators in split-party delegations therefore have a

---

[1] Written survey response from newspaper editor.
[2] Written survey response from newspaper editor.

greater opportunity to pursue overlapping geographic or economic constituencies.

On the geographic dimension, same-state senators present fewer constraints to each other in broadening their appeal across the state, but limitations nonetheless persist. When one senator from the state tries to broaden his appeal to another part of the state that is the home base of a state colleague, the residents of that region may pose the question, "What can you do for us that our other senator is not already doing?" As noted above, Senator Arlen Specter (R-PA) faced this very problem in establishing a footing in western Pennsylvania, which was the home base of his Republican colleague, John Heinz. Fenno (1991, 149–50, 165), describes how Senator Specter was very eager to expand his base of support into western Pennsylvania but could not do so without the explicit support of his colleague. In this case, a senator was unable to establish a base of support that was independent of the other senator who dominated the region.

Whether a senator comes from a same- or split-party delegation will determine the extent to which the two senators compete head to head for support in common geographic areas. If senators are from different parties, then their natural constituencies are less likely to overlap across the state, if that state is divided by partisan affiliation. This means that the core support groups of senators may often be located in different parts of the state. However, senators will not automatically concede territory in their state that is not on its face partisan friendly. Instead, they will try to sell themselves on other dimensions, such as personal governing style, specific issue positions, or securing funds for local projects in the area. This may not ensure wholesale victory in the region or county, but since Senate elections are statewide, any increase in votes will help the senator's chances for reelection.

LEGISLATIVE EFFORTS AND ELECTORAL SUCCESS: OKLAHOMA, OHIO, AND NEW YORK

In the following section, I present case studies of three senators who target voters in specific geographic areas in the state in order to build their reelection coalitions, each in the context of sharing the same state with another senator. The states — Oklahoma, Ohio, and New York — were chosen as examples because they cover different regions of the country, each state has a different internal regional configuration, and the partisan composition of each state differs. The first case, Oklahoma, details how a Republican senator tried to attract support in a Democratic part of the state by securing targeted federal programs and funds for that region. The second case, Ohio, details how two senators from the same party can attract strikingly different levels of support in the state, and how the selection of specific issues can attract crossover party votes in otherwise hostile partisan territory. The third case, New York, details how senators from opposite parties adopted representational agendas that surmounted regional and partisan divisions in the state and produced similar levels of support in common regions in the state.

Oklahoma

During the time period studied here, Oklahoma was represented by a split-party delegation: David Boren (D) was the senior senator, and Don Nickles (R) was the junior senator. Senator Boren had been a popular governor of Oklahoma prior to entering the Senate in 1978 and consistently rated as the most popular elected official in the state. Senator Nickles was elected two years later, in 1980, and the landscape that he faced in building his reelection coalition in his first term presented partisan difficulty for him. The looming presence of Senator Boren as a popular state official meant that if Nickles were to build an enduring majority coalition across the state, it would necessarily have to overlap with Senator Boren's reelection constituency. But the difficulty lay in the fact that the two men differed in their partisanship and their ideology: although Senator Boren was a conservative Democrat, the two senators were still separated by thirty-five points in their ADA ratings. Given that partisan gulf, Senator Nickles did not seek to attract crossover votes with his roll-call voting record; rather, he made use of his institutional positions to appeal to voters on other dimensions. Whereas Senator Boren joined the Agriculture, Finance, and Select Intelligence committees, Senator Nickles joined the Appropriations, Energy, and Select Indian Affairs committees. In this way, Senator Nickles could use the partisan and ideological differences between himself and Senator Boren to establish a separate identity and at the same time expand his reelection base by addressing concrete Oklahoma interests and securing funds for particular regions in the state where he was electorally vulnerable. The strategy that Senator Nickles employed reflects the ways that senators use geographical representation as a means of overcoming or mitigating partisan disadvantages in their state.

Two newspaper articles from the *Tulsa World* detail Senator Nickles' efforts during the 1991–1992 campaign season. The first article points out the ideological divisions between the two senators on campaign finance reform:

> The U.S. Senate approved a non-binding proposal Thursday by Senator David Boren, D-Okla., to remove tax breaks from political action committees and lobbyists and to use the revenue to fund a campaign reform package. Mean-

while, Oklahoma's other U.S. Senator, Don Nickles, helped lead a charge against Boren's plan, calling it welfare for politicians. (Myers 1991, C7)

The second article details Senator Nickles' efforts to attract crossover partisan votes in areas of the state by targeting economic and regional interests:

> Senator Don Nickles, R-Okla., hoping to expand his statewide voter base, last week went into the "no man's land" for Republicans. That is Little Dixie, since statehood the land of Carl Albert, Gene Stipe and other Democrats. . . . Although Nickles has won by landslides in his Senate elections, he has never carried a majority of the state's 77 counties. . . . The Ponca City Republican's strength has been in heavily populated Oklahoma and Tulsa counties, and in Canadian, Cleveland, Garfield, Kay and Payne counties. This year, there are several counties that Nickles might be able to put in to the win column at last. Thursday and Friday, however, Nickles' schedule sent him into the heart of the Democratic Party stronghold in southeastern Oklahoma . . . he hoped he would achieve a major GOP breakthrough and carry a Little Dixie county.
> . . . Because tourism and recreation are major businesses in the Little Dixie counties he visited, Nickles pointed to his work in helping to obtain improvements at McGee Creek in Atoka County and Lake Texoma in Bryan County. He noted his involvement in the establishment of the Sardis Lake Authority in the effort to build a water treatment plant to serve Pushmataha, LeFlore and Latimer counties. Nickles has also been given credit locally for a $7 million loan and grant for a gravity-flow water system to serve an estimated 3,600 residents in McCurtain County. "I have worked as hard for Little Dixie as I have the rest of the state. I would like to carry a county down here." (Martindale 1992, A2)

It is clear that Senator Nickles perceived a benefit to reaching beyond partisan dividing lines to attract votes in counties that were traditionally Democratic.

When the results of Senator Nickles' reelection bid to a third term are compared with Senator Boren's reelection bid to a third term, the partisan divide in the state clearly overlaps with a geographic split in the state. Map 5.1 shows that the two senators had different configurations of electoral support in the state.[3] Senator Boren receives support in almost all counties, regardless of partisan leanings, but Senator Nickles receives his strongest support in the traditionally Republican western sectors of the state.

The patterns in map 5.1 suggest that there is a bounded nature to the extent to which split-party senators can overlap in their electoral coali-

---

[3] I am indebted to Morris Fiorina for the helpful suggestion to compare same-state senators' geographic constituencies in this way.

Map 5.1. Oklahoma Senate Election Returns

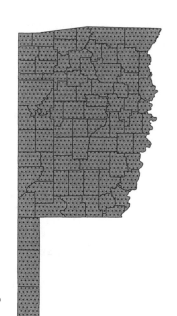

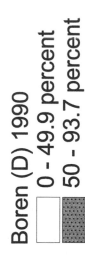

Boren (D) 1990

☐ 0 - 49.9 percent
■ 50 - 93.7 percent

Nickles (R) 1992

☐ 0 - 49.9 percent
▨ 50 - 74.1 percent

tions. When one senator is overwhelmingly popular in a state, it is more difficult for the other senator to develop an equally strong statewide base. Senator Boren had previously overcome partisan disadvantages statewide when he was elected governor, and in the Senate he successfully translated and expanded that electoral coalition to attract a majority of voters in most counties. When Senator Nickles tried to do the same thing, he may have "bumped" up against the presence of Senator Boren in Democratic counties, which made the task of surmounting basic partisan opposition more difficult.

One might argue, then, that Senator Nickles' legislative efforts to attract more support in hostile partisan counties went unrewarded. However, despite the fact that he did not win a majority of votes in the counties in Little Dixie, Senator Nickles did receive more votes there than he had in previous elections and thereby successfully expanded his reelection coalition. (Ervin 1992, A1)

Ohio

In the years between 1987 and 1992, two Democratic senators, John Glenn, who was elected in 1974, and Howard Metzenbaum, who was elected in 1976, represented Ohio. Senator Metzenbaum's home base was Cleveland, whereas Senator Glenn was from Muskingum County in eastern central Ohio. Ohio politics has been traditionally dominated by Cleveland, which has produced most of the statewide office holders in recent times and is a majority Democratic stronghold. One newspaper article described the trend in this way:

> Political leaders elsewhere in the state think Greater Cleveland has more than its share of statewide officeholders. . . . It's an unstated bias against Cleveland area candidates. To downstaters, they represent the worst of the worst . . . [candidates from Cleveland] are major contenders before they even announce for the Senate. And both are running smack into: "Oh no, not another Clevelander."
>
> . . . Despite the grousing, the best political base is in Northeast Ohio. That's why so many candidates from here win offices. The voters in Greater Cleveland win by the numbers—those that count on Election Day. (Sharkey 1993, 7B)

Based on such regional divides, both Senator Metzenbaum and Senator Glenn would be expected to base their reelection coalitions in and around the Cleveland area and expand from there into territory that was traditionally more Republican.

From early on in their Senate careers, the two senators contrasted each other; Senator Glenn was methodical, focused on issues of good government, and moderate in his ideology, while Senator Metzenbaum was more liberal and perceived as a fighter for the consumer and the working-class Ohioan (Fenno 1990, 43–44). Their different reputations stemmed in part from their alternate legislative priorities, as illustrated in a newspaper account of their accomplishments at the end of the 101 (1991–1992) Congress:

> Glenn got $11 million earmarked for universities to figure out ways to get rid of the tiny clams called Zebra mussels, the critters that are clogging water-intake valves and eating fish food in Lake Erie and other Great Lakes. . . . Mr. Checklist (as he is sometimes called) also convinced the Senate and the House that every government agency should have its own chief financial officer to watchdog spending and waste.
>
> . . . Metzenbaum stiffened employer penalties for job-safety violations and expanded the federal government role's in research and treatment of Alzheimer's disease. A third bill seeks to protect workers' interests in cases where companies shut down "overfunded" pension plans. (Staff 1990)

In addition to differences in legislative issue areas, the two senators had divergent voting records. Although their voting records were similar for most party-line votes, over the six year period 1987–1992 Senator Metzenbaum had an average ADA rating of 98, as compared with 78 for Senator Glenn, a difference of 20 percentage points.[4] In brief, both senators used their tools to sell themselves to voters in regions, which were not predisposed to support them. Senator Metzenbaum used his legislative tools to establish a reputation as a senator who attended to his constituents on populist issues, whereas Senator Glenn moderated his voting record and concentrated on more national and nonpartisan policies.

Map 5.2 shows the distribution of votes for Senator Glenn's reelection bid to a fourth term, and Senator Metzenbaum's reelection bid to a third term. In total, Senator Metzenbaum won with 57 percent of the statewide vote, compared with 51 percent for Senator Glenn. Both senators ran against strong challengers in that Senator Metzenbaum faced then Cleveland Mayor George Voinovich (who became governor and is now senator) and Senator Glenn faced Lt. Governor Mike DeWine (now senator). Both senators won in the counties containing the five largest cities in Ohio — Akron, Cleveland, Toledo, Dayton, and Columbus.

The pattern of support that is most striking is that Senator Metzenbaum, the more liberal Democrat, fared considerably better in central

---

[4] This contrast in voting records is yet another example of Uslaner's (1999) more general finding that one senator in a same-party Senate delegation will tend to veer to the extreme of the party distribution to be distinct from a colleague.

Map 5.2. Ohio Senate Election Returns

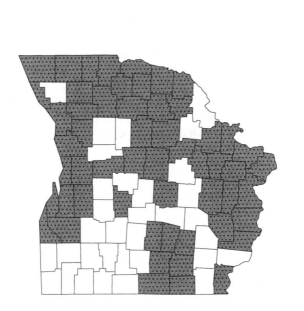

Metzenbaum (D) 1988

□ 0 - 49.9 percent

▨ 50 - 73.9 percent

Glenn (D) 1992

□ 0 - 49.9 percent

▨ 50 - 68.4 percent

and southern Ohio than Senator Glenn, the more moderate Democrat. Metzenbaum's success in the southern and central regions of Ohio is surprising precisely because the Republican party dominates these areas of the state. Overall, Senator Metzenbaum won a majority of the vote in twenty-one counties (out of a total of eighty-eight) in which Glenn failed to win a majority. Moreover, Metzenbaum won these counties by a margin greater than 6 percentage points, which was the difference in their margin of victory statewide.

Senator Metzenbaum managed to penetrate unfriendly partisan territory in much of the southern part of the state where Glenn could not, a pattern that was attributed in part to the issues he chose to champion. One political scientist from Ohio State University, Herbert Asher, said of Metzenbaum that "He has been able to convert his liberalism into a populism that not only benefits people on the bottom rungs of the ladder, but also the middle class. . . . That's why he has been so successful in Ohio; Howard Metzenbaum is a fighter, and a fighter for us — the middle class" (Diemer 1994). Senator Metzenbaum's legislative activism appears to have been a more potent strategy for winning votes in "hostile" territory than Senator Glenn's more subtle approach.

New York

New York represents a state where both senators expanded their initial electoral bases and garnered support in similar regions of the state but did so with contrasting strategies. New York, like Ohio, tends to have a regional split between "upstate" and "downstate." Typically, upstate is considered less urban and more conservative, although it should be noted that four out of the five biggest cities in the state are "upstate." Downstate is considered more liberal and dominated by New York City. Long Island, adjacent to New York City, is often considered to have more in common with upstate than downstate. One *Buffalo News* article about Senator D'Amato's 1992 campaign, entitled "Foul Downstate Politics Defies Newton, Flows Upstream" described the difference in unflattering terms:

> Has there ever been an uglier U.S. Senate race than Robert Abrams vs. Sen. Alfonse D'Amato? . . . It was, to be brutally frank, a race with "downstate" written all over it. . . . [W]hat are nationally decried as the foul pollutants of "New York politics" are really "downstate politics" which fit in perfectly in a fabled cultural world . . . [that] the Manhattan theater people witheringly call the "bridge and tunnel crowd." In New York State, political and cultural pollution usually defies Newton and flows upstream. . . . Crucial to this, of course, is the hilariously inapt knee-jerk condescension to upstate bumpkins

by those who often exemplify the worst that downstate coarseness has to offer." (Simon 1992)

Assuming that this perceived variation exists between these regions of the state, the challenge for both senators would be to develop a reputation that appealed to a cross-section of voters across the state. Because Moynihan was a Democrat and D'Amato was a Republican, that meant each senator had to cross a regional divide.

Senator Moynihan was elected to the Senate in 1976, after serving as U.S. ambassador to the United Nations; he launched his campaign for Senate in the big cities of the state, primarily New York City, but also upstate in Buffalo. Senator D'Amato, on the other hand, was elected to the Senate after serving as supervisor of the town of Hempstead on Long Island, in the downstate region of the state. Both men worked to expand their original electoral coalitions beyond their initial borders. For Moynihan, the natural constituency consisted of the big cities in the state, which were traditionally more Democratic. To offset perceptions that he was a liberal, Moynihan shaped his early career around issues of foreign policy, which was his immediate prior experience and an issue that could help attract more conservative votes. He also focused on Social Security, an issue that affected all of his constituents, regardless of geographic location. Over time, Moynihan developed a reputation as a statesman and a national policymaker in these issue areas, which muted the negative impact of his partisan affiliation in areas of the state that might have been hostile to a Democrat (Editorial staff 1994).

Senator D'Amato, on the other hand, adopted a very different agenda based on his prior experience in the world of Nassau County machine politics. Because Moynihan had been elected first, D'Amato had the task of distinguishing himself in concrete ways from his more senior colleague, something he had already begun in his first Senate campaign. In the Senate, D'Amato used his position on the Appropriations Committee to court the vote in big Democratic cities by providing funds for mass transit, such as subways and trains (Editorial staff 1998). Securing targeted funds for regions all over the state was an effective way of expanding his reelection coalition and penetrating areas that were not favorably disposed toward a Republican. Over the course of his Senate career, Senator D'Amato became known for delivering federal dollars to his home state and acquired the nickname "Senator Pothole" for his mastery of pork-barrel politics (McCarthy 1998). At the same time, D'Amato's Republican partisan affiliation helped secure areas where Moynihan was not as strong, notably upstate New York.

Senator D'Amato took great pride in his efforts and made them a focal point in his reelection campaigns, as noted in two recent articles about the 1998 campaign:

> This time around, D'Amato is likely to face a different sort of campaign, particularly if Ferraro or Schumer is the Democratic nominee: he will be challenged on his record. D'Amato has an eager response to this: "My record? I deliver," he told me as the plane circled the Binghamton [upstate] airport. "See that down there? The runway? I got that extended twelve hundred feet. It cost seventeen million dollars. It was one of the first things I ever worked on. It took me four years to get it." (Klein 1998, 45)

> "There are those who criticize me and say that I deal in small problems. They call me Sen. Pothole," D'Amato said. "But let me tell you, people's problems are not small. And the people who have problems are not small." . . . Indeed, that was the theme the state's junior senator constantly emphasized. He pointed to his involvement in obtaining funds for the Albright-Knox Art Gallery, Roswell Park Cancer Institute, Children's Hospital and Monsignor Adamski housing complex as examples of how he has "fought" for Western New York. (McCarthy 1998)

Indeed, Senator D'Amato believed that by targeting legislative benefits to specific regions in the state he could increase his electoral prospects there.[5]

A comparison of electoral returns for Senator Moynihan's bid for a third term and Senator D'Amato's bid for a third term illustrates how both senators achieved success in securing votes across New York State (map 5.3). Overall, Senator Moynihan received 67 percent statewide, as compared with D'Amato's 49 percent statewide. The two senators both won a majority of the vote in forty-seven counties, but Senator Moynihan won a majority of votes in the counties that include major urban centers, which Senator D'Amato lost. The relative success of both senators in common counties across the state is evidence that their individual strategies of differentiation and coalition building persuaded voters to vote for both of them, even if it meant crossing partisan or geographic lines.

These three case studies suggest that senators incorporate the geographic and demographic divisions within their state into their overall

---

[5] Unfortunately for Senator D'Amato, his 1998 reelection campaign was unsuccessful, and he was beaten by Representative Charles Schumer, a Democrat. Notably, Senator Schumer has chosen to build on his House experience by joining the Judiciary Committee, and he has also taken a seat on the Banking Committee, thereby assuming responsibility for issues that were once "owned" by Senator D'Amato. As we might expect, Senator Schumer's portfolio is likely to look more similar to Senator D'Amato's than to that of his Democratic colleague, Senator Moynihan.

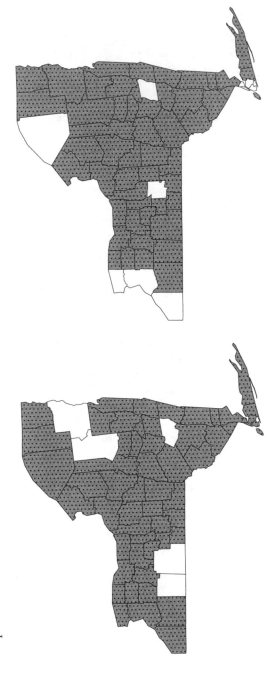

Map 5.3. New York Senate Election Returns

Moynihan (D) 1988
☐ 0 - 49.9 percent
▨ 50 - 85.1 percent

D'Amato (R) 1992
☐ 0 - 49.9 percent
▨ 50 - 67.4 percent

representational agendas, and that voters appear to respond to senators' efforts. In the next section, I expand on the case studies by investigating whether these trends of regional and demographic differentiation are reflected more generally across all senators and the voters in their respective states.

GENERAL PATTERNS OF ELECTORAL SUPPORT FOR SENATORS FROM THE SAME STATE

To study general electoral patterns of support for senators, I constructed a data set with the county-level election returns for both senators, as well as census data on demographic variables, such as the percentage of Blacks, Asians, and Hispanics, income levels, the percentage of women, the percentage of elderly, urban concentration, and the percent of blue-collar workers, all at the county level.

Demographic Patterns of Support

Two forms of analysis are performed on this data. The first analysis is a quantitative model that predicts the difference in vote share between the two senators at the county level as a function of the above demographic variables. This demographic analysis is a modified replication of the work of Jung, Kenny, and Lott (1994), which explains the difference in vote share at the county level between senators from the same state, and the existence of split-party delegations, as a function of campaign platforms and roll-call voting behavior. In their work, they assert that constituents will vote for the candidate who offers the most credible alternative to the other sitting senator. Therefore, whichever candidate has the most distinct platform will garner the most votes and potentially attract support from constituents who are not served by the other sitting senator.[6] In the case of incumbent senators, then, the strength of the challenger is treated here as endogenous to how well the senator has managed to present a credible alternative to a state colleague.

Although I employ a similar rationale, my analysis differs from theirs in two respects.[7] First, because I want to test for differences in electoral support as an indirect consequence of differences in legislative portfo-

---

[6] See also Alesina, Fiorina, and Rosenthal (1991) for a similar argument on the ideological balancing of senators from the same state.

[7] As was explained in more detail in chapter 2, Jung, Kenny, and Lott (1994) assume that senators use roll-call voting as their primary signaling tool to attract support from constituents. The interpretation in this work is that senators use a wide range of legislative tools to build their reelection coalitions, and that roll-call voting is just one of these tools.

lios, I purposely exclude states where one of the senators was a first-time candidate. Candidates who have not yet been elected have not had a chance to use their legislative tools to forge an agenda that is subsequently evaluated by the voters. Therefore, only those states where both senators were incumbents and seeking reelection were included in the sample (n = 29).[8] Second, they studied the 1980, 1982, and 1984 elections, but I use a different set of elections—1986, 1988, 1990, 1992, and 1994—in order to see if their findings hold for the sample of senators included in my study.

The results for states with same-party delegations are displayed in table 5.1, and the results for states with split-party delegations are displayed in table 5.2. For both types of delegations, I find that the coalitions that support senators from the same state do not include the same sectors of the population. Table 5.1 shows that in eleven out of seventeen same-party delegation states, income is a significant divisor of support between the two senators. This is surprising given that income divisions usually tend to occur across parties, not within parties. Yet, in this case, we see evidence that senators from the same party are reaching beyond the strict party core to attract supporters from different economic levels, with one senator leaning toward wealthier voters and the other senator cultivating poorer voters. For example, in a small state like Nebraska, the coalition that supported Senator Jim Exon differed from that which supported Senator Bob Kerrey. Both senators were popular former governors, both are Democrats, and both faced minimal opposition in their reelection campaigns. However, Senator Kerrey proved to be more popular among the elderly, middle-income residents and urban dwellers. In Michigan, where both senators were Democrats, Senator Levin was more popular among upper-income voters while Senator Riegle was more popular among urban voters.[9] In Pennsylvania, a comparison of election results between Senator Heinz and Senator Specter, both Republicans, indicates that Senator Specter was more popular among higher income voters, while Senator Heinz was more popular among urban voters.

In table 5.2, we see that race tends to divide senators from split-party delegations more consistently than income. In eight out of twelve states, the Democratic senator attracted more support from black voters; in

---

[8] Jung, Kenny, and Lott (1994) analyze the election returns from forty-three states. I use the same set of independent variables except that I do not include manufacturing, government employment, and unemployed because theoretically and empirically they do not add a great deal of explanatory power to the model.

[9] Ross Baker (1998) cites an interview with Senator Donald Reigle (D-MI), who mentions this differences in geographic support between himself and Senator Carl Levin (D-MI).

TABLE 5.1
Predicting Differences in Share of Senate Vote by County for Incumbent Senators, 1987–1994: Same-Party Delegations[a]

State	Intercept	Black	Female	Hispanic	Old	Income	Urban	Labor	Adj. R^2
MD (24)	−50.1	−.28**		2.03**	−1.80**	−.0006**	−6.25*	−.57**	.51**
PA (67)	−13.9**	.32**			−.15	.0002**	−3.0**	−.07	.25***
NJ (21)	−29.1**	.19*			.63*	.0004**	.46	−.34	.43**
MI (83)	17.5**	−.08			−.16	−.0004**	4.1**	.03	.11**
IL (102)	−2.7	−.02			.01	−.00002	.51	.01	−.05
NE (93)	−2.1	.03			−.30*	.0004**	−7.5**	.05	.12**
AL (66)	−1.1	−.12**			.32	−.0002	.29	−.008	.12**
OR (36)	−39.0**	2.1			.30	.001**	.60	−.16	.34**
MO (115)	13.9**	−.14**			−.11	.0002	−.05	−.03	.07**
LA (64)	−33.6	.30**			−1.0**	.0005**	4.3*	−.17	.52**
IN (92)	−26.9**	.05			.26	.0004**	−.69	.15*	.12**
OH (88)	14.0**	−.01			−.11	.0002*	.41	.005	.05
MN (87)	17.6**	.46			−.50**	−.000004	−2.6*	−.21**	.42***
WY (23)	−22.0	−.53			.41	.0003	−4.5	−.04	−.04
KS (105)	10.8	−.22	.11		.16	−.0002	.85	−.02	.07**
ND (53)	15.2**	−.04			−.27**	−.0003**	−.40	.01	.11*
WV (55)	−27.9**	−.07			−.37	.002**	−7.3**	−.46**	.34***

***Statistically significant at .01, two-tailed test. **Statistically significant at .05, two-tailed test.
*Statistically significant at .10, two-tailed test.
[a]Senators included in vote share difference:

MD	Sarbanes (D) 88–Mikulski (D) 92	LA	Johnston (D) 90–Breaux (D) 92
PA	Specter (R) 86–Heinz (R) 88	IN	Coats (R) 92–Lugar (R) 94
NJ	Lautenberg (D) 88–Bradley (D) 90	OH	Metzenbaum (D) 88–Glenn (D) 90
MI	Riegle (D) 88–Levin (D) 90	MN	Durenberger (R) 88–Boschwitz (R) 90
IL	Dixon (D) 86–Simon (D) 90	WY	Wallop (R) 88–Simpson (R) 90
NE	Exon (D) 90–Kerrey (D) 94	KS	Kassebaum (R) 90–Dole (R) 92
AL	Heflin (D) 90–Shelby (D) 92	ND	Burdick (D) 88–Conrad (D) 92
OR	Hatfield (R) 90–Packwood (R) 92	WV	Byrd (D) 88–Rockefeller (D) 90
MO	Danforth (R) 88–Bond (R) 92		

two of those states, the Democratic senator also attracted more votes from Hispanic voters. This may indicate that on race and immigration issues, the divisions between the parties are clearer than on economic issues. For example, in Florida, where the delegation was divided, Senator Graham, a Democrat, was more popular among blacks and Hispanics, while Senator Mack, a Republican, was more popular among higher-income voters. In New York, another divided delegation, Senator Moynihan, a Democrat, was more popular among black voters than his colleague, Senator D'Amato, a Republican. In South Carolina, Senator Hollings, a Democrat, was more popular among black voters than his Republican counterpart, Senator Thurmond.

Surprisingly, the percentage of female voters did not exert a statis-

TABLE 5.2
Predicting Differences in Share of Senate Vote by County for Incumbent Senators, 1987–1994: Split-Party Delegations[a]

State	Intercept	Black	Female	Hispanic	Old	Income	Urban	Labor	Adj. R^2
NY (62)	15.6	1.24**			−.11	−.0004*	4.11	−.28	.55***
TX (254)	55.9**			.07	−.02	−.002**	4.9	−.72**	.39***
IA (99)	31.2	2.6**			−1.14**	−.001*	3.3	−.13	.14**
FL (67)	−8.5	.80**		.40**	.25	−.0006*	.31	−.11	.50***
KY (120)	9.8	−.64			.34	−.001*	18.1**	.11	.04*
AZ (15)	41.0**			.01	−.98*	−.0005	−7.4	−.16	.18
CA (58)	−33.8*	1.04*	1.1**	−.09	.53	.0002		.26	.24**
NC (100)	16.9	−.63**			.26	−.0004	9.6**	.65**	.46***
SD (66)	43.9	−.43**			−1.0*	−.0009	−8.4	−.34	.01
SC (46)	20.6	−.69**			−.45	.0004	3.8	.53**	.90***
NM (33)	9.5	−2.4*		.42**	−1.4**	−.0002	−6.5	−.41	.58***
OK (77)	91.2**	.26		−.80**	−.46	−.002**	1.5	−.35*	.62***

***Statistically significant at .01, two-tailed test. **Statistically significant at .05, two-tailed test. *Statistically significant at .10, two-tailed test.

[a] Senators included in vote share difference:

NY	Moynihan (D) 88–D'Amato (R) 92	CA	Cranston (D) 86–Wilson (R) 88
TX	Bentsen (D) 88–Gramm (R) 90	NC	Helms (R) 90–Sanford (D) 92
IA	Harkin (D) 90–Grassley (R) 92	SD	Pressler (R) 90–Daschle (D) 92
FL	Graham (D) 92–Mack (R) 94	SC	Thurmond (R) 90–Hollings (D) 92
KY	McConnell (R) 90–Ford (D) 92	NM	Bingaman (D) 88–Domenici (R) 90
AZ	DeConcini (D) 88–McCain (R) 92	OK	Boren (D) 90–Nickles (R) 92

tically or substantively important effect in any state in the sample, with the exception of Maryland and California. Ironically, in the two states with female senators, Maryland and Kansas, neither female senator appeared to win more support from women than their male counterparts. In Maryland, Senator Paul Sarbanes was more popular among women voters than his female colleague, Senator Barbara Mikulski. In Kansas, Senator Nancy Kassebaum received slightly more support from women than Senator Dole, but the parameter estimate is insignificant. California was the only state to show a significant gender gap in support between two male senators, with the Democrat, Senator Cranston, attracting more support from women than his Republican colleague, Senator Wilson.

The results of the model suggest that senators' efforts to differentiate resonate with voters in their state. In chapter 2, both anecdotal and quantitative evidence was presented to illustrate how senators from the same state specialize in alternate legislative arenas. Even in states with two same-party senators, senators appeal to different sectors of the population. Overall, senators from the same state exhibit systematic patterns of contrast with one another in their legislative work, and these patterns are reflected in differences in support levels from constituent groups.

Geographic Patterns of Support

Using the same data set of electoral returns by county, I constructed maps to show a comparison of the distribution of votes for both senators from a state for the reelection campaigns that occurred during the time period 1986–1994.[10] Essentially, these maps are included to build on the case studies presented earlier to show more general trends across states. Clearly there are many factors that will determine a senator's electoral margins statewide, notably partisanship. Therefore, for the purposes of comparing Senate election returns for two senators from the same state in different time periods, I make the assumption that partisanship at the county level remains constant over time for the majority of the counties in a state. Of all the factors that contribute to a senator's electoral success, strong partisanship at the local level is one of the most stable and enduring. Of course, shifts in partisanship do occur, but they tend to occur over long periods of time and would not be expected to change drastically in a period of six years.

Assuming that a minimum level of partisan strength exists in each

[10] In general, the time period under study for this book is 1986–1994. But because the maps are comparing electoral returns for pairs of senators, I expanded the time frame to include six-year cycles for each member of the state delegations.

county, the expectation is that senators from the same party would receive similar levels of support in the same regions in the state. Likewise,
senators from opposite parties should receive support from voters in
different regions, depending on the partisan distribution in the state.
However, if senators' efforts to contrast themselves do yield benefits by
attracting support from alternative constituent groups and regions in
the state, then the geographic patterns of support should contradict
these expectations.

The maps below are presented to illustrate the distinctive regional
coalitions that support senators from the same state. Most notably,
states with same-party senators exhibit some clear divides between the
two senators, despite their shared party affiliation. One such state is
Oregon; in chapter 2 I documented the distinct legislative portfolios of
the two Republican senators from Oregon. With the exception of the
issue of abortion, Senator Packwood was known to be more conservative, especially on taxes and defense issues, and more nationally focused. Senator Hatfield was known to be more liberal, especially on
defense issues, and more attentive to economic concerns like logging
and forestry, which were dominant in the southeastern section of the
state.

Map 5.4 shows how each senator had regional strength in separate
parts of the state. Both senators were generally strong across the state,
but Senator Packwood was more popular in the rural, eastern part of
the state, and Senator Hatfield was more popular in the urban, western
parts of the state.

In addition to Oregon, Pennsylvania, Michigan, Wyoming, and Nebraska provide more examples of same-party senators with different
regional patterns of support for each senator (maps 5.5–5.8).[11]

In states with split-party delegations, there are more stark regional
divisions, but even so, there is more overlap at the county level than we
might have expected. In Florida, as noted in chapter 2, both senators
carefully constructed separate legislative agendas but overlapped to
serve a major economic interest in the state. Florida is a state where
both senators received close to 70 percent of the vote statewide: Senator
Graham received 65.4 percent, and Senator Mack received 70.5 percent. The two senators each received a majority of the vote in sixty-six
out of sixty-seven counties, and in thirteen of those counties, the difference that separated them was less than the difference statewide.

While the two senators clearly succeeded in overcoming partisan
boundaries among voters, nevertheless, some minor geographic divisions

[11] Other *same-party* Senate delegations in which senators attract support from distinct
regions of the state include New Jersey, Indiana, Louisiana, Alaska, and Illinois.

Map 5.4. Oregon Senate Election Returns

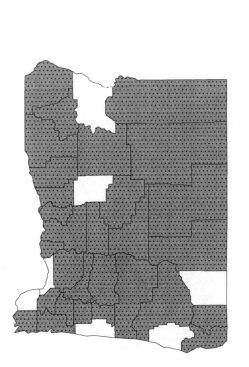

Hatfield (R) 1990

☐ 0 - 49.9 percent

■ 50 - 61.4 percent

Packwood (R) 1992

☐ 0 - 49.9 percent

■ 50 - 75.8 percent

Map 5.5. Pennsylvania Senate Election Returns

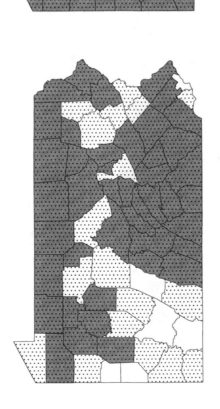

Specter (R) 1986

0 - 49.9 percent

50 - 59.9 percent

60 - 76.7 percent

Heinz (R) 1988

0 - 49.9 percent

50 - 59.9 percent

60 - 87.2 percent

Map 5.6. Michigan Senate Election Returns

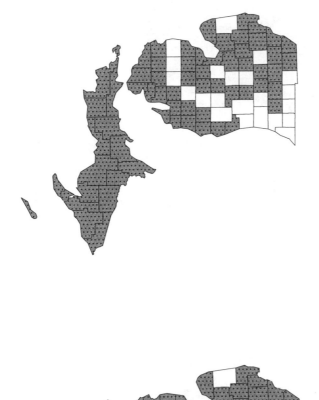

Reigle (D) 1988
0 - 49.9 percent
50 - 75.8 percent

Levin (D) 1990
0 - 49.9 percent
50 - 73.9 percent

Map 5.7. Wyoming Senate Election Returns

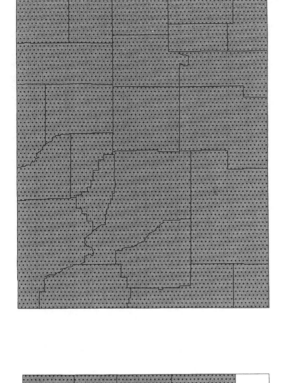

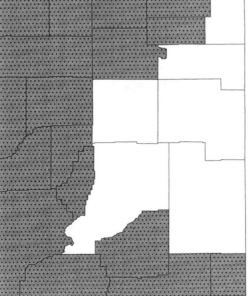

Simpson (R) 1990

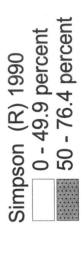

☐ 0 - 49.9 percent

▨ 50 - 76.4 percent

Wallop (R) 1988

☐ 0 - 49.9 percent

▨ 50 - 71.2 percent

Map 5.8. Nebraska Senate Election Returns

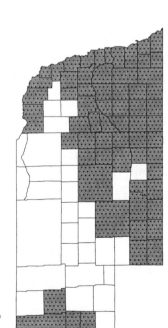

Exon (D) 1990
0 - 49.9 percent
50 - 78 percent

Kerrey (D) 1994
0 - 49.9 percent
50 - 72.9 percent

persisted. Map 5.9 illustrates the electoral returns for both senators. The two senators were relatively equal in popularity across the entire state, despite their contrasting party affiliations, with the exception of northwest Florida, where Senator Mack was more popular than Senator Graham.

In addition to Florida, Texas and South Carolina (maps 5.10 and 5.11) are more examples of states where senators from opposite parties win a majority of votes in common counties.[12]

Taken as a whole, the demographic and geographic patterns of electoral results in states suggest that voters' choices reflect senators' efforts to divide up the representational responsibilities in a state.

CONCLUSION

Comparing the patterns of electoral support for senators from the same state indicates that senators are rewarded for responding to their constituents along multiple dimensions. Senators from the same state select different subsets of interests and opinions to address in their legislative work, and they usually establish different home bases in the state. When senators from the same state do try to expand their original geographic base support, they usually seek out regions and groups that are not already strongly supportive of their state colleague. It is more difficult to attract support from a region of the state, or specific groups within that region, if the other senator has already proven to be attentive to their needs. Under such circumstances, one senator has already achieved recognition and association with the region in the local press, making it more difficult for a state colleague to be given credit for also serving that region.

In this way, the search for an expanded reelection coalition leads senators from the same state to focus on different regions within the state, and hence on different sets of concerns. The smaller the state, the less difference we should see in geographic representation, although small states do contain diverse sets of policy opinions and can have a competitive partisan distribution of voters. The larger a state, in terms of geographic space and population, the more diverse two senators are likely to be in the focus of their legislative work.

The evidence presented in this chapter suggests that senators do not view their states in purely partisan terms, and voters do not merely respond to the partisanship of their senators when expressing their sup-

---

[12] There are other *split-party* Senate delegations, including Iowa, Kentucky, and New Mexico, which exhibit similar patterns of overlap in regional support to those that are shown here.

Map 5.9. Florida Senate Election Returns

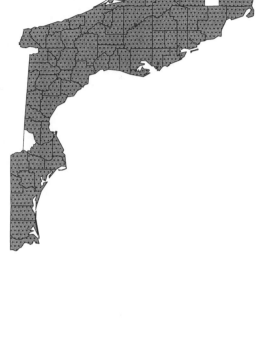

Graham (D) 1992

☐ 0 - 60 percent

▨ 60.1 - 81.8 percent

Mack (R) 1994

☐ 0 - 60 percent

▨ 60.1 - 84.5 percent

Map 5.10. Texas Senate Election Returns

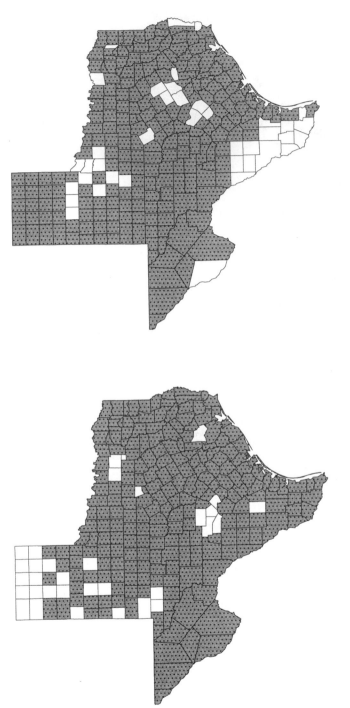

Bentsen (D) 1988
☐ 0 - 49.9 percent
▨ 50 - 90.5 percent

Gramm (R) 1990
☐ 0 - 49.9 percent
▨ 50 - 88.6 percent

Map 5.11. South Carolina Senate Election Returns

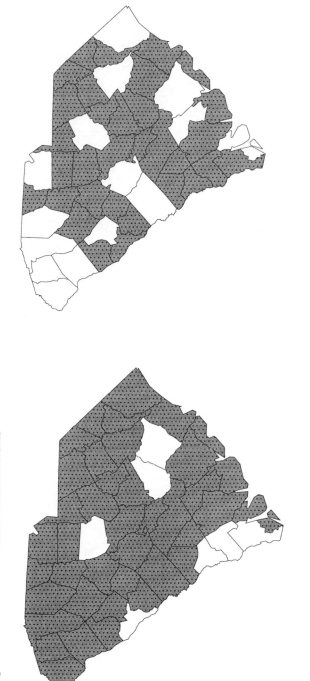

Thurmond (R) 1990

☐ 0 - 49.9 percent
▩ 50 - 75.9 percent

Holllings (D) 1992

☐ 0 - 49.9 percent
▩ 50 - 72.6 percent

port. Senators from the same party and the same state do not fare equally well among the same groups or same regions of the state. In contrast, senators from the same state but opposite parties do often attract the same percentage of support among common groups or in common regions in the state.

Chapter 6

ECONOMIC INTERESTS AND

CAMPAIGN CONTRIBUTIONS

HAVING EXPLORED the dynamics of demographic and regional coalition building in chapter 5, we are left with the question of how senators from the same state build coalitions among economic interests. In one sense, the economic dimension of representation provides the widest range of interests for senators to choose from when constructing their legislative portfolios. Unlike demographic or geographic interests, which can be confined to one particular group in the state, or one particular region, economic issues can affect all constituents in a state. Senators have a wide range of legislative tools to address these broad economic issues or, on a local level, to help secure a federal contract, tax provision, or trade benefit for a specific industry in the state. The combination of the far-reaching impact of economic issues and interests and the institutional powers of the Senate provides a highly effective means of coalition building among voters.

The economic dimension of representation can be conceptualized in two ways. First, economic interests can be defined as constituents' preferences over broad economic policies, such as taxes, welfare, minimum wage, and social security. Such preferences may be strongly linked with constituents' party preferences, based on their views of which party holds the policy positions closest to their own. Likewise, a senator's positions on these broader economic policy issues may reflect the opinions of the senator's party (Erikson, Wright, and McIver 1993). In one way, then, the power of economic policy positions to attract new supporters may be bounded along the partisan lines of a state.

Alternatively, these economic issues may be used to establish a reputation as a populist, or defender of the middle class, or, in contrast, a protector of the business community. Depending on who is seen to benefit from the economic policies that a senator espouses and supports, the senator may attract support from crossover voters because of their perceptions that he is working on their behalf as members of an economic class. The extent to which economic policy positions in general can be used to expand electoral coalitions therefore depends somewhat on how heavily constituents weigh individual economic well-being against broader partisan affiliations.

The second way that economic interests can be defined is more narrow and is based on professional or industrial affiliations. The economic interests of constituents can be identified through their membership in an organized interest group based on their profession, such as farmers or doctors (Bauer, Pool, and Dexter 1963). Likewise, constituents can be employed by a major industry or large company in the state, for example, the steel industry or Boeing, that has a concrete financial stake in legislation that affects their businesses. Senators work to address these economic interests as part of their legislative agenda. The benefits that senators secure for constituents on an economic dimension can help them expand their electoral coalition in the state beyond partisan and geographic borders.

Just as the two-member structure of a Senate delegation can constrain senators on these other dimensions, it also exerts an impact on coalition building using economic issues and interests. Although there are a great number of potential economic interests that each senator can court, not all economic interests are created equal in a given state; some interests are more important to the state's economy — for example, employ more people — than others. Consequently, we would expect convergence on these interests by the two senators: both should be attempting to establish themselves as the "go-to guy" for the same set of major state-based economic interests.

The extent to which senators from the same state compete for support for economic interests is influenced by the interaction of the economic diversity of their state, Senate rules, and whether they share the same party. In states with large numbers of economic interests, two senators will have greater opportunity to attract support from different sets of interests. In states with few major economic interests, notably smaller-population states, senators will have less to choose from and are thereby more likely to court an overlapping set of interests.

Seniority within the delegation, which occurs as a function of staggered elections, and committee selection rules in the Senate, also mitigate the tendency to court the same set of economic interests in the state. Each senator may wish use the opportunities presented by the institution, such as committee selection, to secure an advantageous position to help certain economic interests. By joining relevant committees, senators can incorporate the specific needs of their state's economic interests into their legislative work (Evans 1991; Hall 1996). But as chapter 2 demonstrated, senators from the same state rarely sit on the same committee, especially if they are from the same party. For example, two senators from a soybean-growing state may each wish to help the soybean industry, but only the senator who sits on the Agriculture Committee will have the power to deliver benefits. Unequal institutional positioning does not prevent both senators from trying to serve the interest, but it does place one senator in a more powerful position than a colleague to deliver benefits to a specific industry in the state.

On a national level, the Senate's informal rules on committee selection also constrain a senator's ability to forge a reputation as a champion of economic interests that are spread out across state lines. Joining a particular committee in the Senate places senators in the position of serving national economic interests, such as autos, textiles, oil, banking, and telecommunications, as well as interests in their state that may or may not exist outside the state border. Committee assignment thereby becomes a means of raising money from both state and national economic interests. Some committees in the Senate, such as the Banking Committee and the Energy Committee, are traditionally known as "cash cows," because these committees attract a lot of financial support from wealthy industries (Schiller 1994). If one senator sits on a "cash cow" committee, the other senator from the same state is at the very least discouraged, if not prevented, from also joining that committee. Thus it is rare that two senators from the same state have access to the same strong fundraising base that a particular committee may provide, especially if they are from the same party. This again may weaken the reelection prospects for senators from same-party delegations, notably the junior senator. In sum, the electoral and institutional structures that govern Senate delegations encourage senators from the same state to be responsive to different economic issues and interests, both in their own state and nationwide.

Campaign Contributions as a Measure of Support from Economic Interests

Campaign contributions occur because contributors believe they are purchasing some degree of influence in the policy-making process by supporting particular legislators (Schlozman and Tierney 1986; Denzau and Munger 1986). On this subject, congressional scholars have focused on two aspects of contributing: patterns of campaign contributions and what, if anything, these contributions actually buy. To date, contributor behavior has been explained by comparing group ideology with positions taken by legislators on roll-call votes, and comparing legislators' committee work with the economic interests of the group (Wright 1985; Grier and Munger 1993; Romer and Snyder 1994; Hall and Wayman 1990).

While definite patterns of contributing have been established by these works, the precise quid pro quo that occurs between legislators and contributors has been less definitively demonstrated. Wright (1985) asserts that the timing of campaign contributions by political action committees (PACs) obscures their impact on legislators' roll-call votes. Grenzke (1989) and Wright (1990) argue that lobbying and having the opportunity to present a case to a legislator are a larger determinant of legislators' voting behavior than campaign contributions.

Hall and Wayman (1990) take an alternative approach by focusing on how PAC contributions influence the level of participation by members on specific legislation in committee. They demonstrate that contributions to legislators can produce more effect on bills in committee than on roll-call decisions on bills once they reach the floor.[1] Their framework serves as a useful tool to study the relationship between state-based PACs and senators from the same state because of its emphasis on committee behavior. They suggest that campaign contributions are not just rewards for legislative behavior but can actually exert an anticipatory influence on legislators. When a PAC contributes to a legislator's reelection effort, it can be investing in the legislator for future efforts on its behalf and as such can explain an increase in attentiveness of some legislators to specific interests in their committee jurisdiction.

Most of the above work focuses primarily on the House of Representatives rather than the Senate. If one accepts the argument put forth by Denzau and Munger (1986) that campaign contributions really matter in those cases where the legislator is indifferent toward a proposal, the Senate would be a less attractive place for contributors. Given that a senator's district is an entire state, a unit of representation that is much larger than the average House district, there will be a greater number and diversity of interests with a stake in any given piece of legislation.[2] As a consequence, interest groups and the media are more likely to monitor a senator's roll-call vote behavior on a bill, thereby diminishing the number of roll-call votes about which the senator is indifferent. Therefore, campaign contributors may have less opportunity to purchase influence over legislation on the Senate floor than they do in the House of Representatives.

In fact, Grier and Munger (1993) demonstrate that the patterns of PAC

---

[1] McCarty and Rothenberg (1996) offer an alternative explanation for why we cannot establish a definitive connection between contributions and legislative behavior. They argue that there is no credible enforcement mechanism to ensure that legislators vote the way PACs want them to, or provide access in any way. They demonstrate that PACs keep giving to legislators, even when legislators have not served the PACs interests or have punished them by not granting access, in order to preserve future access and influence.

[2] The notable exceptions are the six states that have the same number of residents as a House district.

contributions do differ between the House and the Senate. Whereas institutional positions, such as committee assignment and seniority, matter in the House, they do not factor significantly in the amount of national PAC contributions made to senators. Rather, a senator's party affiliation and majority/minority status loom large in PAC decisions about how much money to give to specific senators. Snyder (1993) refines this analysis of PAC giving to senators by examining the behavior of what he terms "investor" PACs who seek representation for specific economic interests. He finds that the total amount of investor contributions corresponds to the probability of a senator winning (re)election. He also argues that each senator is viewed as essentially equal to any other senator in terms of the power to provide a return on a contributor's investment.

In this chapter, I combine work on how two senators court economic interests in their state with current findings on the determinants and effects of campaign contributions on legislative behavior. First, I try to construct an alternative measure of "demand behavior" using committee assignments and bill and amendment sponsorship. Second, I measure the reciprocal support that senators receive from organized and unorganized economic interests in their states in terms of the amount of money that an industry or a group contributes to the senator's reelection campaign. These contributions most often come from PACs that are affiliated with the industry or group.

Because this study explores the relationship of senators to their states, I use the contribution behavior of state-based PACs as a measure of electoral support for the senator from state-based economic interests. A state-based PAC is defined as a PAC that is registered in a single state and represents a business or economic interest whose primary location is in that state. Because such PACs represent localized state interests, they are more likely to be financially constrained than national PACs, and thus more likely to seek narrow and concrete compensation for their contributions. Additionally, state-based PACs do not usually seek broad-based (national) economic benefits, therefore they will seek to spend as little as possible to secure desired benefits. The most cost-efficient place for them to seek assistance is from their own senators.

If senators succeed in sending signals that they are working on behalf of different sets of state economic interests, then we should see state-based PACs favoring one senator over the other, depending in large part on which senator exerts more effort to address their specific interest. Using the contribution behavior of state-based PACs is an appropriate way of testing for variation in support among economic interests across senators from the same state. Moreover, it can help explain the choice of different committee assignments among senators from the same state as a function of their desire to signal particular interests in the state that they will be their champions, well before issues get to the Senate floor.

RESEARCH DESIGN

To test the behavior of economic interests in states, I use Federal Election Commission data on campaign contributions and limit the type of PACs to those categorized as economic: corporate, labor union, trade/membership/health, and cooperative. Importantly, because Senate terms span six years, the reelection cycles of senators from the same state will rarely if ever coincide. Subsequently, if the analysis were limited to a single two-year congressional session, I would be unable accurately to compare the relationships of PACs to each senator, since senators invariably receive more campaign contributions across the board during their own reelection cycle. By the same logic, the six-year time period also helps to control for the effects of perceived chances of reelection on the contribution decision. Therefore, I aggregate campaign contributions from state-based PACs over the entire six-year period for those senators from the same state who held office together continuously from 1987 to 1992 (N = 52).

Total contributions from state-based PACs constituted 14 percent of the total amount of economic PAC contributions to the fifty-two senators in this subsample. Although this may seem small as a percentage of all PAC activity, it should be noted that of state-based PAC contributions to all senators, 32 percent was contributed to in-state senators. Rather than treating the behavior of state-based PACs as proxy for the behavior of all PACs, this study seeks to investigate the relationship between state-based PACs and their senators. In order to explore whether a senator's individual characteristics and behavior explain patterns of campaign contributions from state-based PACs, I also include data on senators' party affiliations, ideology (ADA ratings), the number of economic interests in the state as measured by the number of industries generating $500 million or more, seniority within the delegation, the number of bills sponsored, type of committee assignment, and cosponsorship (defined as the percent of bills introduced by either member that were cosponsored by the other senator). The senators in this subsample vary by seniority, party, and ideology, and the states in this subsample vary by same- or split-party delegation and region.[3]

I use membership on four Senate committees to measure the effect of committee assignment: Finance, Appropriations, Armed Services, and

[3] Two states are excluded: Oklahoma, because Senator Boren refused to accept PAC contributions at this time, and Wyoming, because no Wyoming PACs are registered as making contributions during this time.

Agriculture. I chose membership on these committees for two reasons: first, they are generally recognized as providing senators with the greatest opportunity to deliver economic benefits to interests in their states. Second, senators are only allowed one membership among the Finance, Appropriations, or Armed Services committees, thereby diminishing the potential effects of collinearity. Lastly, I coded the electoral vulnerability of the senator during his or her reelection cycle based on reports in *Congressional Quarterly Weekly Report* (1988, 1990, 1992): 0 — safe seat, 1 — favored, 2 — leaning, 3 — too close to call.

SENATE ADVERTISING: HOW SENATORS
ATTRACT INTEREST GROUP SUPPORT

Up to this point, I have argued that senators from the same state exhibit demand behavior by signaling state-based economic interests of their willingness to secure benefits. Senators advertise themselves in a number of ways, which vary according to the group they are trying to attract. For example, if a senator seeks to help a small company in the state, he may not seek widespread publicity but rather inform the president of the company directly. If the industry employs individuals across the state, the senator will seek more public methods of informing constituents by issuing a press release or holding a press conference. The bigger the industry, the more the senator will desire publicity that portrays efforts on behalf of that industry. Chapter 3 demonstrated that media attention is highly correlated with committee assignment, and therefore senators are guaranteed that the publicity they receive will reflect their efforts on behalf of specific economic interests in their state. The benefits of publicity, aside from the obvious name recognition it brings, is that the senator becomes identified with the economic interests, thereby discouraging encroachment by a state colleague. In addition, if the senator is perceived generally as an effective advocate for state interests, then more interest groups may approach the senator for help.

In some cases the connection between committee work and campaign contributions is quite explicit, as described in one newspaper article about Senator D'Amato's (R-NY) actions on behalf of the New York–based securities industry, as well as the more narrowly concentrated sugar interests:

Over the years, the financial industry has provided the most money to Mr. D'Amato's campaigns. . . . He has been a member of the Senate Banking Committee where he has been a strong advocate for measures backed by the securities industry. In 1985, when he was chairman of the securities subcommittee, Mr. D'Amato excluded from legislation he introduced a proposal that would have limited the purchase of junk bonds by federally regulated savings and loans. That same year, Drexel Burnham Lambert, then the top marketer of the high-risk securities, held a fund-raising reception for Mr. D'Amato. . . .

A handful of sugar refiners, including one with a plant in New York, stood to gain $365 million in tariff rebates, and Mr. D'Amato was all for it. With his help, the provision squeaked through the Senate in the summer of 1987. That fall, five years before his next race, Mr. D'Amato received $8,500 in campaign contributions from the sugar refiners. It is from such incidents that Mr. D'Amato, who has cultivated an image as a zealous guardian of constituents' interests, has also gained a reputation as one of the Senate's most aggressive and prolific fund-raisers. (Fritsch 1992)

In characterizing the other senator from New York, Moynihan, and his efforts to represent state economic interests, the media was more generous. One newspaper article described Moynihan's record this way:

Mr. Moynihan has already derived more benefits for his home state from log rolling than from the pork barrel. He is credited with legislation to increase job-related mass transit subsidies and projects ranging from the belated re-painting of the Hell Gate railroad bridge to the planned revival of the 42nd Street trolley.

"We have currency," Mr. Moynihan said. "Everybody needs something from Environment and Public Works. Either something they don't want in their state or something they have to have. Every senator who wants a dam has a committee from which we may want something." And everybody wants something from Finance. (Roberts 1992)

The portrayal might have been softer, but the message still served the same purpose for the senator because it signaled groups in the state that he was working on their behalf. In addition to working in separate issue areas, and adopting distinct governing styles, these two senators also actively courted different economic interests in the state. As such they were on relatively equal footing with New York State PACs: Senator D'Amato received 53 percent of New York PAC contributions while Senator Moynihan received 47 percent. Furthermore, an almost equal number of PACs contributed to Senator D'Amato (119) as contributed to Senator Moynihan (121) (see table 6.1).[4]

---

[4] Careful observers of the Senate will no doubt point out that Senator D'Amato left the Appropriations Committee in 1995 to join the Finance Committee. At the time it was widely noted that he did so as a favor to Senator Dole, who wanted to keep Senator Phil Gramm (R-TX) from joining the Finance Committee and using it as a launching pad for his presidential campaign. In addition, since Senator D'Amato also became chair of the Banking Committee, he could continue credibly to sell himself as a champion of many of the same economic interests that he had always sought to represent.

TABLE 6.1
State-Based PAC Campaign Contributions to Senate Incumbents, 1987–1992

Senator	State	Party	# of State PAC Contributors	# of PACs Who Gave To One Senator	# of PACs Who Gave To Both Senators	Total Amount of PAC Contributions	Percent of PAC $
Stevens	AK	R	4	4	0	3,998	100.0
Murkowski	AK	R	4	0	0	0	0.0
Heflin	AL	D	35	4	24	121,000	.45
Shelby	AL	D	35	7	24	148,075	.55
Pryor	AR	D	19	3	8	27,774	.45
Bumpers	AR	D	19	8	8	33,600	.55
DeConcini	AZ	D	38	14	16	36,000	.39
McCain	AZ	R	38	8	16	56,100	.61
Roth	DE	R	11	3	7	13,750	.67
Biden	DE	D	11	1	7	6,875	.33
Nunn	GA	D	48	5	27	73,470	.26
Fowler	GA	D	48	16	27	209,249	.74
Grassley	IA	R	35	15	11	28,612	.51
Harkin	IA	D	35	9	11	27,555	.49
Dole	KS	R	18	8	4	37,140	.81
Kassebaum	KS	R	18	6	4	8,488	.19
Ford	KY	D	32	5	18	73,950	.51
McConnell	KY	R	32	9	18	69,926	.49
Johnston	LA	D	30	5	21	68,510	.53
Breaux	LA	D	30	4	21	61,794	.47
Kennedy	MA	D	13	10	1	18,757	.79
Kerry	MA	D	13	2	1	5,000	.21
Sarbanes	MD	D	35	4	12	49,500	.36
Mikulski	MD	D	35	19	12	89,012	.64
Cohen	ME	R	4	1	1	7,002	.58
Mitchell	ME	D	4	2	1	5,400	.42
Riegle	MI	D	71	20	35	131,243	.48
Levin	MI	D	71	16	35	138,096	.52
Danforth	MO	R	73	12	53	200,657	.43
Bond	MO	R	73	8	53	264,311	.57
Domenici	NM	R	8	0	6	14,775	.61
Bingaman	NM	D	8	2	6	9,375	.39

TABLE 6.1 (*continued*)

Senator	State	Party	# of State PAC Contributors	# of PACs Who Gave To One Senator	# of PACs Who Gave To Both Senators	Total Amount of PAC Contributions	Percent of PAC $
Bradley	NJ	D	66	9	37	137,904	.35
Lautenberg	NJ	D	66	20	37	259,147	.65
Moynihan	NY	D	151	32	89	293,401	.47
D'Amato	NY	R	151	30	89	333,133	.53
Glenn	OH	D	58	36	13	134,572	.73
Metzenbaum	OH	D	58	10	13	48,975	.27
Hatfield	OR	R	26	11	13	72,028	.72
Packwood	OR	R	26	3	13	28,236	.28
Pell	RI	D	9	2	3	13,365	.44
Chafee	RI	R	9	4	3	17,300	.56
Thurmond	SC	R	15	1	12	33,700	.45
Hollings	SC	D	15	2	12	41,450	.55
Pressler	SD	R	4	1	2	1,250	.36
Daschle	SD	D	4	1	2	2,245	.64
Sasser	TN	D	34	11	17	92,190	.69
Gore	TN	D	34	6	17	42,000	.31
Bentsen	TX	D	190	36	97	336,091	.42
Gramm	TX	R	190	57	97	472,063	.58
Byrd	WV	D	5	0	3	5,100	.27
Rockefeller	WV	D	5	2	3	13,650	.73

Source: Federal Election Commission.

The case of Senators John Danforth and Christopher "Kit" Bond from Missouri illustrates how two senators from the same party attract financial support from disparate economic interests. Senator Bond, interviewed after serving two years into his first term, described himself in the following newspaper article:

Bond has had few opportunities for leadership on big issues. But the senator says: "I've developed a reputation as somebody who will work hard on the issues. And I get approached by a lot of people to take on issues." Asked for examples, Bond mentioned . . . that . . . "the corn growers asked us to take the lead in the Corn Caucus." While Bond's legislative work has extended beyond corn, potatoes and soybeans, he has focused lots of time on agriculture issues. That is because he serves on the Senate Agriculture Committee and says the drought bill and next year's farm bill are important to Missouri. "Obviously, some of the priorities that I have to deal with are defined by the committees I serve on," Bond said. (Koenig 1989)

In this instance, Bond clearly acknowledges his own emphasis on local economic interests and his choice of specializing in his committee work.

An editorial in the same newspaper clearly associates each senator with distinct economic interests that correspond to their committee assignments:

Common Cause recently released a detailed accounting of the honoraria received by all members of Congress. . . . Sen. Danforth spoke before 22 different groups. . . . His fellow Missouri Republican, Sen. Christopher Bond, addressed 52 organizations. . . . The groups paying out the money were mainly corporations or trade associations whose interests are directly affected by what Sen. Danforth, [and] Bond do in the Senate. Sen. Danforth's appearances included talks before insurance, trucking, rail and airline groups. Coincidentally, he is ranking Republican on the Transportation Committee. Sen. Bond cast a wider net. He made paid visits not only to insurers and truckers, but [also] to bankers, contractors, tobacco and almond interests, corn refiners, chemical manufacturers, forest product groups and pork producers. It so happens he is on the Agriculture Committee. (Editorial staff 1989)

The editorial does not say whether these groups were national or locally based, but the message it sends is that each senator is clearly identified with particular economic interests. Although the editorial is critical of Danforth and Bond accepting speaking fees (a practice since prohibited), it is good press for them because it sends the right signals to economic interests that they are working on their behalf. In turn, the PACs affiliated with economic interests will respond by making campaign contributions.

In this case, the junior senator, Senator Bond, attracted more in-state local contributions than his more senior colleague did; Senator Bond received 57 percent of Missouri economic PAC money as compared with 43 percent that went to Senator Danforth. However, Senator Bond received money from slightly fewer PACs (61) than contributed to Senator Danforth (65) (see table 6.1).

The process of coalition building among state-based economic interests is not a static one; senators are constantly looking for more issues and interests to address in order to attract more support. Over time, however, an equilibrium develops between two senators from the same state whereby they establish the boundaries of their portfolios and their electoral coalitions. These boundaries are usually solidified after each senator has secured reelection to at least a second term. However, when one senator leaves the Senate, an opening arises for the other senator to pursue the support of the former colleague's supporters. When such a vacancy occurs, senators weigh the benefits of their seniority on a committee, their existing reputations in specific issue areas, and their relationship with a set of economic interest groups against the costs of starting over on a different committee, with less seniority, and no existing reputation in the issue area. The calculation they arrive at discourages senators from changing course in midcareer merely to fill an opening left by their state colleague.

A case in point is the state of Illinois, represented by two Democrats, Alan Dixon and Paul Simon, from 1985 to 1992. Senator Dixon sat on the Banking Committee and the Agriculture Committee and used those positions to actively address the economic interests of the Chicago business community (e.g., commodity traders) and the farm interests in his state (e.g., soybean farmers). His Democratic colleague, Senator Paul Simon, sat on the Judiciary and Labor and Human Resources committees, where he specialized in constitutional law, immigration, and education. When Senator Dixon was defeated in the primary in March 1992, the *Chicago Tribune* wrote that his defeat would leave a large gap in the set of Illinois interests that were directly represented in the Senate:

> Dixon was considered the detail man for Illinois projects moving through the Senate, "the mover, the shaker," as one GOP lobbyist described him. . . . The Chicago futures industry . . . is nervous: It depends on Dixon's position on the Banking and Urban Affairs Committee to block competition from the New York markets and efforts by the Securities and Exchange Commission to take over its regulation. . . . David Yudin, the City of Chicago's lobbyist in Washington, said Dixon's committee position made him "tremendously helpful on a lot of issues, particularly transportation, housing, a lot of urban issues. He will be missed on this." (Locin and Dellios 1992)

A later article suggested that Senator Simon would have to pick up the slack and now attend to interests that he had not previously served:

> Simon seems eager to tackle his new role as the senior senator. His conversion from dabbler to doer is timely, given the departure of hands-on Democratic Sen. Alan Dixon. Simon has emerged as a more forceful figure in the Senate since his re-election two years ago. . . . Now, not only does Simon, a new Deal liberal, suddenly become the more moderate of Illinois's two senators, he is also thrust into the unlikely position of having to deliver for the state's demanding political and business interests. (Hardy 1992, C4)

With the departure of his same party colleague, Senator Simon was free to pursue and respond to specific economic interests in an effort to expand his reelection constituency and serve his state. Despite this open-ing, Senator Simon did not actually shift committee assignments or signif-icantly alter his legislative portfolio and governing style. He did use his seniority in the Senate to facilitate approval for specific projects in Illi-nois, but the actual extent to which he sought the support of Senator Dixon's old coalition was limited.[5]

CONTRIBUTIONS FROM STATE-BASED PACs
DO THEY RESPOND TO SENATORS' SIGNALS?

Senators from the same state have a strong incentive to establish con-trasting reputations among groups and constituents. To do so, senators use all the legislative tools available to them, above and beyond roll-call voting, to serve different economic interests in the state. In return, sena-tors solicit campaign contributions from different sets of PACs who rep-resent these economic interests. In this section, data on state-based PAC contributions, state demographics, and senators' ideology and institu-tional positions are all used to test two hypotheses.

Hypothesis 1 states that if investor PACs seek only to buy roll-call votes, then they should contribute the same amount of money to sena-tors from the same party and the same state, controlling for probability of winning reelection. In contrast, state PACs seeking a commitment on roll-call votes should not contribute the same amount of money to sena-tors from that state who are from different parties.

Hypothesis 2 states that if investor PACs are seeking some other form of compensation, like a provision inserted in committee bill, or sponsor-ship of a specific bill or amendment by the senator, then PACs will seek out the senator who is the best position to secure that compensation. In this case, we should see state PACs contributing more money to one senator over the other, regardless of party, because it is a more efficient investment than disbursing money over two senators.

A simple examination of state-based PAC contributions to their sena-tors provides some evidence to refute hypothesis 1. As table 6.1 illus-trates, state-based PACs do not uniformly contribute the same amount of money to each senator from the state, and some PACs contribute to only one senator and exclude the other. Furthermore, PACs clearly ap-pear to be investing in one senator over the other but do not appear to be investing based on party affiliation.

To test my hypotheses more systematically, I constructed two ordi-

[5] For additional discussion on this type of "division of labor," see Lee and Oppenheimer (1999).

nary least squares regression models. In the first model, I seek to explain the variance in the total amount of money contributed by state-based PACs to each senator, controlling for whether the delegation was a same- or split-party delegation; the number of economic interests in the state; the total number of bills a senator introduces; membership on the Finance, Appropriations, Armed Services, or Agriculture Committee; whether the senator was the senior or junior senator; the difficulty of the campaign; and the ideology of the senator.[6]

The second model seeks to explain the variance in the number of state-based PACs that give to both senators, using the same set of variables. The purpose of this model is to test for any patterns associated with the breadth of support that a senator receives in the state. In cases where the total amount of state-based PAC contributions is in part driven by a few PACs that make large contributions, the number of state-based PACs may be a better indicator of the diversity of support sought by, and given to, an individual senator. This is especially important for explaining the different number and types of economic interests that offer support to one or both senators from the same state.

The results of both models imply that hypothesis 1 should be rejected and that hypothesis 2 is supported: state-based PACs clearly invest differently in senators. For example, sharing the same party affiliation with the other senator from the state decreases the total amount of contributions by $49,352 (table 6.2).

The size of the state's economy also influences the total amount of state-based PAC contributions: for each additional large industry, total contributions increase by $6,327.[7] A senator's institutional behavior seems to influence PAC contributions as well. For each additional bill a senator introduces, total contributions decrease by $476; again, this may indicate that PACs do not want to invest in a senator that is over-extended. The degree of vulnerability in the reelection cycle does not appear to affect the total amount of contributions to a senator, and neither does seniority within the state delegation.

With respect to committee assignments, my results diverge from those of Grier and Munger (1993) in that I find statistically significant effects associated with sitting on the Finance, Appropriations, and, to a lesser extent, Agriculture committees.[8] All three committee memberships in-

---

[6] I exclude cosponsorship from the model because it is highly correlated with sharing the same party affiliation (.45).

[7] This seems to contradict Snyder's (1993) finding that the size of a state does not correlate with the total amount of investor contributions. State size and number of $500 million industries are highly correlated (.89).

[8] One explanation for the lack of effects associated with sitting on the Armed Services

TABLE 6.2
Total Amount of State-Based PAC Campaign Contributions to Senators,
1987–1992 (in dollars)

Intercept	56349.0**
	(27418.7)
Shared party affiliation	−49352.0***
	(16049.0)
Senior senator	−12923.0
	(16121.2)
Campaign difficulty	−4394.0
	(8539.0)
Ideology	−382.1
	(393.9)
Party affiliation	−23843.0
	(25103.3)
Size of state economy	6327.3***
	(473.1)
Number of bills introduced	−475.7***
	(167.5)
Appropriations Committee	39570.0**
	(20057.1)
Finance Committee	51801.0**
	(21035.7)
Armed Services Committee	10539.0
	(22124.0)
Agriculture Committee	32291.0*
	(22689.4)
Adj. R^2	.78
prob > F	.0001
N	52

Standard errors in parentheses. ***Statistically significant at .01, one-tailed test. **Statistically significant at .05, one-tailed test. *Statistically significant at .10, one-tailed test.

Committee is the time period under study. From 1989 to 1992, defense spending was reduced due to the end of the cold war. In the area most likely to be affected by congressional action, local base closing, the only opportunity for congressional intervention was a single roll-call vote on an externally prepared list of bases to be closed.

crease the total amount of state-based PAC contributions by, respectively, $51,801, $39,570, and $32,291. It is important to note again that Senate rules (and customs) usually prohibit two senators from the same state from sitting together on the Finance or Appropriations committees.[9] At the very least, then, these results provide support for the assertion that state-based PACs are making choices about how much money to contribute to their senators based on their *different* committee assignments.

The results of the second model, which seeks to explain the total number of state-based PACs that contribute funds to a senator, reveal that the same set of variables exert an effect on both the amount of money that a senator receives from state PACs and the number of PACs that contribute to a senator's campaign (table 6.3).

In sum, the results of this analysis lend support to the assertion that state-based PACs do not invest equally in senators from the same state, especially when the senators share the same party affiliation. Rather, a PAC's contribution decision to invest more heavily in one senator over the other within a Senate delegation appears to vary with a senator's institutional position and willingness to address the PAC's specific economic interest. So even if the exact quid pro quo cannot be identified, these results support earlier work that suggests that PACs believe they are buying the services, or access to services, that senators are selling.

CONCLUSION

In this chapter I have tried to combine two subfields of congressional scholarship: campaign contributions and the dynamics of representation within a Senate delegation. In examining the behavior of state-based economic PACs, I found support for the assertion that campaign contributors react to the signaling behavior of senators from their state who, using their institutional positions, demonstrate a concrete commitment to them. Importantly, a senator's party affiliation does not seem to be a major indicator of the amount of funds he will receive from state-based PACs. In states with both same- and split-party Senate delegations, PACs choose among the senators based on committee position and observed attentiveness to their economic interests.

One implication of these results is that, regardless of the same- or split-party composition of the Senate delegation, senators represent a wider range of economic interests in their state than would be expected if they merely followed traditional partisan lines. Senators seek out dif-

[9] Both party caucuses in the Senate have an incentive to limit the extent to which a single state wields influence on these committees.

TABLE 6.3
Total Number of State-Based PACS that Contributed to Senators, 1987–1992

Intercept	14.0
	(11.0)
Shared party affiliation	−22.0***
	(5.0)
Senior senator	−2.0
	(5.0)
Campaign difficulty	−2.0
	(2.0)
Ideology (ACU ratings)	0.0
	(0.0)
Party affiliation	−14.0**
	(8.0)
Size of state economy	2.0***
	(.13)
Number of bills introduced	−.11**
	(.05)
Appropriations Committee	15.0**
	(6.0)
Finance Committee	21.0**
	(6.0)
Armed Services Committee	5.0
	(6.0)
Agriculture Committee	6.0
	(6.0)
Adj. R^2	.84
prob > F	.001
N	52

Standard errors in parentheses. ***Statistically significant at .01, one-tailed test. **Statistically significant at .05, one-tailed test. *Statistically significant at .10, one-tailed test.

ferent sets of economic groups to form the foundation of their electoral coalitions. But is this really expanded representation if the two senators are merely choosing between a set of elite economic interests (as represented by economic PACs)? Would senators work as hard to address these state-based economic interests without the promise of potential rewards in the form of campaign contributions?

Presuming that senators have a vested stake in establishing their effectiveness as "senators," one might argue that they would attend to these interests anyway. On the other hand, given the sheer number of economic interests in a state, and, in many cases, the narrow base of the interest, a senator could address far fewer interests and still create a distinct reputation among constituents as a hard worker for the state. At some level, then, the contributions that state-based economic interest groups provide to senators do secure preferential treatment in the form of specialized attention to their needs.

Still, this may only be a problem for representation if two conditions are met. First, if senators are addressing specific economic interests in the state in response to campaign contributions at the expense of their average constituents, they are providing unequal representation. However, disproportionate representation on this dimension is by no means certain; for each elite economic interest that a senator serves, any number of constituents may benefit in the form of job opportunities or an expanded tax base. It is entirely possible that constituents accrue benefits from their senators' behavior even if it is not directed primarily at them.

Second, problems arise for representation if senators, in the course of serving local economic interests, are neglecting their other responsibilities, such as national policy. But the multidimensional nature of representation precludes that from happening. Senators are constantly forced to vote on national issues, in several committees, and on the Senate floor. Even if senators wanted to neglect national policy, the structure of the Senate makes it impossible for them to do so. Moreover, senators are judged in part on their roll-call voting record, in close association with their party affiliation, which means they cannot afford to abdicate their responsibility to address national concerns.

Therefore, it is difficult to argue that the relationship between state-based PAC campaign contributions and senators' legislative actions to benefit those interests necessarily results in disproportionate representation. In fact, competition for support among economic interest groups is an important mechanism in ensuring greater diversification among senators from the same state.

Chapter 7

RETHINKING SENATE REPRESENTATION

O VER TWO HUNDRED years ago, James Madison, Alexander Hamilton, and John Jay brilliantly made the case for an American constitutional government. In a series of newspaper articles that eventually formed the classic book *The Federalist Papers*, these authors extolled the virtues of a bicameral legislature and justified the need for a Senate to check the popular excesses of democratic government. Writing in *Federalist* 62, Madison boldly proclaimed: "The necessity of a Senate is not less indicated by the propensity of all single and numerous assemblies to yield to the impulse of sudden and violent passions, and to be seduced by factious leaders into intemperate and pernicious resolutions" (Rossiter 1961, 379).

Throughout *The Federalist Papers*, the framers made the argument that the Senate would be the antidote against direct democracy. Being directly elected by the people for short two-year terms and comprising a large group of members, the House posed the risk of a democracy that would run out of control. Based on the fears of the framers, it was much more likely that the House rather than the Senate, with its six-year terms, indirect selection by state legislatures, and staggered elections, would mirror the opinions of the general population. In their eyes, the Senate was the chamber that would be deliberative in nature and more likely to check the passions of ordinary citizens.

During the debates for the ratification of the Constitution, these early political leaders allotted the same number of senators for each state in order to counter the inequality that existed between large and small states in the House of Representatives. It was a pragmatic compromise, and the allotment of *two* senators for each state attracted little attention at the time. Although they did not fully appreciate the momentous impact of the number of senators they awarded to each state, in choosing two senators per state our constitutional framers laid the groundwork for a system of dual representation in the Senate. As I have argued in this book, choosing two senators for each state profoundly altered the character of the Senate, the day-to-day conduct of our senators, and the nature of representation in American democracy.

In this chapter I step back from the details of how dual representation influences Senate behavior and look more generally at its normative consequences. In examining the United States Senate, I have found that dual representation affects a broad range of activities: roll-call voting, committee selection, bill and amendment sponsorship, media strategies, campaign contributions, and campaign behavior. With such a wide range of consequences, dual representation suggests that the current framework that we use to evaluate our senators, and legislators more generally, requires revision. The remainder of this chapter outlines why we need to rethink our conception of representation and how doing so reveals that our elected legislators do a better job of representing citizens than is typically thought.

Broadening our Concept of Senate Representation

One of the overriding arguments in this book is that the current model that we use to measure and assess Senate representation is flawed because it invariably leads us to conclude that the senator does an incomplete job, and that states are not adequately represented in the Senate. Most studies of legislative representation use roll-call voting as the main indicator of senators' responsiveness to constituent opinion and interests (Bullock and Brady 1983; J. Wright 1985; G. Wright 1989; Shapiro et al. 1990; Erikson 1990; Grofman, Griffin, and Berry 1995; Bernstein 1991). This framework is limited in that it overlooks the fact that senators engage in a wide range of legislative activities on which they spend their time and resources, of which roll-call voting takes the least amount of time. Included among these activities are committee selection, bill sponsorship and cosponsorship, publicity efforts, electoral coalition building, and the solicitation of campaign contributions. As Hall (1996) has argued, limiting our scope of study to the activity that takes the least amount of a legislator's time leads us to draw an incomplete picture of the legislative process. If senators view their jobs as multidimensional and use the different legislative tools available to them to accomplish the task of representation, then congressional scholars have an obligation to study the full range of their activities.

Moreover, the definition of constituent interest needs to be refined in the context of the larger debate about what comprises representation of interests, a debate that is embodied in Hanna Pitkin's 1967 classic, *On the Concept of Representation*. In that work, Pitkin makes the claim that the dichotomy of "trustee or delegate" is an inadequate conceptual framework to guide the study of legislative representation. As an alternative, she offers the following definition:

> representing here means acting in the interest of the represented, in a manner responsive to them. The representative must act independently; his action must involve discretion and judgement; he must be the one who acts. The

represented must also be conceived of as capable of independent action and judgement, not merely being taken care of. And, despite the resulting potential for conflict between representative and represented about what is to be done, that conflict must not normally take place. The representative must act in such a way that there is no conflict, or if it occurs an explanation is called for. He must not be found persistently at odds with the wishes of the represented without good reason in terms of their interest, without a good explanation of why their wishes are not in accord with their interest. (209–10)

The results of this study yield a picture consistent with Pitkin's conception of representation in that senators act as both trustees and delegates. Each state has a set of economic interests and preferences over policies that vary in importance across constituents. It is impossible for a single senator to address all economic interests and policy areas that affect a state because there are simply not enough resources in terms of time, staff, and opportunity to do so adequately. A senator adjusts to limited resources by constructing an agenda that targets a subset of interests and opinions held by residents in the state. In that sense, senators act as trustees in that their legislative portfolios are the reflection of their decisions as to which interests and opinions they will advocate in the Senate.

The very fact that two senators from the same state choose different sets of interests to represent indicates that they have a certain amount of flexibility in defining what they view to be the state's interests. But that flexibility is limited because senators ultimately have to face the judgment of the voters every six years. Voters evaluate a senator based on his reputation, which rests in part on his legislative portfolio, and elections can thereby serve as a referendum on the senator's selective view of the state's interests. Senators may set the agenda for what will be represented in their state, but their choices are a reflection of what they anticipate constituents would desire. In this way, constituents hold senators accountable as delegates, who are supposed to act in their stead at the federal level.

In addition, our method of studying representation does not take into account the environment in which senators construct their representational agendas. Senators build their careers and represent their states in the context of sharing their state with another colleague who has the same geographic constituency. A "limited resources" explanation would predict that both senators would target their efforts toward the same set of dominant interests and opinions in the state. After all, it is logical to expect that senators who share the same geographic constituency would choose the same representational agenda. However, the evidence in this work suggests just the opposite: senators from the same state choose to represent different sets of interests and opinions in their legislative work.

A more complete explanation of Senate representation takes into account the structure of Senate elections and the institutional arrangements that exist within the Senate. These two factors create an inequality of opportunity between senators from the same state to address the same set of issues effectively. Staggered Senate elections produce a condition whereby the senator who is elected first will have seniority over a state colleague. Consequently, the senior senator has the opportunity to make choices about which interests to address through committee assignments before the junior senator even arrives in the Senate.

Upon arriving in the Senate, the junior senator faces constraints on pursuing the same set of issues and interests as a senior colleague. Even if the junior senator wants to join the same committees as the senior colleague, the rules and practices of the Senate make it difficult for two senators from the same state to secure the same committee assignments. This is especially true of senators from the same state and the same party, who are effectively prohibited by the party caucuses from joining the same major Senate committees. Because senators from the same state differ in seniority and committee assignments, they have *unequal institutional opportunity and clout to legislate in the same issue areas*.

In turn, differences in committee assignments are reflected in the publicity that senators receive for their legislative efforts because the local and national media take their cues from committee jurisdictions in awarding coverage to senators on specific issues. Media coverage is a crucial instrument that senators use to build reputations among their constituents, and senators benefit from media coverage that focuses exclusively on their legislative record. The more "solo" coverage a senator receives, the more likely it is for constituents to evaluate the senator favorably, as an effective legislator. Subsequently, the incentive to attract individualized media coverage helps sustain the differences between same state senators in their legislative portfolios.

Interest groups also respond to senators' committee assignments in that they tend to seek help from the senator who is in the best position to advance their goals, and affiliated PACs generally reward senators' efforts with campaign contributions. Without the institutional power to accomplish legislative action on behalf of a particular interest group, senators find it difficult to sell themselves as credible advocates. It is therefore a more productive and efficient strategy for same-state senators to court the state interest groups whose concerns fall under their separate committee jurisdictions. In this way, the incentive to attract interest group and campaign contributor support also sustains differentiation between senators from the same state.

Ultimately, it is the sum total of the legislative efforts of both senators from a single state that explains the degree of representation that state receives at the federal level. By expanding our scope of study from a single senator to a two-member delegation, and recognizing that representation has multiple dimensions, scholars can better measure legislative representation in the United States Senate.

SENATE REPRESENTATION IS
BETTER THAN WE THINK

If we incorporate the two-person nature of Senate delegations and the multidimensionality of legislative behavior into our evaluation of Senate representation, we can conclude that representation in the U.S. Senate is better than it is commonly believed to be. When two senators from the same state are viewed as a pair, it is clear that their combined representational agendas include a wide range of the interests and opinions that exist among constituents in their state. Moreover, framing Senate representation as a multidimensional activity can provide a more comprehensive evaluation of the ways in which states are included in federal policy making.

For example, if a state is represented by a split-party delegation, we might assume that the state's clout is diluted by the fact that the two senators oppose each other on party-line roll-call votes. But if we were to examine other legislative activities, such as bill and amendment sponsorship, we might find that two senators from opposite parties are more likely to work together than their same-party counterparts on issues relevant to their states. Because they have starkly different roll-call voting records, senators in split-party delegations face less pressure to contrast their legislative portfolios and can therefore afford to address the same issues more frequently than senators in same-party delegations.

Similarly, we might assume that because senators in a same-party delegation have similar roll-call voting records, voters who do not share their party affiliation are not represented in the Senate. But it would be a mistake to conclude that same-state, same-party senators represent only their partisan constituents. Senators are risk-averse, and for that reason, senators from the same state and the same party will not rely on the same set of core partisan voters. Instead, they will seek out the widest possible base of support, including voters who are not in their own party. But because they can be easily confused with one another, senators from the same party and the same state often go in opposite directions and address separate state issues when they construct their legislative portfolios. In doing so, they each reach out to different sets of voters, and in the process, they represent constituents outside the confines of their party affiliation.

Also intrinsic to judging the quality of representation is judging the job of the instruments that constituents can use to hold their senators accountable. It is often argued that senators spend too much time seeking publicity and fund raising and too little time legislating, a scenario that is ultimately detrimental to representation. But on further examination, that assertion can be refuted, at least in part. If we take a hard look at what senators actually spend their days doing and allocate their resources toward, we discover that they do exert a great deal of energy trying to give voice to the policy views of their constituents, and address their geographic and economic interests. Although attracting media attention is of paramount importance to senators, it is not just because they are "media hounds" and may wish to run for president someday. Rather, senators recognize that drawing media attention is crucial to establishing a reputation among their constituents, a reputation that is in large part built on concrete legislative work.

Interest group support is also fundamental to senators' reelection success, and there is no question that much of their time is spent seeking such funds from national and local groups. But the decisions that interest groups make about contributing to a senator can be revealing as to the senator's effectiveness. At least at the local level, there is evidence that such campaign contributions from interest groups correspond to the legislative choices that senators make on behalf of specific interests *in their states*. While it is true that senators actively represent a selected subset of interests, and they are rewarded for doing so, it is only a problem if their actions do not benefit their states.

The Institutional Effects of States as Multimember Districts

The observed behavior of senators from the same state that has been documented throughout this book is not unique to the United States. Candidates and legislators in countries that have legislatures with multimember districts exhibit similar patterns of behavior. In particular, Chile and Japan each have legislative districts with two or more seats per district. A brief study of the legislatures in these two countries helps to illustrate the effects of dual-member districts on candidate strategy, legislative choices, and even the organization of the legislatures themselves. Making a comparison of this sort helps reinforce the argument that the U.S. Senate should be viewed as an institution with multimember districts.

The works of Jay Dow (1998) and Eric Magar, Marc Rosenblum, and David Samuels (1998) both examine the results of electoral reforms on the 1989 general elections in Chile, which were the first post–Pinochet dictatorship elections to be held in that country. Chile has a dual-member Senate district, where two senators are simultaneously elected from the same geographic space, under an open-list proportional representation system. Parties nominate up to two candidates per Senate district, and seats are awarded based on the percentage of votes the party receives nationwide.[1] However, in order for each candidate nominated from a single party to win a Senate seat, that party has to attract double the number of votes as the next highest party. Since such a margin of victory is highly unlikely, the usual result is that only one of the party's nominees wins a Senate seat from the district.

In their works, Dow and Magar, Rosenblum, and Samuels assert that the structure of the electoral system creates an incentive for two candidates nominated by the same party for the same district to contrast themselves as much as possible within the limits of the party's policy positions. Rather than adopting campaign platforms that appeal to the median voter in a district, each candidate for the Senate adopts a more extreme position (right or left) of the party in order to attract the majority of the party's voters in a given district. This strategy is a direct outgrowth of the fact that the candidate is competing against another candidate from the same party, as well as all other party candidates.

Although U.S. senators from the same state are not simultaneously elected, they behave in ways that are similar to the behavior of legislators in Chile. First, Senate candidates try to adopt campaign platforms that create a readily identifiable image, one that is noticeably different from the other sitting incumbent senator. Second, senators from the same state and the same party do not pursue the same set of voters; rather, they contrast themselves, ideologically, as liberals or conservatives, and they actively court different regions of the state. Once elected, U.S. senators from the same state and the same party adopt alternative representational agendas in order to create separate reputations as strong advocates for their state, which helps them attract and maintain different electoral coalitions.

In addition to Chile, Japan also serves as an illustrative example of how sharing the same geographic constituency can influence legislative representation. In particular, the work of McCubbins and Rosenbluth (1995) details the ways in which the multimember structure of districts influences legislative and electoral behavior in Japan. The Japanese leg-

---

[1] For an expanded description of the allocation of Senate seats in Chile, see Dow (1998, 3).

islature (the Diet) includes multimember districts, with a minimum of two legislators per district, which encourages parties to "run more than one candidate in each district to attempt to win a majority" (38). Because voters have multiple choices, political parties must find a way to distinguish the candidates who run under the party label in the same district. To meet this challenge, political parties encourage and support differentiation among their same-party candidates along several dimensions. Candidates are encouraged to develop a personal following that is based on an individual reputation for securing goods and services for particular constituencies in their districts. McCubbins and Rosenbluth argue that Japanese public policy is more particularistic and distributive than we might expect of a strong party system because of the way that district seats are allocated. In other words, the range of constituents who receive targeted goods and services from the legislature is expanded because of intraparty competition at the district level.

The multimember structure of legislative districts in Japan translates into legislative arrangements that are designed to sustain the advantages of incumbency. For instance, the majority party has Policy Affairs Research Councils (PARCs), which serve to filter legislative proposals to the larger legislative body. As McCubbins and Rosenbluth point out, the party ensures that their members from the same district receive assignments to different PARCs because "differentiation in PARC affiliations allows LDP members from the same district to build different personal vote coalitions" (1995, 50). In this way, the Japanese legislative committee system is geared toward enabling members of the same party and the same district to differentiate their legislative portfolios.

Even though the U.S. Senate is not a strong majority-party institution, it encourages differentiation between senators from the same state in a way that is similar to the Diet. Parties in the U.S. Senate informally but systematically prohibit senators from the same state and the same party from sitting on the same committees. The motivation is somewhat different: in the case of Japan, the party wants to maximize its chances of winning seats in a single district so it differentiates its candidates; in the case of the United States, parties want to prevent states from exerting disproportionate influence in the issues that fall under the jurisdiction of a single committee. Yet, despite alternative motivations, the effect of having two legislators who represent the same geographic and electoral space produces these institutional arrangements in legislatures in both countries.

In the United States, senators from the same state are not simultaneously elected and do not compete directly against each other in an election. Nonetheless, their behavior strongly resembles that of legislators in other countries who do compete directly against one another for the right to represent the same geographic constituency. One implication of this pattern of behavior is that the structural effects of having two legislators who share the same district may not be contingent upon simultaneous competitive elections. In other words, merely holding the same level of office and sharing the same pool of potential supporters may be sufficient to encourage differentiation across legislators from the same district.

BENEFITS AND COSTS OF DUAL REPRESENTATION

The systematic tendencies of senators from the same state to adopt contrasting legislative portfolios, and thereby build distinct electoral coalitions in their state, produce both benefits and costs for American democracy. Dual representation is much like divided government in the sense that it is a way to maximize the strength of diverse interests in the political process. With two senators for each state, voters can opt for two partisan viewpoints by voting for one Democratic senator and one Republican senator. Or, voters can sustain divisions in representation by voting for senators with different geographic bases in the state. By selecting senators who promise to address different sets of economic interests in the state, voters can maximize the amount of benefits that the state receives within the federal system. Furthermore, voters can choose two senators with differing perspectives — for example, one senator who is more nationally oriented and the other who pays closer attention to state needs.

The act of selecting two senators who differ from each other does not require an outright comparison on the part of voters. Senators, by virtue of their choices to pursue alternate agendas, provide a set of contrasts to which voters respond. It is unrealistic to believe that an individual voter literally brings his assessment of one senator into the voting booth when voting on the other senator's reelection. But whether the voter chooses to reelect an incumbent senator will be based on a positive evaluation of the senator's job performance. A senator's job performance rating will rest on how well the senator manages to establish an independent identity, which in turn rests on the ability to create contrast with the other incumbent senator. Indirectly, then, when voters reelect incumbent senators, they are tacitly approving of the ways that their two senators, assessed as a team, represent the state.

Even challengers who are running for the Senate for the first time incorporate the dual structure of Senate delegations into their campaign strategies. Because there are factors other than partisanship that determine the outcome of Senate elections, Senate candidates conduct multifaceted campaigns. In addition to appealing to core party supporters, a candidate's platform also emphasizes personal characteristics and policy positions. If candidates have prior governing experience, they will undoubtedly make their governing record a focal point of the campaign (Sellers 1998). In particular, they will venture to particular regions in the state that they have helped and try to focus local attention on their efforts. Candidates will do the same with issue positions: in attempting to attract votes in a state, they will try to cultivate constituencies by highlighting their policy positions when they coincide with the preferred policy stances of the voters. A candidate makes choices about which elements to emphasize: for example, a candidate who visits a blue-collar conservative region will emphasize efforts to protect industry but not necessarily reveal a prochoice stance. Such selective campaigning is not merely smoke and mirrors; it reflects the complicated nature of representing a state on multiple dimensions.

The existence of another sitting senator compounds the numerous other challenges in waging a successful campaign for the Senate. Consider a challenger who is running against an incumbent senator: the task is to formulate a campaign agenda that will attract support from a majority of the voters. To run a campaign that promises merely to mirror the efforts of the incumbent senator leaves a candidate vulnerable to the charge of offering nothing new or different. Assuming that most, if not all, Senate candidates are risk-averse to losing, it makes sense for them to adopt a campaign platform that emphasizes a separate and distinct agenda for the future. The problem that they run into in devising such a platform is that there is *another* incumbent senator who, assuming he is a capable senator, already serves specific interests and issues in the state that differ from those served by the senator who is being challenged. The process of composing a Senate campaign therefore requires that a challenger also consider the other incumbent senator's agenda. In one sense, then, challengers for Senate seats perceive a benefit to contrasting themselves with both senators from the state, not just their campaign opponent.

This type of positioning by Senate candidates is somewhat similar to the campaign strategies that might have been employed by senators in the nineteenth century. When candidates had to sell themselves to state legislatures, they had the incentive to distinguish themselves from the other sitting senator in order to appeal to divisions within the state legislature. When delegations were primarily single-party, notably in the very early and very late parts of the nineteenth century (Brunell and Grofman 1998, 394), parties also had the same incentive to support senators with different portfolios. If the party did not differentiate its Senate candidates this way, then the opposition party in the state could mount a challenge against at least one of the senators for failing to address interests outside that senator's party's purview. If, on the other hand, both senators, even in the same party, covered all the geographic and economic bases in the state, the party would be less vulnerable to a successful challenge by an opposite-party candidate. The modern-day equivalent of such a strategy is that a candidate for Senate is not likely to present himself as a clone of the other sitting senator, even if they are from the same party.[2] In this way, campaign platforms, which often serve as the basis for legislative agendas in the Senate, can be the seeds of differentiation among senators from the same state.

However, the multiple number of senators for each state also brings with it some unavoidable difficulties, especially in holding senators accountable for their actions. Just as divided government makes it hard to assign responsibility for public policy outcomes, a two-person delegation makes it hard for constituents in a state to hold senators accountable for advocating on their behalf in the policy process. When a state receives a federal grant, for instance, or a controversial policy is enacted that benefits the state, both senators presumably will have voted on these measures and could claim credit for them. On the other hand, if the policy outcome is negative, such as storing nuclear waste in Nevada or losing the Supercollider project, neither senator is likely to be held accountable. As much as senators work to distinguish themselves, and as clearly as the media might portray differences between them, there will inevitably be a certain level of confusion among constituents about their senators.

Although senators have a constant incentive to represent their states well because such behavior can make reelection easier, only a small number of constituents pay constant and close attention to senators' records, so it is possible for senators to engage in the minimum level of activism on behalf of their state. In other words, the subset of state interests and opinions that are addressed in the senator's legislative portfolio might be less than adequate to satisfy the state's needs. Furthermore, senators might actually be tempted to act against the interest of the majority in their state if such an action benefited an important

---

[2] Even in reelection campaigns, incumbent senators perceive some pressure to demonstrate their differences from the other senator from the state. Richard Fenno (1989, 136–37) describes how Senator Quayle and his advisers compared his image to that of the governor and the other senator from his state when he sought reelection: "but we haven't talked about what we are going to send through the pipeline. Who is Dan Quayle? What are we going to market? [Governor] Bowen is the country doctor. [Senator] Lugar is the intellectual. What is Dan Quayle? What is the theme that we will use to package the candidate? We ought to think about that so all of us can start pushing that theme — in legislation, in press releases, in warding off the opposition."

economic interest or campaign contributor. A single act of "shirking" may not amount to much, and the chances are small that it will be discovered by the local press or the average constituent. However, repeated acts of shirking over the course of six years might produce a record that is not responsive to the best interests of the state.

However, by its very construct, dual representation also provides powerful protection against such repeated inattentiveness and shirking because every senator knows that a state colleague is simultaneously acting on behalf of the state. For example, when a vote takes place on the Senate floor that has a direct impact on a state and one senator votes to preserve the state's interest, the other senator is unlikely to vote against the colleague, even if ideology, partisanship, or campaign backers might lead him to do so. In this case, it is not a benefit for the senators to contrast themselves. But the degree to which having two senators from the same state keeps them both more accountable can be more general than a single vote. If one senator from a state is very active and considered a strong and productive legislator, the other senator will be under more pressure to show legislative accomplishment. Failing to emerge from the shadow of a more prominent state colleague can render a senator more vulnerable to a strong challenger in the next reelection campaign. Consequently, the dual nature of a Senate delegation exerts pressure on both senators to serve their states in a responsible fashion, but in contrasting issue areas and with different governing styles.

The inherent competition between two senators from the same state also may produce negative outcomes for the state if the competition reaches the point where the two senators are unable to work together. In such cases, they will not be able to present a united front to their colleagues, or the administration, and may lose valuable federal aid for the state. Even if their working relationship is tenable, two senators may see it more in their own individual interest to seek a benefit for the state on their own or, more simply, have divergent views on the best strategy for securing a favorable outcome for the state. Both senators have the same constitutional obligation to represent their state and can easily assert their prerogative to do so in a way that they see fit, even if it contradicts the preferences of their colleague. In this way, the same incentives for differentiation in a Senate delegation can weaken the delegation's capacity to work as a team on behalf of the state.

Constituents and interest groups may also take advantage of the fact that there are two senators from their state by playing one senator off the other to get attention and secure a policy goal. For example, a senator who is not otherwise disposed to helping an particular group in the state faces the real possibility that the group will then turn to the state colleague. This manipulation of the two-person nature of Senate delegations by state groups injects conflict into the relationship between the two senators because one senator is taking action on behalf of a state interest, which may force the other senator to actively oppose the interest. In addition, it necessarily multiplies the number of decision points in the legislative process, increases the risk of decisions taking longer than necessary, and raises the probability that decisions by one senator will be overturned or opposed by the other senator from the delegation. The opposite but no less detrimental effect is that senators from the same state will team up to ignore or bury a controversial issue that they do not want to take a position on.

Despite the problems associated with dual representation, such as decreased accountability and potential conflict within a Senate delegation, the total benefits of having two senators who represent the same geographic constituency outweigh the total costs. Though there will be overlap across a Senate delegation, the tendency for senators from the same state to diversify their legislative portfolios expands the range of state opinions and interests that are given voice in federal policymaking. Although our legislative system does not always function efficiently or productively, the competitive structure of Senate delegations does create the potential for broad and responsive representation in the United States Senate.

Appendix A

MEASUREMENT OF VARIABLES

SENIORITY	Number of terms served in the Senate
REELECTION	Dummy variable coded 1 if the senator was up for reelection and 0 if not
STATE POPULATION SIZE	State population in millions
SIZE OF STATE ECONOMY	Number of industries in the state generating $500 million in income
IDEOLOGICAL DIFFERENCE	Absolute difference in Americans for Democratic Action (ADA) ratings
PARTY AFFILIATION	Dummy variable coded 1 if the senator was a Democrat and 0 if the senator was a Republican
SHARED PARTY AFFILIATION	Dummy variable coded 1 if the senator shared the same party affiliation as his or her state colleague and 0 if not
NUMBER OF COMMITTEE ASSIGNMENTS	Number of standing committee assignments
CHAIRMAN	Dummy variable coded 1 if the senator was a committee chair and 0 if not
DIFFERENCE IN YEARS SERVED	Absolute difference in the number of years that the two senators have held office in the Senate
NUMBER OF YEARS AS CONGRESSIONAL TEAM	Number of years that the two senators worked together when one was in the House of Representatives
PRESIDENTIAL CANDIDATE	Dummy variable coded 1 if the senator ran for or was considered as a potential presidential candidate and 0 if not
FORMER MEMBER OF HOUSE	Dummy variable coded 1 if the senator had served in the House prior to entering the Senate and 0 if not
FORMER GOVERNOR	Dummy variable coded 1 if the senator had served as governor prior to entering the Senate and 0 if not
STATE COLLEAGUE ISSUE MENTIONS	Number of constituents' like or dislike mentions about the other sitting senator from the state

STATE COLLEAGUE MEDIA	Number of newspaper articles mentioning the other sitting senator from the state
JUDICIARY COMMITTEE	Dummy variable coded 1 if the senator was a member of the Senate Judiciary Committee and 0 if not
LABOR COMMITTEE	Dummy variable coded 1 if the senator was a member of the Senate Labor and Human Resources Committee and 0 if not
ENERGY COMMITTEE	A dummy variable coded 1 if the senator was a member of the Senate Energy Committee and 0 if not
EPW COMMITTEE	Dummy variable coded 1 if the senator was a member of the Senate Environment and Public Works Committee and 0 if not
FINANCE COMMITTEE	Dummy variable coded 1 if the senator was a member of the Senate Finance Committee and 0 if not
AGRICULTURE COMMITTEE	Dummy variable coded 1 if the senator was a member of the Senate Agriculture Committee and 0 if not
ARMED SERVICES COMMITTEE	Dummy variable coded 1 if the senator was a member of the Senate Armed Services Committee and 0 if not
FOREIGN RELATIONS COMMITTEE	Dummy variable coded 1 if the senator was a member of the Senate Foreign Relations Committee and 0 if not
PERCENT COSPONSORSHIP	Percent of the total number of bills introduced by either senator from the same state that were cosponsored by his or her state colleague.
CAMPAIGN DIFFICULTY	Electoral vulnerability of the senator during his or her reelection cycle based on reports in *Congressional Quarterly Weekly Report*: 0-safe seat, 1-favored, 2-leaning, 3-too close to call

Appendix B

QUESTIONNAIRE MAILED TO NEWSPAPER
EDITORS AND REPORTERS

SAMPLE FOR OREGON

Please answer the following questions about Senators Hatfield and Packwood as completely as you can. Your time and input is greatly appreciated.

1. In general, I would say:
      (circle one)
   Senator Hatfield was more issue-oriented (focused primarily on national issues).
   Senator Hatfield was more constituency-oriented (focused primarily on state issues).

      (circle one)
   Senator Packwood was more issue-oriented (focused primarily on national issues).
   Senator Packwood was more constituency-oriented (focused primarily on state issues).

2. How closely would you say Senator Hatfield and Packwood agreed on state issues? Evaluate their agreement on a scale of 1 to 10, 1 being little or no agreement and 10 being total agreement. _____

3. How closely would you say Senator Hatfield and Packwood agreed on national issues? Evaluate their agreement on a scale of 1 to 10, 1 being little or no agreement and 10 being total agreement. _____

4. How well would you say Senators Hatfield and Packwood represented the voters of Oregon? (circle one)

   Very well   Well   Fairly well   Not well at all

5. In general, please rate the legislative skills of each senator:
                    (circle one)   (circle one)
   SENATOR HATFIELD   SENATOR PACKWOOD
   Got his bills passed   Y N   Got his bills passed   Y N

Influenced Senate debate	Y N	Influenced Senate debate	Y N
Voiced state views in the Senate	Y N	Voiced state views in the Senate	Y N
Procured Federal dollars for the state	Y N	Procured Federal money for the state	Y N

6. Did Senators Hatfield and Packwood tend to work together?
        (circle one)
        Yes   No

    If you answered "yes" to the above question, on what type of issues
        did they tend to work together?
                State issues   National issues

7. In what ways are Senator Hatfield and Packwood similar? In what
    ways are they distinct? (use back of sheet if necessary)
                Similarities   *Differences*

Appendix C

NEWSPAPER ARTICLES BY SUBJECT MATTER, STATE, AND SENATOR

Texas

Subject Matter	1987–1988		1989–1990		1991–1992	
	Bentsen	Gramm	Bentsen	Gramm	Bentsen	Gramm
Foreign policy/ Defense	54	30	44	37	32	31
Judiciary	29	41	23	49	17	19
Education	4	5	7	0	0	2
Environment/ Energy	35	16	18	19	30	10
Infrastructure	6	5	16	4	23	5
Health	16	2	22	0	28	0
Welfare/ Labor	17	8	4	3	22	0
Agriculture	5	4	5	10	4	1
Budget/Tax/ Trade	105	45	105	25	135	19
Banking/ Housing	16	16	12	24	12	9
State politics/ issues	146	44	72	172	61	22
Presidential	640	43	33	24	146	140
Pork	12	12	11	15	11	10
Other	87	54	69	54	81	37
Total	1,171	225	442	436	601	305

NEW YORK

Subject Matter	1987–1988		1989–1990		1991–1992	
	Moynihan	D'Amato	Moynihan	D'Amato	Moynihan	D'Amato
Foreign policy/ Defense	19	64	47	87	13	55
Judiciary	21	70	23	78	14	56
Education	2	0	0	3	0	3
Environment/ Energy	36	25	4	18	10	22
Infrastructure	17	6	6	14	20	14
Health	4	2	4	2	1	19
Welfare/ Labor	55	6	34	5	14	6
Agriculture	0	0	0	0	0	0
Budget/Tax/ Trade	14	18	31	15	19	13
Banking/ Housing	5	27	2	123	1	85
State politics/ issues	98	122	64	294	39	461
Presidential	29	34	3	7	23	25
Pork	3	8	0	9	2	15
Other	53	54	25	69	30	136
Total	361	436	244	729	186	910

FLORIDA

Subject Matter	1987–1988		1989–1990		1991–1992	
	Graham	Chiles	Graham	Mack	Graham	Mack
Foreign policy/ Defense	21	11	20	15	26	25
Judiciary	128	35	83	32	39	27
Education	26	21	21	7	14	6
Environment/ Energy	66	8	43	7	33	11
Infrastructure	11	2	6	6	5	4
Health	11	30	27	10	25	15
Welfare/ Labor	15	15	10	5	7	7
Agriculture	13	3	3	2	0	1
Budget/Tax/ Trade	27	48	28	11	32	16
Banking/ Housing	23	5	25	12	19	8
State politics/ issues	217	166	116	78	123	64
Presidential	41	30	13	6	49	20
Pork	6	2	6	2	6	4
Other	63	21	62	23	64	36
Total	668	398	463	216	445	244

MINNESOTA

Subject Matter	1987–1988		1989–1990		1991–1992	
	Durenberger	Boschwitz	Durenberger	Boschwitz	Durenberger	Wellstone
Foreign policy/ Defense	85	42	36	44	22	56
Judiciary	18	14	11	25	21	21
Education	2	1	1	7	8	5
Environment/ Energy	45	6	30	19	11	27
Infrastructure	5	1	0	0	8	0
Health	38	2	26	4	16	7
Welfare/ Labor	13	5	3	11	6	9
Agriculture	8	34	0	31	3	0
Budget/Tax/ Trade	20	27	12	33	14	15
Banking/ Housing	6	2	3	8	0	1
State politics/ issues	291	79	293	473	147	199
Presidential	30	15	3	15	11	36
Pork	4	2	1	2	0	0
Other	106	54	109	146	80	148
Total	671	285	528	838	347	523

Nebraska

Subject Matter	1987–1988		1989–1990		1992–1992	
	Exon	Karnes	Exon	Kerrey	Exon	Kerrey
Foreign policy/ Defense	81	45	122	94	103	96
Judiciary	27	46	21	36	46	28
Education	11	10	6	33	8	20
Environment/ Energy	46	34	137	78	41	76
Infrastructure	48	3	42	5	13	24
Health	6	11	10	28	5	107
Welfare/ Labor	2	3	13	10	5	45
Agriculture	46	110	22	100	17	73
Budget/Tax/ Trade	51	35	64	32	25	44
Banking/ Housing	10	29	16	51	6	39
State politics/ issues	149	796	605	609	115	195
Presidential	46	52	2	21	14	619
Pork	25	36	9	12	0	16
Other	109	249	26	91	40	8
Total	657	1,459	1,099	1,200	438	1,472

CALIFORNIA

Subject Matter	1987–1988		1989–1990		1991–1992	
	Cranston	Wilson	Cranston	Wilson	Cranston	Seymour
Foreign policy/ Defense	53	78	89	54	50	18
Judiciary	39	66	19	97	20	36
Education	5	0	0	14	0	1
Environment/ Energy	29	53	40	66	12	51
Infrastructure	3	14	5	9	0	8
Health	12	17	8	2	1	3
Welfare/ Labor	11	6	7	8	0	15
Agriculture	1	13	0	4	1	2
Budget/Tax/ Trade	8	20	18	13	5	6
Banking/ Housing	24	5	222	10	91	2
State politics/ issues	146	163	146	810	135	362
Presidential	35	28	0	36	7	25
Pork	0	7	0	2	0	5
Other	33	67	46	107	27	42
Total	438	637	598	1,232	349	577

REFERENCES

Abramowitz, Alan, and Jeff Segal. 1992. *Senate Elections*. Ann Arbor: University of Michigan Press.

Adams, Greg D. 1996. "Legislative Effects of Single-Member vs. Multi-Member Districts." *American Journal of Political Science* 40: 129–44.

Alesina, Alberto, Morris P. Fiorina, and Howard Rosenthal. 1991. "Why Are There So Many Split Senate Delegations? A Model of Opposite Party Advantage." Manuscript.

Arnold, R. Douglas. 1990. *The Logic of Congressional Action*. New Haven: Yale University Press.

———. 1999. "Congress and the Press." Manuscript.

Baker, Ross. 1998. "Factors Influencing the Political Relationships of Same-State Senators." Manuscript.

Bartels, Larry M. 1988. *Presidential Primaries and the Dynamics of Public Choice*. Princeton: Princeton University Press.

———. 1991. "Constituency Opinion and Congressional Policy Making: The Reagan Defense Buildup." *American Political Science Review* 85: 457–74.

Bauer, Raymond, Ithiel de Sola Pool, and Lewis Dexter. 1963. *American Business and Public Policy*. New York: Atherton Press.

Berelson, Bernard R., Paul F. Lazarsfeld, and William N. McPhee. 1954. *Voting*. Chicago: University of Chicago Press.

Berke, Richard L. 1998. "In Campaign '98, Being an Insider Is Back in." *New York Times*, July 13.

Bernstein, Robert A. 1991. "Ideological Deviation and Support for Reelection." *Western Political Quarterly* 42: 987–1003.

———. 1992. "Determinants of Differences in Feelings toward Senators Representing the Same State." *Western Political Quarterly* 44: 703–23.

Binder, Sarah, Forest Maltzman, and Lee Sigelman. 1998. "Senators' Home State Reputations: Why Do Constituents Love Bill Cohen So Much More than Al D'Amato?" *Legislative Studies Quarterly* 28: 545–60.

Born, Richard. 1997. "Causal Linkages between Constituents' Evaluations of Their Federal Legislators." *American Politics Quarterly* 25: 179–202.

Brown, Mike. 1990. "The Senate Race: McConnell Uses Tools of Incumbency," *Louisville Courier-Journal*, November 1.

Brunell, Thomas L., and Bernard Grofman. 1998. "Explaining Divided Senate Delegations 1788–1994: A Realignment Approach." *American Political Science Review* 92: 391–401

Bullock, Charles S., and David W. Brady. 1983. "Party, Constituency, and Roll-call Voting in the U.S. Senate." *Legislative Studies Quarterly* 8: 29–44.

Bureau of Economic Analysis, Department of Commerce. 1991. "Total Personal Income by Major Source & Earnings by Industry, 1969–1990." Washington, DC.

Campbell, Angus, Philip E. Converse, Warren E. Miller, and Donald E. Stokes. 1960. *The American Voter*. New York: Wiley.

Carmines, Edward G., and James A. Stimson. 1989. *Issue Evolution*. Princeton: Princeton University Press.

Carroll, James R. 1998. "McConnell, Lugar want to cut off tobacco aid — Proposal would buy out farmers, kill price supports. *Louisville Courier-Journal*, May 18.

Clines, Frances X., and Warren Weaver Jr. 1982. "Who Laughs Last," *New York Times*, April 3.

Clymer, Adam. 1992. "Change in the Senate: Moynihan Preparing for a Wider Stage." *New York Times*, December 6.

Congressional Quarterly Weekly Report. 1988. "Election Guide 1988." Washington, DC: Congressional Quarterly Inc. 46: 2880–2954.

———. 1990. "Countdown to November." Washington, DC: Congressional Quarterly Inc. 46: 3286–3358.

———. 1992. "The Trails End." Washington, DC: Congressional Quarterly Inc. 50: 3344–354.

Congressional Research Service. 1988. *Digest of Public General Bills and Resolutions*. Washington, DC: Government Printing Office.

Converse, Philip E. 1964. "The Nature of Belief Systems in Mass Publics." In *Ideology and Discontent*, ed. David E. Apter. New York: Free Press.

Cook, Timothy E. 1986. "House Members as Newsmakers: the Effects of Televising Congress." *Legislative Studies Quarterly* 11: 203–26.

———. 1989. *Making Laws and Making News*. Washington, DC: Brookings Institution.

Cox, Gary W. 1997. *Making Votes Count: Strategic Coordination in the World's Electoral Systems*. Cambridge: Cambridge University Press.

Cross, Al. 1989. "Ford, McConnell Differ on Whether Current Congress Will Pass Legislation on Acid Rain." *Courier-Journal*, February 18.

Dahl, David. 1989a. "Graham and Mack Make Up: Now a Senate Odd Couple." *St. Petersburg Times*, April 12.

———. 1989b. "Florida's Senators Split 9 of 16 Votes." *St. Petersburg Times*. December 17.

Dao, James. 1998. "Legislating at 50 Paces: The 2 Democratic Senators from New Jersey." *New York Times*, April 26.

Deering, Christopher J., and Steven S. Smith. 1997. *Committees in Congress*. Washington, DC: Congressional Quarterly Press.

Denzau, Arthur, and Michael Munger. 1986. "Legislators and Interest Groups: How Unorganized Interests Get Represented." *American Political Science Review* 80: 89–106.

Dexter, Lewis Anthony. 1969. *The Sociology of Politics*. Chicago: Rand McNally.

Diemer, Tom. 1994. "Howard's End: Metzenbaum Was True to Form through His Last Days in the Senate." *Cleveland Plain Dealer* December 4.

Dougan, William, and Michael Munger. 1989. "The Rationality of Ideology." *Journal of Law and Economics* 32: 119–42.

Dow, Jay K. 1998. "A Spatial Analysis of Candidate in Dual Member Districts: The 1989 Chilean Senatorial Elections." *Public Choice* 97: 451–74.

Dow Jones News Retrieval Service, 1987–1992.

Downs, Anthony. 1957. *An Economic Theory of Democracy*. New York: Harper.

Editorial Staff. 1989. "The Limits of Their Convictions." *St. Louis Post-Dispatch*, December 6.

Editorial Staff. 1994. "Re-Elect Senator Moynihan: He Delivers for the Nation and New York." *Buffalo News*, October 24.

Editorial Staff. 1998. "Senate Takes Right Road on Mass-Transit Funds." *Buffalo News*, March 7.

Erikson, Robert S. 1990. "Roll Calls, Reputations, and Representation in the U.S. Senate." *Legislative Studies Quarterly* 4: 623–42.

Erikson, Robert S., Gerald C. Wright, and John P. McIver. 1993. *Statehouse Democracy: Public Opinion and Policy in the American States*. New York: Cambridge University Press.

Ervin, Chuck. 1992. "Nickles Roars to Re-election." *Tulsa World*, November 4.

Evans, Lawrence C. 1991. *Leadership in Committee*. Ann Arbor: University of Michigan Press.

Farrand, Max. 1966. *The Records of the Federal Convention of 1787*. New Haven: Yale University Press.

Fenno, Richard F., Jr. 1973. *Congressmen in Committees*. Boston: Little, Brown.

———. 1978. *Home Style*. New York: Scott, Foresman and Company.

———. 1986. "Adjusting to the United States Senate." In *Congress and Policy Changes*, ed. Gerald C. Wright, Jr., Leroy R. Rieselback, and Lawrence C. Dodd. New York: Agathon Press.

———. 1989. *The Making of Senator: Dan Quayle*. Washington, DC: Congressional Quarterly Press.

———. 1990. *The Presidential Odyssey of John Glenn*. Washington, DC: Congressional Quarterly Press.

———. 1991. *Learning to Legislate: The Senate Education of Arlen Specter*. Washington, DC: Congressional Quarterly Press.

———. 1992. *When Incumbency Fails: The Senate Career of Mark Andrews*. Washington, DC: Congressional Quarterly Press.

———. 1996 *Senators on the Campaign Trail*. Norman: University of Oklahoma Press.

Fiorina, Morris P. 1977. *Congress: Keystone of the Washington Establishment*. New Haven: Yale University Press.

Franklin, Charles H. 1993. "Senate Incumbent Visibility over the Election Cycle." *Legislative Studies Quarterly* 2: 271–90.

Fritsch, Jane. 1992. "D'Amato Serves as a Magnet for Funds." *New York Times*.

Gale Research Company. 1986. *The 1986 IMS Directory of Publications*. Detroit: Gale Research Company.

Goodwin, Christopher. 1997. "Reassessing the Local News." Ph.D. dissertation, Brown University.

Gray, Virginia, and David Lowery. 1995. "The Population Ecology of Gucci Gulch, or the Natural Regulation of Interest Group Numbers in the American States." *American Journal of Political Science* 39: 1–29.

Grenzke, Janet. 1989. "PACs and the Congressional Supermarket: The Currency Is Complex." *American Journal of Political Science* 33: 1–24.

Grier, Kevin, and Michael Munger. 1993. "Corporate, Labor and Trade Association Contributions to the U.S. House and Senate, 1978–1986." *Journal of Politics* 55: 614–43.

Grofman, Bernard, Robert Griffin, and Gregory Berry. 1995. "House Members Who Become Senators: Learning from a 'Natural Experiment in Representation." *Legislative Studies Quarterly* 4: 513–29.

Hall, Richard L. 1996. *Participation in Congress.* New Haven: Yale University Press.

Hall, Richard L., and Frank Wayman. 1990. "Buying Time: Moneyed Interests and the Mobilization of Bias in Congressional Committees." *American Political Science Review* 84: 797–820.

Hardy, Thomas. 1992. "Clinton, Simon Could Offer Illinois Republicans a Seat." *Chicago Tribune,* November 15.

Haynes, George H. 1960. *The Senate of the United States: Its History and Practice.* New York: Russell & Russell.

Herrick, Rebekah, and Sue Thomas. 1993. "Split Delegations in the United States Senate: 1920–1988." *Social Science Journal* 30: 69–81.

Hess, Stephen. 1981. *The Washington Reporters.* Washington, DC: Brookings Institution.

———. 1986. *The Ultimate Insiders: U.S. Senators in the National Media.* Washington, DC: Brookings Institution.

Hibbing, John R., and John R. Alford. 1990. "Constituency Population and Representation in the U.S. Senate." *Legislative Studies Quarterly* 15: 581–98.

Hibbing, John R., and Sara C. Brandes. 1983. "State Population and the Electoral Success of U.S. Senators." *American Journal of Political Science* 27: 808–19.

Hill, Gail Kinsey, and Steve Suo. 1995. "Oregon Faces Loss of Clout in D.C." *Portland Oregonian,* September 12.

Hill, Kim Quaile, Stephen Hanna, and Sahar Shafqat. 1997. "The Liberal-Conservative Ideology of U.S. Senators: A New Measure." *American Journal of Political Science* 41: 1395–1413.

Jones, Mary Lynn. 1997. "Torricelli, Lautenberg Joust for Media Limelight." *Washington, DC Hill,* November 5.

Jung, Gi-Ryong, Lawrence W. Kenny, and John R. Lott, Jr. 1994. "An Explanation for Why Senators from the Same State Vote Differently So Frequently." *Journal of Public Economics* 54: 65–96.

Kahn, Kim F. 1993. "Incumbency and the News Media in U.S. Senate Elections." *Political Research Quarterly* 46: 715–40.

Kalt, Joseph P., and Mark A. Zupan. 1990. "The Apparent Ideological Behavior of Legislators: Testing for the Principle-Agent Slack in Political Institutions." *Journal of Law and Economics* 33: 103–31.

Kesssler, Daniel, and Keith Krehbiel. 1996. "The Dynamics of Cosponsorship." *American Political Science Review* 90: 555–66.

Key, V. O. 1949 (1970). *Southern Politics in State and Nation.* Knoxville: University of Tennessee Press.

Klein, Joe. 1998. "The Soul of the New Machine." *The New Yorker,* June 1.

Koenig, Robert L. 1989. "Not a Showhorse Bond Prefers to Be Known as a Workhorse." *St. Louis Post-Dispatch*, May 21.

Krehbiel, Keith. 1995. "Cosponsorship from A to Z." *American Journal of Political Science* 39: 906–23.

Lee, Frances, and Bruce I. Oppenheimer. 1997. "Senate Apportionment: Competitiveness and Partisan Advantage." *Legislative Studies Quarterly* 22: 3–24.

———. 1999. *Sizing Up The Senate: Unequal Consequences of Equal Representation*. University of Chicago Press.

Levy, Dena. 1996. "Mapping the Effects of Previous Experience: The Transition and Legislative Activities of First-Term Senators." Ph.D. dissertation, University of Iowa.

Locin, Mitchell, and Hugh Dellios. 1992. "Dixon's Washington Cohorts Feel Loss, Too." *Chicago Tribune*, March 19.

Lott, John R. Jr., and W. Robert Reed. 1989. "Shirking and Sorting in a Model of Finite-Lived Politicians." *Public Choice* 74: 125–49.

Lowery, David, and Virginia Gray. 1995. "The Population Ecology of Gucci Gulch, or the Natural Regulation of Interest Group Numbers in the American States." *American Journal of Political Science* 39: 1–29.

McCarthy, Robert J. 1998. "D'Amato Points to Successes in Visit Here." *Buffalo News*, May 18.

McCarty, Nolan, and Lawrence Rothenberg. 1996. "Commitment and the Campaign Contribution Contract." *American Journal of Political Science* 40: 872–904.

McCubbins, Mathew D., and Frances McCall Rosenbluth. 1995. "Party Provisions for Personal Politics: Dividing the Vote in Japan." In *Structure and Policy in Japan and the United States*, ed. Peter Cowhey and Mathew McCubbins. New York: Cambridge University Press.

Magar, Eric, Marc R. Rosenblum, and David Samuels. 1998. "On the Absence of Centripetal Incentives in Double-Member Districts: The Case of Chile." *Comparative Political Studies* 31: 714–39.

Martindale, Rob. 1992. "Diving into Little Dixie: Nickles Tries to Give GOP at Least a Toehold." *Tulsa World*, April 26.

Matthews, Donald. 1960. *U.S. Senators and Their World*. Chapel Hill: University North Carolina Press.

Miller, Warren, and Donald Stokes. 1963. "Constituency Influence in Congress." *American Political Science Review* 57: 45–56.

Mohr, Lawrence B. 1990. *Understanding Significance Testing*. London: Sage Publications.

Myers, Jim. 1991. "Nickles Helps Lead Way against Boren's PAC Tax-Break Proposal. *Tulsa World*, May 17.

Neal, Steve. 1986. "Senators Dixon and Simon Wouldn't Turn Down Promotions." *Chicago Tribune*, May 15.

Nie, Norman, Sidney Verba, and John Petrocik. 1976. *The Changing American Voter*. Cambridge: Harvard University Press.

Obmascik, Mark. 1991. "Wilderness Compromise Is Unveiled, Wirth Gives in on Water Issue." *Denver Post*. May 11.

Oppenheimer, Bruce I. 1996. "The Representational Experience: The Effect of State Population on Senator-Constituency Linkages." *American Journal of Political Science* 40: 1280–99.

Page, Benjamin I., and Robert Y. Shapiro. 1992. *The Rational Public.* Chicago: University of Chicago Press.

Pitkin, Hanna. 1967. *On the Concept of Representation.* Berkeley: University of California Press.

Popkin, Samuel L. 1991. *The Reasoning Voter.* Chicago: University of Chicago Press.

Powell, Lynda W. 1990. "Explaining Senate Elections: The Basis of Split Delegations and Party Polarizations." Manuscript.

Riker, William H. 1955. "The Senate and American Federalism." *American Political Science Review* 49: 452–69.

Roberts, Sam. 1992. "For the Real Potholes, See Moynihan." *New York Times,* December 7.

Romer, Thomas, and James M. Snyder Jr. 1994. "An Empirical Investigation of the Dynamics of PAC Contributions." *American Journal of Political Science* 38: 745–69.

Rossiter, Clinton, ed. 1961. *The Federalist Papers.* New York: Mentor Books.

Schiller, Wendy J. 1994. "Constituent Expectations and Agenda Setting in the U.S. Senate." Paper delivered at the annual meetings of the Midwest Political Science Association.

———. 1995. "Senators as Political Entrepreneurs: Using Bill Sponsorship to Shape Legislative Agendas." *American Journal of Political Science* 1: 186–203.

Schlozman, Kay Lehman, and John T. Tierney. 1986. *Organized Interests and American Democracy.* New York: Harper and Row.

Segura, Gary M., and Stephen P. Nicholson. 1995. "Sequential Choices and Partisan Transitions in U.S. Senate Delegations: 1972–1988." *Journal of Politics* 57: 86–100.

Sellers, Patrick. 1998. "Strategy and Background in Congressional Campaigns." *American Political Science Review* 92:159–71.

Shapiro, Catherine R., David W. Brady, Richard Brody, and John A. Ferejohn. 1990. "Linking Constituency Opinion and Senate Voting Scores: A Hybrid Explanation." *Legislative Studies Quarterly* 15: 599–622.

Sharkey Mary Anne. 1993. "Northeast Ohio Is Where the Senatorial Votes Are." *Cleveland Plain-Dealer,* May 26.

Shepsle, Kenneth A. 1979. "Institutional Arrangements and Equilibrium in Multidimensional Voting Models." *American Journal of Political Science* 23: 27–59.

Shepsle, Kenneth A., and Barry R. Weingast. 1981. "Political Preferences for the Pork Barrel: A Generalization." *American Journal of Political Science* 25: 96–111.

Simon, Jeff. 1992. "Foul Downstate Politics Defies Newton." *Buffalo News,* November 8.

Sinclair, Barbara. 1989. *Transformation of the U.S. Senate.* Baltimore: Johns Hopkins University Press.

———. 1990. "Washington Behavior and Home-State Reputation: The Impact of National Prominence on Senators' Images." *Legislative Studies Quarterly* 15: 475–93.

Smith, Steven. 1989. *Call to Order*. Washington, DC: Brookings Institution.

Snyder, James M. Jr. 1993. "The Market for Campaign Contributions: Evidence for the U.S. Senate 1980–1986." *Economics and Politics* 5: 219–40.

Squire, Peverill. 1988. "Who Gets National News Coverage in the U.S. Senate." *American Politics Quarterly* 16: 139–56.

Staff. 1990. "Ohio's Senators Look as Busy as Candidates." *Cleveland Plain Dealer*, November 4.

Stimson, James A., Michael B. Mackuen, and Robert S. Erikson. 1995. "Dynamic Representation." *American Political Science Review* 89: 543–565.

Swanstrom, Roy. 1988. *The United States Senate 1787–1801*. Washington, DC: Government Printing Office.

Swift, Elaine K. 1996. *The Making of an American Senate*. Ann Arbor: University of Michigan Press.

Tidmarch, Charles M., and John J. Pitney Jr. 1985. "Covering Congress." *Polity* 17: 463–83.

United States Department of Commerce, Census Bureau. 1988. *The Statistical Abstract*. Washington, DC: Government Printing Office.

Uslaner, Eric M. 1999. *The Movers and the Shirkers*. University of Michigan Press.

Wattenberg, Martin P. 1996. *The Decline of American Political Parties 1952–1994*. Cambridge: Harvard University Press.

Weaver, David, and G. C. Wilhoit. 1980. "News Media Coverage of U.S. Senators in Four Congresses 1953–1974." *Journalism Monographs* 67. Lexington: Association for Education in Journalism.

West, Darrell. 1994. "Political Advertising and News Coverage in the 1992 California U.S. Senate Campaigns." *Journal of Politics* 56: 1053–75.

West, Darrell, and Burdett C. Loomis. 1998. *The Sound of Money: How Political Interests Get What They Want*. New York: W. W. Norton.

Westlye, Mark. 1991. *Senate Elections and Campaign Intensity*. Baltimore: Johns Hopkins University Press.

Williams, Dick. 1992. "Is Fowler Back to Old Self?" *Atlanta Constitution*, January 21.

Wilson, Rick K., and Cheryl D. Young. 1997. "Cosponsorship in the U.S. Congress." *Legislative Studies Quarterly* 22: 25–43.

Wood, Gordon S. 1998. *The Creation of the American Republic, 1776–1787*. Chapel Hill: University of North Carolina Press.

Wright, Gerald C. Jr. 1989. "Policy Voting in the U.S. Senate: Who is Represented?" *Legislative Studies Quarterly* 14: 465–82.

Wright, Gerald C. Jr., and Michael Berkman. 1986. "Candidates and Policy in United States Senate Elections." *American Political Science Review* 80: 567–90.

Wright, John. 1985. "PACs, Contributions, and Roll Calls: An Organizational Perspective." *American Political Science Review* 79: 400–14.

————. 1990. "Contributions, Lobbying, and Committee Voting in the U.S. House of Representatives." *American Political Science Review* 84: 417–38.

Zaller, John. 1992. *The Nature and Origins of Mass Opinion*. New York: Cambridge University Press.

Zuckerman, Jill. 1997. "Under Fire on Hill, Kerry Shuffles Staff." *Boston Globe*, April 28.

INDEX

Adams, Greg D., 4n
Agriculture Committee, Senate: effect of
  membership on campaign contributions
  and farm, interests, 153, 154, 157 (table 6.2), on media coverage, 83–85, on
  public opinion, 109; seniority, 93
Alabama Senate Delegation
  —Heflin, Howell: state PAC contributions to, 151 (table 6.1); demographic
  patterns of support for, 129 (table 5.1)
  —Shelby, Richard: state PAC contributions to, 151 (table 6.1); demographic
  patterns of support for, 129 (table
  5.1); switching party affiliation, 39
Alaska Senate Delegation
  —Murkowski, Frank: competition with
  state colleague, 28–29; state PAC
  contributions to, 151 (table 6.1);
  —Stevens, Ted: competition with state
  colleague, 28–29; state PAC contributions to, 151 (table 6.1)
Appropriations Committee, Senate: effect
  of membership on state PAC contributions, 156, 157 (table 6.2), 158, on constituent evaluations, 109, on media
  coverage of senators, 9, on state colleague's committee selection, 48–53
Arizona Senate Delegation
  —DeConcini, Dennis: demographic patterns of support for, 130 (table 5.2);
  state PAC contributions to, 151 (table
  6.1)
  —McCain, John: demographic patterns
  of support for, 130 (table 5.2); state
  PAC, contributions to, 151 (table 6.1)
Arkansas Senate Delegation
  —Bumpers, Dale: state PAC contributions to, 151 (table 6.1)
  —Pryor, David: state PAC contributions
  to, 151 (table 6.1)
Armed Services Committee, Senate: effect
  of membership on constituent evaluations, 109, on media coverage of senators, 68, 83–85, on state PAC
  contributions to, senators, 156n, 157
  (table 6.2)

Arnold, Douglas R., 66
Asher, Herbert, 123
Atlanta Constitution, 68, 70

Baker, Ross, 25, 128n
Banking Committee, Senate: effect of
  membership on state PAC contributions
  to senators, 145, 154
Bartels, Larry M., 97n
Bernstein, Robert A., 96–97
Binder, Sarah, 95–96, 97n
Born, Richard, 96
Buffalo News, 123

California Senate Delegation
  —Boxer, Barbara, 25
  —Cranston, Alan: constituent evalua-
  tion of, 106, 107, 108; demographic
  patterns of, support for, 130 (table
  5.2), 131; media coverage (Los Angeles Times) of, 184, (appendix C)
  —Feinstein, Dianne, 25
  —Seymour, John: media coverage of,
  184 (appendix C)
  —Wilson, Pete: constituent evaluation
  of, 106, 107, 108; demographic patterns, of support for, 130 (table 5.2),
  131; media coverage (Los Angeles
  Times) of, 184, (appendix C)
Chicago Tribune, 154
Colorado Senate Delegation
  —Brown, Hank: cooperation with state
  colleague, 53; role as senior senator,
  108
  —Nighthorse-Campbell, Ben, switching
  party affiliation, 39
  —Wirth, Tim: cooperation with state
  colleague, 53
Committees, Senate: assignment to, 25–26,
  43–44, 147; effect of Appropriations seat
  within, delegation, 48–53; selection of,
  43–53, 99–101, 109–10, 144–45. See
  also, individual Senate committees
Constituent evaluation of senators: 95–
  101; issue-based, 101–104; effect of
  home-style on, 104–110; role in senators'

Constituent evaluation of senators (*cont.*)
  legislative agenda setting, 8, 27. *See also*
  Media, Coverage
Constitutional Convention: Great Compromise, 14; meeting of, 6; debate on
  number of, senators per state, 14–15,
  17, 161, on per capita voting, 15, on
  size of, Senate membership, 13–14, 17
Cook, Timothy E., 26
Courier-Journal, 79

D'Amato, Alfonse: constitutent evaluation
  of, 109–10; signaling behavior to cam-
  paign, contributors, 149–51. *See also*
  New York Senate Delegation
Delaware, Senate Delegation
  — Biden, Joseph: state PAC contribu-
    tions to, 151 (table 6.1)
  — Roth, William: state PAC contribu-
    tions to, 151 (table 6.1)
Demographic Representation: concept of,
  5, 8–9, 113–14; statewide patterns of
  support for, senators, 127–131
Denzau, Arthur, 146
Dixon, Alan: signaling behavior to cam-
  paign contributors, 154–55. *See also* Il-
  linois Senate, Delegation
Dow, Jay K., 6n, 167
Dual Representation: concept of, 4–6, 12–
  17, 161–162, 169–173. *See also* indi-
  vidual, Senate delegations

Economic Representation: concept of, 9,
  22, 27, 143–45; impact of campaign
  contributions, on roll call votes, 145–
  46; measured by campaign contributions to senators, 145–48; patterns of
  state PAC contributions, 152–53, 155–
  58; senators' signaling, behavior, 149–
  50, 152–55; state political actions committees (PACs), 9, 27, 146–48, 151–52
Elections, Senate: campaigns, 93–99; effect of Seventeenth Amendment on, 19;
  effects of, state partisanship in, 95–97;
  mode of, 13–14, 19; public canvass in,
  18–19, 114–16; role of state legislatures in, 14–17, 20; staggered nature of,
  23–24, 26, 144
Energy Committee, Senate: effect of membership on overall campaign contributions, 145

Federalist Papers, 161
Fenno, Richard F. Jr., 22, 171n
Finance Committee, Senate: effect of
  membership on state PAC contributions
  to senators, 156, 157 (table 6.2), 158,
  on media coverage of senators, 8, 99
Fiorina, Morris P., 118n
Florida Senate Delegation
  — Chiles, Lawton: retirement of, 35n
  — Graham, Bob: constituent evaluation
    of, 106, 107, 108; demographic pat-
    terns of support for, 130 (table 5.2);
    geographic patterns of support for,
    132, 138–139 (Map 5.9); legislative
    comparison to state colleague, 35–37;
    media coverage (*St. Petersburg Times*)
    of, 181 (appendix C)
  — Mack, Connie: constituent evalua-
    tion of, 106, 107, 108; demographic
    patterns of support for, 130 (table
    5.2); geographic patterns of sup-
    port for, 132, 138–139 (Map 5.9);
    legislative comparison to state,
    colleague, 35–37; media coverage
    (*St. Petersburg Times*) of, 181
    (appendix C)
Foreign Relations Committee, Senate, effect of membership on media coverage
  of, senators, 80, 81 (table 3.6), 82–84,
  85 (table 3.7)
Franklin, Charles H., 27, 95, 98, 101

Geographic Representation: case studies
  of, 115–126; concept of, 8–9, 22, 114–
  115; patterns of support for senators,
  131–141
Georgia Senate Delegation
  — Fowler, Wyche: constituent evaluation
    of, 106, 107, 108; media coverage
    (*Atlanta Constitution*) of, 68, 69 (fig-
    ure 3.1), 70–71; state PAC contribu-
    tions to, 151 (table 6.1)
  — Nunn, Sam: constituent evaluation of,
    106, 107, 108; media coverage (*At-
    lanta Constitution*) of, 68, 69 (figure
    3.1), 70–71; state PAC contributions
    to, 151 (table 6.1)
Ghorum, Nathaniel, 15
Gramm, Phil, 150n. *See also* Texas Senate
  Delegation
Gray, Virginia, 23

Grenzke, Janet, 146
Grier, Kevin, 146, 156

Hall, Richard L., 146, 162
Hamilton, Alexander, 161
Hess, Stephen, 26

Illinois Senate Delegation
— Dixon, Alan: constituent evaluation of, 106, 107; demographic patterns of support for, 129 (table 5.1); media coverage *(Chicago Tribune)* of, 63, 71, 73, 74 (figure 3.3), 75–76; signaling behavior to campaign contributors, 154–55
— Simon, Paul: constituent evaluation of, 106, 107; demographic patterns of support, 129 (table 5.1); media coverage *(Chicago Tribune)* of, 63, 71, 73, 74 (figure 3.3), 75–76; signaling behavior to campaign contributors, 154–55
Indiana Senate Delegation
— Coats, Daniel: demographic patterns of support for, 129 (table 5.1)
— Lugar, Richard: demographic patterns of support for, 129 (table 5.1)
Iowa Senate Delegation
— Grassley, Charles: demographic patterns of support for, 130 (table 5.2); state PAC contributions to, 151 (table 6.1)
— Harkin, Tom: demographic patterns of support for, 130 (table 5.2); state PAC contributions to, 151 (table 6.1)

Jay, John, 161
Judiciary Committee, Senate: effect of membership on constituent evaluation, 99–100 (table, 4.1), on media coverage, 73, 75, 80–82, 83–85
Jung, Gi-Yong, 9n, 127

Kalt, Joseph P., 38n
Kansas Senate Delegation
— Dole, Robert J.: demographic patterns of support for, 129 (table 5.1), 131; state PAC contributions to, 151 (table 6.1)
— Kassebaum, Nancy: demographic patterns of support for, 129 (table 5.1),

131; state PAC contributions to, 151 (table 6.1)
Kenny, Lawrence W., 9n, 127
Kentucky Senate Delegation
— Ford, Wendell: constituent evaluation of, 106, 107; demographic patterns of support for, 130 (table 5.2); media *(Courier-Journal)* coverage of, 76, 77 (figure 3.4), 78–79; state PAC contributions to, 151 (table 6.1)
— McConnell, Mitch: constituent evaluation of, 106, 107; demographic patterns of support for, 130, (table 5.2); media *(Courier-Journal)* coverage of, 76, 77 (figure 3.4), 78–79; state PAC contributions to, 151 (table 6.1)
Kerrey, Robert, 109. *See also* Nebraska Senate Delegation
Kerry, John, 109. *See also* Massachusetts Senate Delegation
Key, V. O., 112
King, Rufus, 14

Labor and Human Resources Committee, Senate: effect of membership on media, coverage of senators, 83–85
Legislative Agenda Setting: encroachment by state colleague, 54–55, 79; media effects on, 65; role of bill and amendment sponsorship and cosponsorship in, 4, 7, 37, 53–58; role of roll-call voting in, 4, 7, 37–43; similarity of, within delegations, 38–43, 145–46; strategy of, 4–5
Lott, John R., 9n, 38, 127
Louisiana Senate Delegation
— Breaux, John: demographic patterns of support for, 129 (table 5.1), state PAC, contributions to, 151 (table 6.1)
— Johnston, Bennett: demographic patterns of support, 129 (table 5.1); state PAC, contributions to, 151 (table 6.1)
Lowery, David, 23

Madison, James, 161
Magar, Eric, 167
Maine Senate Delegation
— Cohen, William: state PAC contributions to, 151 (table 6.1)
— Mitchell, George: state PAC contributions to, 151 (table 6.1)

Maltzman, Forrest, 95–96, 97n
Martin, Alexander, 15
Maryland Senate Delegation
— Mikulski, Barbara: demographic patterns of support for, 129 (table 5.1), 131; state PAC contributions to, 151 (table 6.1)
— Sarbanes, Paul: demographic patterns of support for, 129 (table 5.1), 131; state PAC contributions to, 151 (table 6.1)
Massachusetts Senate Delegation
— Kennedy, Edward M.: comparison to Kerry, 20n, 73; constituent evaluation of, 107, 108; media coverage *(Boston Globe)* of, 71, 72 (figure 3.2); state PAC contributions to, 151 (table 6.1)
— Kerry, John: comparison to Kennedy, 20n, 73; constituent evaluation of, 107, 108; media coverage *(Boston Globe)* of, 71, 72 (figure 3.2); state PAC contributions to, 151 (table 6.1)
McCarty, Nolan, 146n
McCubbins, Matthew D., 6n, 167–68
Media Coverage of Senators: case studies of local media coverage in Georgia, Massachusetts, Illinois, and Kentucky, 68–80; effect on constituent evaluations, 99–104; patterns of local coverage, 7–8, 26–27, 80–87; patterns of national coverage, 7–8, 26–27, 63, 65; senators' efforts to attract publicity, 63–65. *See also,* individual state delegations
Michigan Senate Delegation
— Levin, Carl: demographic patterns of support for, 128, 129 (table 5.1); geographic patterns of support for, 135 (map 5.6); state PAC contributions to, 151, (table 6.1)
— Riegle, Donald: demographic patterns of support for, 128, 129 (table 5.1); geographic patterns of support, 135 (map 5.6); state PAC contributions to, 151 (table 6.1)
Miller, Warren, 88
Minnesota Senate Delegation
— Boschwitz, Rudy: constituent evaluation of, 106, 108; demographic patterns of, support for, 129 (table 6.1); media coverage *(Star-Tribune)* of, 182 (appendix C)

— Durenberger, Dave: constituent evaluation of, 106, 108; electoral patterns of, support for, 129 (table 6.1); media coverage *(Star-Tribune)* of, 182 (appendix C)
— Wellstone, Paul: adaptation to the Senate, 92; constituent evaluation of, 106, 108; media coverage *(Star-Tribune)* of, 182 (appendix C)
Missouri Senate Delegation
— Bond, Christopher 'Kit': cooperation with state colleague, 30; demographic, patterns of support for, 129 (table 5.1); signaling behavior to campaign contributors, 152–53; state PAC contributions to, 151 (table 6.1)
— Danforth, John: cooperation with state colleague, 30; demographic patterns, of support for, 129 (table 5.1); state PAC contributions to, 151 (table 6.1); signaling, behavior to campaign contributors, 152–53
Montana Senate Delegation
— Baucus, Max: comparison to state colleague, 115
— Melcher, John: comparison to state colleague, 115
Morris, Gouverneur, 14–15
Moynihan, Daniel P.: signaling behavior to campaign contributors, 150–151. *See also* New York Senate Delegation
Multimember Districts: states as, 3–6; comparison to, Chile, 166–67; Japan, 166–68. *See, also* Dual Representation
Munger, Michael, 146, 156

Nebraska Senate Delegation
— Exon, James: constituent evaluation of, 106, 107, 108; demographic patterns of, support for, 128–129 (table 5.1); geographic patterns of support for, 137 (map 5.8); media coverage, *(World-Tribune)* of, 183 (appendix C); state PAC contributions to, 151 (table 6.1)
— Karnes, David: constituent evaluation of, 106, 107, 108; media, coverage *(World-Tribune)* of, 183 (appendix C)
— Kerrey, Robert: constituent evaluation of, 106, 107, 108; demographic patterns of support for, 128–129 (table

5.1); geographic patterns of support for, 137 (Map 5.8); media coverage *(World-Tribune)* of, 183 (appendix C); state PAC contributions to, 151 (table 6.1)

New Hampshire Senate Delegation
— Rudman, Warren: bill cosponsorship, 30
— Smith, Bob: bill sponsorship, 29–30

New Jersey Senate Delegation
— Bradley, Bill: state PAC contributions to, 152 (table 6.1); demographic patterns of support for, 129 (table 5.1)
— Lautenberg, Frank: demographic patterns of support for, 129 (table 5.1); feud with Torricelli, 12; state PAC contributions to, 152 (table 6.1)
— Torricelli, Robert: feud with Lautenberg, 12

New Mexico Senate Delegation
— Bingaman, Jeff: demographic patterns of support for, 130 (table 5.2); state PAC contributions to, 151 (table 6.1)
— Domenici, Pete: demographic patterns of support for, 130 (table 5.2); state PAC contributions to, 151 (table 6.1)

New York Senate Delegation
— D'Amato Alfonse: constituent evaluation of, 105; geographic patterns of support for, 123–125, 126 (map 5.3), 27; demographic patterns of support for, 129, 130 (table 5.2); media coverage *(Newsday)* of, 180 (appendix C); signaling behavior to campaign contributors, 149–50; spotlight with state colleague, 3; state PAC contributions to, 152 (table 6.1). *See also* individual name
— Moynihan, Daniel P.: constituent evaluation of, 105; geographic patterns of support for, 123–125, 126 (map 5.3), 27; demographic patterns of support for, 129, 130 (table 5.2); media coverage *(Newsday)* of, 180 (appendix C); signaling behavior to campaign contributors, 149–50; spotlight with state colleague, 3; state PAC contributions to, 152 (table 6.1). *See also* individual name
— Schumer, Charles, 125n

North Dakota Senate Delegation
— Burdick, Quentin: demographic patterns of support for, 129 (table 5.1)
— Conrad, Kent: demographic patterns of support for, 129 (table 5.1)

Ohio Senate Delegation
— Glenn, John: demographic patterns of support, 129 (table 5.1); geographic patterns of support, 120–21, 122 (map 5.2), 123; state PAC contributions to, 152 (table 6.1)
— Metzenbaum, Howard: demographic patterns of support, 129 (table 5.1); geographic patterns of support, 120–21, 122 (map 5.2), 123; state PAC contributions to, 152 (table 6.1)

Oklahoma Senate Delegation
— Boren, David: demographic patterns of support for, 130 (table 5.2); geographic patterns of support for, 117–18, 119 (map 5.1), 120
— Nickles, Don: demographic patterns of support for, 130 (table 5.2); geographic patterns of support for, 117–18, 119 (map 5.1), 120

Oregon Senate Delegation
— Hatfield, Mark: demographic patterns of support for, 129 (table 5.1); geographic patterns of support, 132, 133 (map 5.4); legislative comparison to state colleague, 33–35, 37, 49; state PAC contributions to, 152 (table 6.1)
— Packwood, Robert: demographic patterns of support for, 129 (table 5.1); geographic patterns of support, 132, 133 (map 5.4); legislative comparison to state colleague, 33–35, 37, 49; state PAC contributions to, 152 (table 6.1)

Page, Benjamin I., 4, 97
Partisan Composition of Senate Delegation: effect on Senate careers, 18–20, on bill, sponsorship, 54–55, on committee selection, 46–48, on constituent evaluation, 106–108, on cosponsorship, 56–57, on legislative similarity index, 58–62, on media coverage, 81, 82 (table 3.6), on reputation building, 91, 95–97, 97n, 100 (table 4.1), 102, 103 (table 4.2), effect on state PAC contributions

Partisan Composition of Senate Delegation (*cont.*)
to senators, 156, 157 (table, 6.2) 158, 159 (table 6.3); interaction with geographic representation, 115–116, 131–38; interaction with demographic representation, 128–131

Partisan Representation: 21, 165–66; in legislative behavior, 39–43; party as voting cue, 88–89. *See also* state partisanship

Party Caucuses, Senate, 25–26, 43–44

Pennsylvania Senate Delegation
—Heinz, John: geographic competition with state colleague, 115, 116; demographic, patterns of support for, 128, 129 (table 5.1); geographic patterns of support for, 134, (map 5.5.)
—Maclay, William, 16
—Morris, Robert, 16
—Specter, Arlen: geographic competition with state colleague, 115, 116; demographic patterns of support for, 128, 129 (table 5.1); geographic patterns of support for, 134 (map 5.5.)

Pitkin, Hanna, 162–63
Popkin, Samuel L., 89
Public opinion of senators. *See* Constituent Evaluation of senators

Quayle, Dan, 171n

Randolph, Edmund, 13
Representation. *See* Senate Representation
Rhode Island Senate Delegation
—Chafee, John: state PAC contributions to, 152 (table 6.1)
—Pell, Claiborne: state PAC contributions to, 152 (table 6.1)

Riker, Willliam H., 18, 19
Root, Elihu, 19
Rosenblum, Marc R., 167
Rosenbluth, Frances, 167–168
Rothenberg, Lawrence, 146n
Rules Committee, Senate, 76

Samuels, David, 167
Sellers, Patrick, 94
Senate Delegations: cooperation within, 29–31; junior/senior dichotomy, 24,

108–109, 164; legislative similarity index 7, 58–62. *See also* Partisan Composition of Senate delegations; individual state delegations

Senate Election Study 1988–1992: as measure of constituent evaluation of senators, 10, 95–96, 97, 98, 99

Senate Representation: multidimensionality of, 5, 21, 162–66, 169–73. *See also* economic, representation; geographic representation; partisan representation

Senate Reputations: component of Senate careers, 27–28, 88–89; constituent awareness of, 95–110; in a two-member district, 90–91; role of media in, 92–93, 99–104; use of legislative agendas in, 91–92

Shapiro, Robert Y., 94, 97
Sigelman, Lee, 95–96, 97n
Simon, Paul, 147, 156. *See also* Illinois Senate Delegation
Sinclair, Barbara, 27, 95, 98
Snyder, James M. Jr., 110
South Carolina Senate Delegation
—Hollings, Fritz: demographic patterns of support for, 129, 130 (table 5.2); geographic patterns of support for, 141 (map 5.11); state PAC contributions to, 152 (table 6.1)
—Thurmond, Strom: demographic patterns of support for, 129, 130 (table 5.2); geographic patterns of support for, 141 (map 5.11); state PAC contributions to, 152 (table 6.1)

South Dakota Senate Delegation
—Daschle, Thomas: demographic patterns of support for, 130 (table 5.2); home style of, 21; state PAC contributions to, 152 (table 6.1)
—Pressler, Larry: demographic patterns of support for, 130 (table 5.2); state PAC contributions to, 152 (table 6.1)

State Legislatures: role in selection of senators, 14–17, 20

State Partisanship, 95–97, 114–16. *See also* Partisan Composition of Senate Delegation

Stokes, Donald, 88
Swanstrom, Roy, 15–16

Tennessee Senate Delegation
— Gore, Albert: state PAC contributions to, 152 (table 6.1)
— Sasser, James: state PAC contributions to, 152 (table 6.1)
Texas Senate Delegation
— Bentsen, Lloyd: constituent evaluation of, 106, 107, 108; demographic patterns of support for, 130 (table 5.2); geographic patterns of support, 140 (map 5.10); media coverage *(Houston Chronicle)* of, 179 (appendix C)
— Gramm, Phil: constituent evaluation of, 106, 107, 108; demographic patterns of support, 130 (table 5.2); geographic patterns of support, 140 (Map 5.10); media coverage *(Houston Chronicle)* of, 179 (appendix C). *See also* individual name
Tulsa World, 117–18

Uslaner, Eric M., 38, 107, 121n

Vermont Senate Delegation
— Jeffords, James: legislative differentiation from state colleague, 24–25, 47

— Leahy, Patrick: legislative differentiation from state colleague, 24–25, 47

Wayman, Frank, 146
West Virginia Senate Delegation
— Byrd, Robert C.: demographic patterns of support for, 129 (table 5.1); state PAC contributions to, 152 (table 6.1)
— Rockefeller, John D.: demographic patterns of support for, 129 (table 5.1); state PAC contributions to, 152 (table 6.1)
Wood, Gordon S., 15
Wright, John, 146
Wyoming Senate Delegation
— Simpson, Alan: demographic patterns of support for, 129 (table 5.1); geographic patterns of support for, 136 (map 5.7)
— Wallop, Malcolm: demographic patterns of support for, 129 (table 5.1); geographic patterns of support for, 136 (map 5.7)

Zupan, Mark A., 38n